RECLAIMING SOVEREIGNTY

i

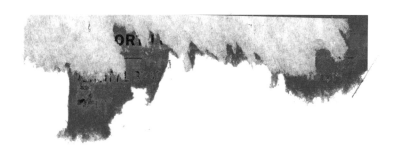

RECLAIMING SOVEREIGNTY

Edited by

LAURA BRACE AND JOHN HOFFMAN

PINTER
London and Washington

PINTER

A Cassell imprint

Wellington House, 125 Strand, London WC2R 0BB, England
PO Box 605, Herndon, Virginia 20172, USA

First published 1997
© The editors and contributors 1997

British Library Cataloguing-in-Publication Data
A catalogue record for this book is available from the British Library.
ISBN 1–85567–456–4

Typeset by BookEns Ltd, Royston, Herts.
Printed and bound in Great Britain by Creative Print and Design (Wales), Ebbw Vale

Contents

About the Contributors

R. L. Borthwick is a Senior Lecturer at Leicester University who teaches British and American government. His publications include *British Politics in Perspective* (which he edited with Professor J. E. Spence in 1984) and *Long to Reign Over Us? The Future of the British Monarchy*, 1994. He has written widely on the Commons, Lords and the committee system, and has recently contributed to a volume on British prime ministers entitled *Church to Major* edited by D. Shell and R. Hodder-Williams.

Laura Brace is a lecturer in the Department of Politics, University of Leicester. She is working on a book *The Idea of Property in Seventeenth Century England: Tithes, Rights and the Individual* which will be published by Manchester University Press, and has just published an article on Gerrard Winstanley.

Anthony Carty was recently appointed Professor of International Law at the University of Derby, and has published extensively in the field. In 1986 he wrote a book entitled *The Decay of International Law?*, and more recently published *Perestroika and International Law: Anglo–Soviet Approaches to International Law* with G. Danilenko. He has also edited a volume entitled *Law and Development*.

Robert Garner is a lecturer at the University of Leicester who has published widely on British politics, animal rights and environmental politics. In 1993 he wrote *Animals, Politics and Morality* and *British Political Parties Today* (with Richard Kelly), and in 1995 his *Environmental Politics* was published. He is currently working on a book on animal protection policies in Britain and the USA and is conducting a research project on animal welfare funded by the RSPCA.

John Hoffman is Reader in the Department of Politics, University of Leicester. He has written widely on questions of political and state theory. His most recent book is *Beyond the State*, published by Polity Press in

1995. His other works include *Marxism and the Theory of Praxis* (1975), *The Gramscian Challenge* (1984) and *State, Power and Democracy* (1988).

Stephen Hopkins is a lecturer at the University of Leicester who teaches French, Italian and Irish politics. He is currently completing a doctoral thesis on a comparative study of French and Italian trade unions. He has written a paper on contemporary developments within the Irish republican movement and published an article on the organizational and political evolution of the Workers' Party of Ireland in the *Journal of Communist Studies*.

Philip Lynch is a lecturer in the Politics Department at the University of Leicester and Deputy Director, Centre for European Politics and Institutions. He has written on Britain and European integration and the question of the nation and nation-state in British politics. His book *The Politics of Nationhood* is forthcoming with Macmillan. He is coeditor of and contributor to *Reforming the European Union* (Longman) which will appear after the Inter-Governmental Conference (probably early 1998).

Julia O'Connell Davidson is a Reader in the Department of Sociology at the University of Leicester. She has researched and written on the effect of privatization on employment relations in the utilities. She published *Privatisation and Employment Relations* and is coauthor of a recent methods textbook, *Methods, Sex and Madness*. She is currently working on the question of prostitution in Europe and sex tourism and child prostitution in South-east Asia, Latin America and the Caribbean.

J. E. Spence was formerly Head of Department and Professor of Politics at the University of Leicester. He has published extensively on Southern and South Africa and frequently broadcasts on the topic. He recently edited a volume entitled *Change in South Africa*, published by the Royal Institute for International Affairs in 1994. He has also written a good deal on international relations and edited the *British Journal of International Studies*.

Lucy Taylor has just completed her doctoral thesis on social mobilization and political participation in Chile and Argentina. She contributed a chapter on Latin American political studies to the edited volume *The State of the Academy: New Reflections on Political Studies*, published in 1995. A paper on human rights in Chile was written in 1993 and she has also published work on civil society and political participation.

David Welsh has taught at the University of Cape Town since 1963. He is currently Professor of Southern African Studies in the Political

Studies Department. His major publications include *The Roots of Segregation* (Oxford, 1971) and *South Africa's Options* (with F. Van Zyl Slabbert; published by David Philip, 1979). His particular research interests are South African politics and the politics of divided societies.

Gillian Youngs is an independent researcher currently dividing her time between the UK and Hong Kong. Her interests are conceptual and theoretical aspects of the relationship between political, economic and cultural dimensions of global relations. Her publications include *From International Relations to Global Relations: A Conceptual Challenge* (Cambridge: Polity Press, forthcoming); and, as coeditor with Eleonore Kofman, *Globalization: Theory and Practice* (London: Pinter, 1996).

Introduction: Reclaiming Sovereignty

LAURA BRACE AND JOHN HOFFMAN

In 1969 a book was published which sought to defend sovereignty (Stankiewicz, 1969). Today most people would want to know what sovereignty is before deciding whether it should be defended or not. As the contributions to this volume make clear, sovereignty is a highly ambiguous and contested concept, and there has been no attempt to impose a uniform definition upon the diversity of argument which these contributions express.

However we do believe that the question of the state provides a way of focusing and organizing this diversity. Central to current debates about sovereignty is the relationship between sovereignty and the state. Some take it for granted that sovereignty is a concept which only applies to the state. But there is a growing body of literature (which we have tried to reflect in the contributions to this volume) which challenges the sovereignty–state equation.

Here it is argued that sovereignty is social rather than state-centred in its orientation, and there are those who would go even further. It is not enough, they contend, to 'extend' sovereignty from men to women; from 'insiders' to 'outsiders', from the haves to the have-nots. Are animals not also sovereign? What about the natural world in general?

No volume on sovereignty can appear today which does not give some consideration to the question of whether sovereignty can and should be extended in this way. All who have contributed to this volume believe that the concept is worth taking seriously; but if the idea is worth reclaiming, then we need to be aware of its numerous dimensions. Making readers aware of this diversity is the central objective of this volume.

Part 1 links sovereignty to the state, either as a self-evident assumption or as a relationship which deserves to be challenged. Part 2 focuses on international developments within political economy and law, where there is growing evidence to suggest that the traditional sovereignty–state nexus should be questioned. In Part 3 we examine the case for linking sovereignty to the self, to popular organizations outside the state, to the position of prostitute women and to the wider world of nature.

The traditional concept

John Hoffman opens Part 1 by arguing that it is the traditional link between the state and sovereignty which lies at the heart of the contested and ambiguous nature of the concept itself. He notes that whereas many 'domestic' political scientists no longer use the concepts of state and sovereignty within their academic discourse, 'realist' thinkers within international relations (IR) believe that sovereignty will be protected from contention as long as it is confined to a world of *inter-state* relationships. Hoffman provides a critique of James (an eminent IR theorist), contending that paradox and ambiguity are unavoidable as long as the concept of sovereignty is linked to the state. Treating sovereignty as a purely modern development aggravates rather than resolves this problem and, Hoffman argues, some postmodern critiques of sovereignty are unconvincing because they accept rather than challenge the sovereignty–state relationship.

Bob Borthwick examines the problem of sovereignty within both a state-centred and a national context. In Britain, he argues, sovereignty has traditionally been seen as a question of parliamentary competence, and he explores the various challenges currently confronting parliamentary sovereignty in Britain: control over the executive, membership of the EU; the assertiveness of the courts, and the use of referendums.

Philip Lynch argues that in order to assess the complex impact of the EU, sovereignty should be understood as a 'multi-dimensional' concept and analysed in conjunction with autonomy. European integration challenges the sovereign nation-state, although the EU does not fit into traditional models of either state or international organization. The 'Europeanization' of key areas of domestic policy affects the location of sovereign power within the state, strengthening the executive in some respects, but also involving a range of actors in policy-making. Individual and popular sovereignty have been extended by legislation affecting individual rights, but weakened by the EU's democracy and legitimacy deficit. Although the legal authority of state institutions is undermined by membership of the EU, states may manage interdependence more effectively and achieve previously unattainable policy goals by 'pooling' sovereignty.

In Chapter 4, Stephen Hopkins tackles the problem of sovereignty within the deeply divided polity of Northern Ireland. He charts the failure of British and Irish attempts at state-building rooted in the competing visions of sovereignty and self-determination. He explores in particular the problems created by a permanent unionist majority during the Stormont era and the implications of such 'hegemonic control' for notions of consent and self-determination.

His analysis of the Anglo–Irish Agreement raises the problem of whether a 'sovereign power' can also act as a 'neutral arbiter'; can the 'Irish dimension' simply be grafted on to a traditional, unitary notion of sovereignty? Hopkins argues that the attempt is bound to produce ambivalence, and so stalemate. He detects the same ambivalence at the heart of the Downing Street Declaration and the Framework Documents which continue to work with traditional constitutional doctrines whilst aiming at a flexible approach to the sovereignty of Northern Ireland and its constitutional status. The fundamental issue of contested sovereignty remains unresolved.

How does the question of sovereignty affect the conduct and policies of deeply divided states? Jack Spence and David Welsh examine the role that the concept has played in South Africa. Both point out how South Africa was able historically to combine racial oligarchy with formally accredited state sovereignty. The new constitution, forged through negotiation and compromise in the 1990s, has ushered in a transition to liberal democracy; but Welsh, who focuses his analysis specifically upon domestic policy, fears that ANC preference for a unitary over a federalist constitution may mean that a monolithic and majoritarian form of state sovereignty will result.

Spence in his examination of foreign policy notes how in the postwar world, sovereignty has been increasingly linked to legitimacy, democracy and human rights. He argues that only the new South Africa can be said to conform to a normative concept of sovereignty which emphasizes responsibility and accountability. A major challenge facing the postapartheid South Africa then is this: can the government use its prestige and resources to strengthen this normative notion of sovereignty throughout the rest of Africa where corruption and civil war are endemic? Spence finds some grounds for optimism although he warns that the new South Africa is not immune from the constraints which a globalized world places upon all states.

International perspectives

Part 2 looks at the question of sovereignty in the light of international perspectives on the problem. What effect do international institutions and developments have on the notion of sovereignty as a state concept? Anthony Carty argues that the notion of state sovereignty poses an insoluble problem for international lawyers. It is generally accepted that states may be constrained by treaty obligations. These are deemed legal commitments into which states voluntarily enter and which, therefore, do not impair state sovereignty. However, no legal authority exists which can go beyond the state's own interpretation of its legal obligations.

This dilemma is acutely illustrated by two very recent examples affecting the unresolved problem of war. In July 1996 the International Court of Justice reaffirmed the right of states to continue to develop nuclear weapons if these states themselves believe that such weapons are necessary to further their national security. With respect to Bosnia-Herzegovina the United Nations has proved unable to afford it protection because the UN structure is still completely undermined by the legal power of member states, particularly the major players, to interpret the extent of their legal duties for themselves.

Gillian Youngs argues that when we focus on political economy, it becomes clear why the notion of state sovereignty in terms of distinct and exclusive boundaries is so problematic. The fact that the USA emerged as the dominant power in the West after the Second World War cannot be understood in terms simply of its position as a *state*. Its hegemony, she argues, springs from economic as well as political factors. Market forces have become increasingly relevant to an understanding of political power and the revolution in communications technology has radically altered our perceptions of 'boundaries'. International and national differences interact and merge in a way that means that the economic security of one country depends more and more upon forces acting beyond state borders.

Youngs shows graphically how the world is now increasingly unequal but argues that we need to identify divisions within as well as across states. Liberal concepts of state sovereignty cannot help us get to grips with political developments across the globe – in the Pacific countries, for example, where the development of a Chinese diaspora is a particularly dramatic example of globalizing trends. We should not assume that transnational influences will necessarily take a state-centred or even a conventional economic form. Both Youngs and Carty are convinced that a simple equation of sovereignty with the state fails to explain the challenges facing the contemporary international world.

Extending the concept

In Part 3 the argument shifts away from the state and the international realm to the question of society and nature. Laura Brace draws upon the contrasting arguments of Hobbes and Winstanley to distinguish between self-sovereignty as a territory and as a domain. In the case of Hobbes, she argues, the individual is conceived in territorial and statist terms — a competitor who looks suspiciously upon others from the position of a pre-existing self. A fortress is created through boundaries which exclude rivals in a world of conflict and force, and the boundary metaphor here implies a masculinist sense of separation and fear of engulfment.

For Winstanley, by way of contrast, the sovereign self identifies with wholeness. It is the Fall which creates separation, fear and disorder and, as a consequence, the enclosure of the earth as private property. Winstanley's emphasis upon a relational view of sovereignty makes his work valuable for feminists, in Brace's view. Relationships imply individuality within wholeness. Whereas Winstanley identifies 'imagination' with selfishness, an 'imaginary domain' can be conceived as an awareness of context through which individuals project different and plural identities. Sovereignty requires the acceptance both of boundaries and of community.

Lucy Taylor argues for a theoretical approach to the study of democracy and transition in Latin America which takes account of the complexity of the idea of sovereignty. Using Chile as an example, she examines what happens to the concepts of sovereignty and citizenship under authoritarian regimes and in the transition to democracy. Her conclusions paint a nuanced and carefully shaded picture. She finds evidence of formal sovereignty existing in a kind of suspended animation, even under Pinochet's oppressive regime, and in the political activity of democratic movements opposed to the military rule, she identifies a more informal strand of sovereignty based on people acting as 'subjected citizens' outside the formal political arena associated with traditional notions of unitary and state-centred sovereignty.

She insists on the need to take a flexible view of sovereignty, and to be wary of limiting the concept to its formal dimension and attaching it too firmly to the state. The return of democracy to Chile has involved the political parties co-opting the issues which had mobilized social movements under Pinochet, leading to a dramatic decline in participatory politics. We need to look beyond the formal mechanisms of sovereign power, and this is bound to involve looking beyond the state and granting sovereignty to the individual citizen.

Julia O'Connell Davidson uses the example of prostitution and sex tourism to interrogate the power relations that lie behind the idea of self-sovereignty and its exercise within a specific social context. Drawing on her extensive research carried out with Jacqueline Sanchez Taylor in Latin America, Thailand and the Caribbean, she explores the implications of relying on a liberal vision of an 'unencumbered' self for an understanding of sovereignty.

She analyses the stories clients tell themselves, and in particular the way in which they impose a contract which relies on the prostitute relinquishing sovereignty over her own person. The idea that she can give up her inner framework of sovereignty in this way rests on the assumption that she is already excluded from the community of 'true' sovereign individuals. Her exploration of the cost of this exclusion, and also of the psychologically damaging tensions embedded in *inclusion*, reveals the gendered, racialized and economic relations of power which underpin the masculinist notion of a sovereign individual.

Robert Garner brings this volume to a close by challenging the very idea of sovereignty as a human-centred project. A new generation of scholars have argued for a notion of sovereignty which contests what Garner calls the 'moral orthodoxy' — the idea that animals (though valuable in themselves) can be sacrificed if this is absolutely necessary for the interests of humans. He notes that critics of the moral orthodoxy divide between utilitarians and 'rights' theorists. Utilitarians believe that humans and animals enjoy the same moral status because they can *both* feel pain and pleasure, whereas animal rights theorists such as Regan argue that a common sentiency between humans and animals is not enough. Because some animals at least have a mental ability which makes them equally autonomous to humans, they should also be seen as sovereign.

Neither utilitarian nor rights-oriented critics of the moral orthodoxy would necessarily endorse what Garner calls an 'ecocentric' argument that extends sovereignty to nature as a whole. Although it would be valuable to have the kind of environmental ethic for which ecocentrics strive, the idea that nonsentient parts of nature should be deemed sovereign is not, so far at least, credible. It may even, Garner argues, lead to the sacrifice of human sovereignty in order to preserve natural sovereignty.

However we conceptualize sovereignty — as a statist idea, a social concept or a notion which extends to at least parts of nature — it remains central to contemporary political concerns. By arguing that we should reclaim sovereignty, we are suggesting that whatever the diversity which surrounds the concept, it is a debate which we should continue to take seriously.

Reference

Stankiewicz, W. J. (ed.) (1969) *In Defense of Sovereignty*. New York: Oxford University Press.

PART 1

TRADITIONAL PERSPECTIVES: SOVEREIGNTY AND THE STATE

Is it Time to Detach Sovereignty from the State?

JOHN HOFFMAN

Sovereignty, it is generally agreed, is a highly ambiguous term. It is tempting to liken it to democracy as a concept capable of a wide range of conflicting and mutually exclusive meanings. Indeed as with democracy, the term is so ambiguous that some have been tempted to give it up.

Three strategies for tackling this problem of ambiguity will be considered. The first seeks to insulate sovereignty from disagreement by identifying it exclusively with the role of the state as an external actor. The second tries to clarify the notion of sovereignty by limiting it to the modern state, or (in one particular variant of this argument) to the state under capitalism. A third position accepts the contentious nature of sovereignty given the dualistic and paradoxical character of the state, but takes the view that there is no way of resolving the contention, since the term itself is simply indefinable.

I shall argue that each of these responses is unsatisfactory as a way of tackling the question of ambiguity, and in each case the reason is the same. None embraces an argument for detaching sovereignty from the state.

The ambiguity problem

It might be thought that if sovereignty is a thoroughly ambiguous term, then the concept should be abandoned, and as two recent works on sovereignty remind us, this proposition has been considered by some. Bartelson quotes E. H. Carr's famous prediction (just before the Second World War) that all that can be said with certainty about the future of sovereignty is that the concept will become increasingly blurred and indistinct, and Bartelson also recalls Benn's contention (made not long after the Second World War) that so 'Protean' a word ought to be given up (Bartelson, 1995: 13). (Cynthia) Weber cites Haas to the same effect (1995: 1). Even more recently, Newman has concluded that the concept is 'so ambiguous and distorted that it is now a barrier to analysis' (1996: 15).

Yet like democracy, the term remains in political currency however much some political scientists may deplore its ambiguity. In fact the term has become increasingly central to contemporary political debate — both in analysing developments in the post-Cold War period and in the fierce argument over the future direction of the European Union (EU). In Britain, for example, the question of sovereignty has entered the public arena with a vengeance. While Newman argues that some consider sovereignty to be anachronistic in the wake of the Maastricht Treaty of 1992 (1996: 1), others (rather more typically) prefer to *redefine* the term.

James had already noted in 1986 that even when ridicule was heaped upon those who feared that the EU would undermine British sovereignty, this critique was offered in the name of 'the greater sovereignty of a united Europe' (1986: 1, 250). A more recent variant of this position exhorts British politicians to spend less time stressing 'a hopelessly outdated and inflated view of sovereignty' on the grounds that greater involvement in and sympathy for the EU would actually increase British sovereignty (Taylor, 1991: 79–80). Newman himself acknowledges that if we identify sovereignty with overall state power, then it could be argued that sovereignty might actually be increased through greater integration with the EU (1996: 13).

The contestability of the term is, it seems to me, undeniable. In Gallie's classic formulation, contestability arises when different meanings of the same term are expounded and evoked through conflicting sources of evidence, logic and rationality (1955: 188, 193). Yet acknowledging the contestability of the concept of sovereignty does not mean that we should give it up. On the contrary, we should try to understand why this contestability arises. Hinsley, whose seminal arguments on sovereignty will be looked at later, has noted that sovereignty becomes a source of great preoccupation and conflict when there is rapid change 'in the scope of government or in the nature of society or in both' (cited by Biersteker and Weber, 1996: 8). An increase in the contentious nature of sovereignty reveals increasing ambiguity and argument over politics in general.

Ironically the contention over sovereignty extends to the question of contestability itself since there are those who argue that the term is not as contestable as it seems. Weber quotes Walker, who contends that the concept has only been challenged on the margins 'by constitutional lawyers and other connoisseurs of fine lines' (Weber, 1995: 2). Indeed Bartelson finds that the concept is essentially *un*contested as the foundation of modern political discourse, but that it is essentially contested 'as to its meaning within the same discourse' (Bartelson, 1995: 14). The argument seems bizarre, for how can sovereignty be both contested and uncontested at the same time?

The two faces of the state

I will argue that what makes sovereignty a singularly contentious concept is its linkage with the state. Indeed it is this historic association with the state which explains why even the contention surrounding the concept of sovereignty is itself contentious.

James has argued that scholars have been puzzled and confused about the nature of sovereignty 'ever since they witnessed the emergence of the state' (1986: 3). Hinsley's now classic analysis of sovereignty is premised on the assumption that the origin and history of the concept is 'closely linked with the nature, origin and history of the state' (1986: 2). In defining sovereignty as the idea that there is a 'final and absolute political authority in the community', he takes it for granted that this final and absolute authority is a state. The state, he insists, is a necessary condition for the concept itself.

Recent commentators seem to agree. Bartelson argues that it is sovereignty which makes a state a state, and Weber identifies sovereignty as a 'referent' or 'ground' for statehood. She opens the first chapter of her book with the question: 'can one say anything about statehood without beginning by deciding what sovereignty is' (1995: 1). So closely linked are the two notions that she finds it legitimate to run them together as 'sovereign statehood' (1995: 2–3) – the term which James also uses in his analysis of the concept.

Bartelson and Weber suggest therefore that as long as the state is taken for granted, then contestability and *un*contestability exist side by side. On the one hand (as it has recently been argued) where the state is 'privileged', sovereignty is treated as if it were unproblematic (Murphy, 1996: 104); on the other hand, *within* statecentric discourse, the meaning of sovereignty is contested. Theorists might for example argue about whether sovereignty can be identified in a democratic or in a federal state, but the linkage between sovereignty and the state itself remains uncontested.

The problem with this line of argument is that it seems to ignore the fact that for at least two decades since the Second World War, the state itself became a highly contested term. In the 1950s and 1960s a whole range of theorists – from behaviouralists to linguistic philosophers, from radical democrats to pluralists – all contended that the state represented a problematic term within political theory. The state was linked to sovereignty, and the view was taken that political theory should dispense with the conceptual services of *both*. Thus Easton argued in *The Political System* that the elusive nature of the state is integrally linked to the elusive nature of sovereignty. The state has served as a 'myth' in the struggle for national unity because it has been tied to the 'ultimate power of sovereignty' (1953: 108). Neither should form part of a rigorous political theory.

How then is it possible to suggest that sovereignty has continued to enjoy a 'foundational' status in modern political science, given this conceptual onslaught against the state? Easton himself provides the answer. The state, he argues, has led a double life. While its usage within internal or domestic politics ought to be abandoned, the term has never disappeared as a concept identifying what Easton calls 'the unified actors in the international arena'. Here all continue, Easton comments, to recognize the concept as a legitimate abbreviation for the nation-state (1981: 304).

Easton acknowledges implicitly what some of his critics have made brutally clear — that his celebrated definition of the political system as 'the authoritative allocation of values for society as a whole' simply breaks down when applied to international organizations. In the words of one of his commentators, Easton's notion of politics as a 'global system' is so 'shadowy' and 'indeterminate' as to be of questionable utility (Nicholson and Reynolds, 1967: 24–5, 29). Hence his critique of the state is a limited one. Whatever might be said about the state domestically, externally it is still alive and kicking!

Indeed behaviouralists in general suffer a certain schizophrenia when addressing the question of the state at the international level. On the one hand the state (in general) is denounced as a concept which is ideological, ambiguous, elusive and incoherent. On the other hand behaviouralists concede that no analysis of international politics is possible unless we assume that states are the key actors on the international scene. Thus Kaplan, as a major architect of behaviouralism within international relations (IR), identifies the variables of his international system in terms of *states*. Although he and Bull fiercely debated the respective merits of behavioural and classical (realist) IR theory, both assumed that states are the most important actors within international relations (Taylor, 1978: 190–3; Hollis and Smith, 1990: 31).

This schizophrenic attitude is borne out in Nettl's often-cited argument for the state 'as a conceptual variable'. Writing in 1967 Nettl links the state and sovereignty as concepts which have both fallen out of favour in the social sciences. At the same time he comments that whatever may have happened to the state internally, 'there have been few challenges to both its sovereignty *and* its autonomy in "foreign affairs"' (1967–8: 564). A concept which is highly contestable within societies seems perfectly straightforward when sandwiched between them. Thus even in societies (Nettl instances Britain and the USA) which have a low degree of what he calls 'stateness', the extrasocial or international role of the state remains 'invariant'. Britain, for example, may be stateless domestically, but it is uncontestably statist and sovereign in its international relations (1967–8: 564).

This dichotomy between the state domestically and the state externally explains why sovereignty has been both contested and uncontested, and it is a dichotomy which lies at the heart of James's realist analysis of the 'sovereign state'.

James's no-nonsense realism

James echoes the positions of Easton and Nettl noted above by arguing that what has plunged political theory into an intellectual quagmire has been its focus on the internal nature of the state (1986: 3). To avoid ambiguity and contention, James has a simple solution: avoid examining the state as a domestic actor! Political thinkers have found themselves in a conceptual cul-de-sac because, as James puts it, they have 'almost always been directing themselves to the domestic political scene' (1986: 7).

Conceptual difficulties can be dissolved if we follow two prescriptions. The first is to focus on what James calls the 'practice of states' – on what states actually do. A clear view will emerge if we remember (as he puts it magisterially) that the 'meaning of sovereignty' is what the states say it is (1986: 8). The second prescription is to stick to international relations, and this means giving political theory itself a wide berth. In seeking to tackle the question of 'sovereign statehood', James argues, 'the work of the political theorists will find no place' in his argument (1986: 8). The claim sounds fantastic (how can you analyse sovereign statehood without theory?) until we recall that as a realist, James adopts a statecentric view of politics.

In this view, a *theory* of politics can only be a theory of the state. When Wight posed his famous question – 'why is there no international theory?' – his answer was that political theory is 'the tradition of speculation about the state'. No international theory is possible unless we assume that a world state can emerge in which the sovereignty of the domestic state is replicated at the international level (1966: 18, 22). States are to be taken as given. They are sovereign because they say they are, and by restricting ourselves to an analysis of the state's *external* relationships, we can avoid the ambiguity and contention fomented by the state's turbulent domesticity.

While James allows that nonsovereign states are possible (for example states which exist within federal constitutions like that of the USA), sovereignty without the state is not. Sovereignty derives from the constitutional independence or separateness of states, and sovereignty is the attribute which qualifies the state for what James calls international actorhood (1986: 8, 9, 22).

Form without content?

In James's view, sovereignty is essentially a 'formal' question. As 'a matter of fact' either it exists or it does not. Constitutional independence – the attribute of sovereignty – should not be taken to imply a parity of economic or political power (1986: 49) nor should we assume that constitutional independence brings with it political independence if by that term we mean a capacity to ignore external constraint. The point appears to be a formal one. In terms of constitutional law, the sovereign state is 'in control of its own destiny' – 'a clear and straightforward reflection of the fact that it is constitutionally independent' (1986: 53–4).

If we were to identify sovereignty with more 'substantive' factors like popular loyalty, legitimacy, democracy, military prowess or the rule of law then, James argues, we would be plunged into the kind of contention which has bedeviled discussions of sovereignty within a domestic context. Thus even membership of the United Nations is deemed a consequence of, rather than a criterion for, sovereignty. Rights in international law accrue to states which are *already* sovereign. Puppet states can therefore be sovereign since in formal terms they are constitutionally independent, even though James concedes that this independence may be much more of a formality than in most cases. The point is however that 'sovereignty while it does not usually end in formalities, always starts there' (1986: 143).

The problem with this argument is this. How do we explain the way in which states *acquire* sovereignty if, as James insists, recognition by other states does not have a 'constitutive' effect? What then counts as evidence for the existence of sovereignty? This problem becomes acute when contention arises not because the political theorists have created it, but because the existence of sovereignty itself is a matter of international dispute. James finds it tempting to argue that 'in most circumstances', normally, usually, and in the vast majority of cases (1986: 58, 80) the question of identifying sovereignty is a straightforward factual matter. But what of those cases (however few) where disagreement persists?

To his credit, James is willing to engage with the hardest of cases – where contention is explicit and particular states are subject to international aversion. Thus divided states like the two Germanies during the Cold War period or pariah states like South Africa and its 'tribal homelands' in the time of apartheid can be considered 'sovereign' since 'factually speaking' they enjoyed constitutional independence. The Rhodesian case is a particularly important one, for James concedes that this was a state which came into existence in an unlawful and unconstitutional manner and was not recognized by any other state during its 14 years of existence. Yet he argues that with Smith's unilateral declaration of independence in 1965, a new sovereign state 'bearing the name of Rhodesia' emerged (1986: 156).

At one point James argues that sovereignty expresses 'a legal rather than a physical reality' (1986: 40), but he accepts that where sovereignty is almost universally contested, as in the Rhodesia case, other factors come into play. 'Ultimately', as he puts it, a sovereign state's existence depends upon its ability to keep its enemies at bay. This 'ultimate point is rarely reached but, if it is, the legal claim to sovereignty will be as nothing in the absence of an ability to defend it by force of arms' (1986: 41). In other words 'more material characteristics' become relevant (1986: 93), and central among them is the state's capacity to exercise effective physical force. It is this physical reality rather than the law which 'ultimately' counts. Form depends upon 'content', and the formal capacity to exercise sovereignty rests upon a state's ability to defend its territory by force of arms.

The centrality of physical force is crucial. It explains why – to take two of the examples which James himself discusses – Bangladesh succeeded in becoming a sovereign state because it was able (with the help of India) to compel the Pakistani forces in the east to surrender. On the other hand Biafra failed to emerge as a sovereign state, despite the fact that it was relatively large, populous and enjoyed external recognition. Why? Because it *was overwhelmed by the Nigerian government's 'superior strength' (1986: 78, 82). It is true that the substance of sovereignty can (in James's words) 'move away from the form to a considerable degree without the form having to be called into question' (1986: 74), but ultimately, as James concedes, it is the 'physical reality', the capacity to impose rule by force, which is decisive in identifying sovereign statehood.

The problem of the state

James's attempt to sustain a purely formal (and legalistic) view of sovereignty fails. In cases of serious contestation he is obliged to concede that ultimately sovereignty depends upon the capacity to rule through force. His view of sovereignty turns therefore upon the Weberian view of the state as an institution which claims a monopoly of legitimate force. I have argued elsewhere that force is the central category within Weber's definition (Max not Cynthia) (Hoffman, 1995: ch. 3), and when all is said and done, it lies at the heart of James's view of sovereignty.

But once we identify sovereignty with the state's claim to exercise a monopoly of legitimate force, then we highlight its problematic and contentious character. Exercising force is only necessary because it is impossible to resolve conflicts of interest through negotiation and arbitration. On this Hinsley's commentary is most revealing. He argues that in stateless societies, there is no central symbol or instrument of rule. What he calls 'single leadership' is the mark of the presence of the state (1986: 7). Sovereign *one-ness* excludes difference and plurality, and, as Hobbes classically demonstrates, the only way in which a multiplicity of wills can become 'one' is through force.

Hinsley comments that in stateless societies the resort to force by political leaders is tacitly avoided, and this point is borne out, for example, by Clastres in his argument that the Amerindian chief who sought to issue a command backed by sanctions of physical force would be met by certain refusal and a denial of further recognition. In what Clastres calls 'society against the state', it is the community rather than the individual leader who remains the locus of power (1977: 131, 175). Hinsley notes that where force is used in stateless societies, it is met with equal force and the notion of 'defeat' is normally absent. Even if one party to a violent conflict is defeated, no attempt is made to establish 'political dominance' (1986: 8). This point is confirmed by those anthropological studies of stateless societies which argue that even where outbreaks of force occur, this force is not used as a 'means of dominating others' (Mair, 1962: 12). The same point is also argued with regard to the use of force in international society, conceived as an 'anarchical' or stateless order (Bull, 1977: 62, 132).

In stateless societies force is not used as a method of resolving conflicts, and it has therefore no real political significance. The point has been well made that whereas conflict implies a dispersal of activity among multiple actors, *force* (in a political sense) implies concentration, unity and domination (Nicholson, 1984: 34–45). The use of force to resolve a conflict involves suppressing the identity of one of the parties to a dispute so that the victor 'triumphs', and as Hinsley has noted, defeat is tied to domination (1986: 8). An important distinction follows which has an important bearing on both the peculiarity of the state and the contested character of its sovereignty.

If 'singular' political leaderships in states seek to impose their will through force, it is crucial to identify the 'pressures' which are utilized in stateless societies to secure order. Hinsley is again right to argue that in a stateless society, authority rests upon 'psychological and moral coercion' rather than force (1986: 16). This is a crucial point. As I have argued elsewhere (Hoffman, 1995: 87–90), coercion of a psychological and moral kind imposes sanctions for noncompliance, but it does not undermine the freedom of choice and subjective identity of targeted individuals in the way that force does. Force (in a statist context) has to be focused, monopolized and expressed in a manner which entrenches domination and hierarchy. In stateless societies, as Hinsley points out, there may be coercion, but we can still legitimately refer to 'the will of the community'; on the other hand, the king in a state either has might (i.e. force) or does not rule (Hinsley, 1986: 17).

In contrasting the mechanisms for securing order in a stateless with that of a state-centred society, Hinsley provides the conceptual tools (even if he does not himself employ them) for demonstrating the problematic character of sovereignty in the context of the state. For if state sovereignty involves the imposition of force as a method of resolving conflict, then we have an institution which is inherently divisive in character. The sovereign state claims a monopoly of legitimate force because, and only because, sections of a fractured community resort to force of their own and contest the legitimacy of the force they resist. If 'dissidents', criminals and terrorists accepted the state's monopoly of legitimate force, then it would not have to be used against them. Hence the paradoxical character of the state. The community in whose name state sovereignty is exercised does not actually exist, since we can take it for granted that the state's aspiration to exercise a monopoly of legitimate force is necessarily rejected by those against whom it is targeted. Built into the very institution of the state is the ambiguity and contention which bedevils the concept of sovereignty.

James identifies sovereignty (as we have seen) with the capacity of the state to exercise force, and he justifies the sovereign status of the Rhodesian state on the grounds that legitimacy rested upon 'a significant congruence between the decisions of those who purport to rule and the actual behaviour of their alleged subjects' (1986: 155–6, 158). However what is generally true of the state was particularly true of the Smith regime: its legitimacy was sharply contested, its force countered and opposed, and it could only rule by marginalizing and excluding a section of the community – the 'criminals', 'terrorists', 'people of violence', in a word, the 'others' who rejected it. The final and absolute authority of the sovereign state exists because, and only because, it is radically and fundamentally challenged.

Sovereignty and the modern state

But it might be objected that it is unnecessary to detach sovereignty from all states, since sovereignty inheres only in states of a particular kind. It is sometimes argued that sovereignty is the product of the modern state alone.

Thus Hinsley takes the view that although the state is necessary for sovereignty, it is not sufficient. Sovereignty requires two additional features. On the one hand the state and society must be distinct, and on the other they must interpenetrate so that the forms and outlook of the state are recognized and welcomed to some degree by the community (1986: 21). The definition of sovereignty as 'final and absolute authority in the political community' rules out 'segmentary' states on the grounds that in the latter, final and absolute authority either is nowhere explicitly identified (as in federal states) or is seen to reside elsewhere (as in theocratic and imperial states).

For sovereign power to exist in the political community, this power must be seen as absolute and illimitable, and for this to be possible, the 'body politic' (i.e. the state and society) must be composed of both rulers and ruled (Hinsley, 1986: 121). State and society cannot interpenetrate (and mutually influence one another) unless they constitute 'a single personality' (1986: 125). What (in Hinsley's view) makes Hobbes's account of sovereignty even more consistent than that of Bodin's is the way in which he rejects any 'dualism' between the prince and the people by arguing that in every true political society, the authority, will and action of the ruler is the authority, will and action of every individual (1986: 125, 142–3).

Hinsley's argument is basically that sovereignty can only arise in a state where individuals as citizens authorize their rulers to act on their behalf. Support for this position is widespread. Even though Rosenberg is critical of traditional statist views, he argues that sovereignty comes about only when the rise of a capitalist division of labour makes it possible for the state to be 'abstracted' as a 'purely political' public institution (1994: 87). Like Onuf (1991: 426), he sees sovereignty as a quintessentially modern phenomenon.

It is certainly true that the *modern* state or the state under capitalism has features which differentiate it from states in the past. As Rosenberg emphasizes, under capitalism the state becomes *abstracted* from society so that the extraction of a surplus now appears to be the private activity of individuals rather than the public activity of the state. He draws upon Marx to good effect to argue that the individual egalitarianism within a capitalist society is both a modern phenomenon as well as being one which masks the domination and despotism of property.

Hinsley also argues that sovereignty has to be 'abstract' (1986: 142), although he does not endorse the connotation of repression and mystification which the concept of 'abstraction' has in Marxist theory. But whether the equation of sovereignty and the modern state is expressed sympathetically (as in D'Entreves, 1967: 23; Forsyth, 1987: 506), or pejoratively, the argument remains vulnerable nevertheless. The point is that the modern state accentuates and highlights a problem with sovereignty which has existed all along. I have already argued that the state in general asserts a monopoly of legitimate force which it does not and cannot possess, and it is in this notion of a 'monopoly' that the essence of state sovereignty lies. The assertion of monopoly is linked to the use of force as the state's ultimate method of resolving conflict. Force in this sense requires (as I have argued) concentration and hierarchy so that when Roberts speaks of the 'presence of supreme authority' as the differentiating quality of the state, he captures the absolutist and exclusionary attribute central to state sovereignty in all its forms (1979: 32).

I would certainly accept that sovereignty in premodern states is embryonic and undeveloped. Traditional empires like the Roman confined universalizing concepts to their own territories while medieval theorists could only construct a much more universal notion of law and sovereignty by identifying the impersonal rule of law with the power of God. Modern statecraft by contrast employs a notion which is both universal and secular, and is thus able to recognize the sovereignty of all states however different these states happen to be in their outlook or the resources they command.

The point is that by locating sovereignty solely within the modern state, we run the risk of idealizing this state-form and taking its misleading appearances at face value. It is true that in the modern state individuals as citizens are held to authorize the institution which acts on their behalf, but this liberal norm simply serves to aggravate the paradox of an institution which rules in the name of those it 'forces to be free'. The modern state brings to a head a problem which has existed in the state from the start – that of securing order and community through division and suppression. It is the assertion of a monopoly of legitimate *force* which creates the problem.

We have already noted Hinsley's argument that the sovereign state both is separate from and yet interpenetrates society. The more the autonomy and the impersonality of the state is stressed, the more problematic its sovereignty becomes. On the one hand sovereignty is seen as universal in its jurisdiction. On the other hand what makes sovereignty explicit is the fact that it is public rather than private – that it is *separate* from the society it penetrates. Parekh has argued that the state–society relationship has baffled political theorists for the past four centuries and continues to resist adequate conceptualization (1990: 248–9). He is understandably confused, since what is private is itself determined by what is public, and essential to the particularity of state sovereignty is that it has a hand in everything.

These paradoxes express in a sharp and explicit manner the problem of seeking order through force, unity through division, community through exclusion. The problem of sovereignty is the problem of the state itself.

Sovereignty and meaning

There is a final difficulty which we need to tackle in making the case for detaching sovereignty from the state. Some writers of a postmodernist persuasion have rightly identified the link between sovereignty and the state as the source of sovereignty's conceptual problems, but they have then argued that this makes the concept indefinable.

Thus Bartelson and (Cynthia) Weber see the state as embodying the dualisms and divides which paralyse the analysis of state sovereignty. Both focus in particular upon a domestic/international divide which implies that while the sovereign state stands for order, civilization and rationality, the international system is the 'other' — the alien outsider whose turbulent anarchy and incoherent plurality permanently threaten the state (Bartelson, 1995: 42).

Weber argues that as a result of this domestic/international divide, sovereign practices are 'self-referential', by which she means that diplomats constitute and generate the very communities which they then invoke as justification for their actions. The boundaries of these communities are thus contrived, as evidenced by the fact that they are ceaselessly transgressed. In the case of domestic communities this is by groups like criminals, illegal aliens, the homeless, refugees, and the like, who as 'outsiders' are the particular target of statist force. Internationally these transgressions are continuously threatened by nuclear weaponry, environmental pollution and demands for regional security (Weber, 1995: 10).

Yet what prevents postmodernists like Bartelson and Weber from detaching sovereignty from the state is their argument that sovereignty is so contestable as to be indefinable. Any attempt to say what sovereignty is will replicate the very 'act of closure' which creates the arbitrariness of the state and its contestable boundaries in the first place (Weber, 1995: 9). We can only challenge the foundational role of sovereignty if we abandon the whole practice of trying to 'define' concepts (Bartelson, 1995: 49).

The 'discourse' of the sovereign state, it is argued, embraces the very nature of knowledge and meaning. To be sovereign is to decide what counts as the truth, and it is because, in Bartelson's view, sovereignty is a precondition for knowledge, that it is inherently indefinable. A precondition for knowledge cannot at the same time be part of that knowledge itself. Bartelson likens sovereignty to Kant's notion of the parergon in aesthetic discourse. The parergon is a frame which does the framing. It is neither inside nor outside of discourse since it is the condition for the possibility of both (1995: 51). The domestic/ international divide, like all the other divides which give sovereignty its identity, resembles a 'line in water'. It is fluid and unstable, and it would be futile and self-defeating to try to capture (and thus define) it.

The practice of defining things assumes, Bartelson argues, that 'language ought to be a transparent medium for representing what takes place in the world outside the knowing subject' (1995: 15). Whether sovereignty represents a reality 'out there' or is simply a set of juridical rules for identifying independent states, all definitions assume a representational relationship between language and the world beyond it (1995: 7). Weber argues along the same lines. States embody what she calls a 'logic of representation' in which language is tied to some 'empirical referent, foundation or ground that is always the basis for speech' (Weber, 1995: 7). The logic of representation demands that the sovereign constructs a foundation 'which does not exist except as a fiction' (1995: 7).

It is certainly true, as Bartelson and Weber argue, that states are metaphysical and elusive since the communities they purport to represent are indeed fluid and unstable. Bartelson rightly links the assertion of absolutist truths with the sovereign pretensions of the state (1995: 18). But it does not follow that all theory *has to be* absolutist and dogmatic any more than it follows that the pursuit of order can only be undertaken by the state. On the contrary. I have already suggested (with some help from Hinsley) that stateless societies are characterized by an order which is all the more effective and meaningful by virtue of the fact that it is not 'imposed' by an institution claiming to exercise a monopoly of legitimate force (see also Hoffman, 1995: 38). The notion of a stateless society as an irrational and chaotic disorder is a statist myth. In stateless societies rules can only be enforced through consensus, negotiation and arbitration – practices that involve the recognition of differences, the acceptance of plurality and the accommodation of conflict. What is excluded from stateless practices is the kind of monolithicity, oneness and abstraction that is characterized by the violence of the state as it seeks to impose 'unity' from on high.

To challenge the state, therefore, we need to understand how order and cohesion arise from stateless mechanisms (that elsewhere I have called 'governmental', 1995: 40–2). This positive evaluation of statelessness must influence our concept of knowledge. If we are right to link absolutist and abstract thought with the state (and the dualisms which statism generates), why can't we have a notion of truth and representation which embodies the plurality, fluidity and diversity associated with stateless practice? Why should we assume (as Bartelson and Weber appear to) that unless the truth is timeless, it is nonexistent; that if reality is complex and fluid, it cannot be represented; that if thinking is sensitive to change and historicity, then it cannot be transparent?

On the one hand Bartelson and Weber fiercely (and rightly) condemn 'modernist' views of the truth, knowledge and sovereignty as static, timeless and 'foundational'. On the other hand they continue to embrace modernist concepts in inverted form. It is true that sovereignty is tied to knowledge, discourse and truth. But why should we assume that knowledge, discourse and the truth have to be infused with the absolutism and 'essentialism' of the state? Take the critique of representation. Harding has argued that we can and should aim to produce 'less partial and perverse representations' of reality without having to assert 'the absolute, complete, universal or eternal adequacy of these representations' (1990: 100). The abstract dualisms which Bartelson and Weber rightly associate with the state can be challenged not by inverting them but by positing a stateless and 'governmental' approach (in the place of a statist one) to the question of knowledge and sovereignty.

The point is that the state is perfectly real. If its dualisms are (as postmodernists rightly allege) abstract, elusive, metaphysical and arbitrary, this is because the state itself is a contradictory institution which vainly seeks to impose unity upon diversity by invoking a homogenous 'community' which does not exist. Indeed unless we define the state in these terms (and how else can we grasp its elusive and contentious reality?), it is impossible to begin the process of detaching it from sovereignty. When Bartelson argues that 'we must abandon the quest for timeless foundations and essences in political philosophy' (1995: 48), he fails to see that this can only be done if we begin to look beyond the state.

A poststatist view of sovereignty

What makes sovereignty ambiguous and problematic is the contra- dictory character of the state. The state is the source of those absolutist dualisms which have paralysed the conceptual analysis of sovereignty (even, as we have seen, in the work of no-nonsense realists like James). A recent analysis seeks to distinguish analytically the state and sovereignty, but still persists in seeing the two entities as 'mutually constitutive' (Biersteker and Weber, 1996: 11). If we define sovereignty 'as a political entity's externally recognized right to exercise final authority over its affairs' (1996: 12), it is clear that the link between state and sovereignty remains.

But if the state is the source of sovereignty's conceptual problems (as I have argued), then why not ask what the concept might mean in a world without the state – in a world in which conflicts of interest are resolved without force; where differences are respected (even welcomed), and where pluralistic identities have to be accommodated? What makes the modern or liberal state significant in analysing sovereignty is that it raises, however unwittingly, the prospect and possibility of statelessness by enshrining the self-governing individual as its legitimating norm. In the same way that modernity makes postmodernity possible, so *liberal* statism enables us to look beyond the state to a world in which human survival itself increasingly requires governmental rather than statist methods of resolving conflicts of interest.

The point is that it is not enough to denounce state sovereignty. We can only move beyond its abstract divides through identifying a stateless world which celebrates diversity, explicitly recognizes pluralism and focuses upon difference as the heart of individual identity. While conflicts of interests are inherent in social relationships, they can be resolved without the need for an institution seeking to claim a monopoly of legitimate force. On this argument the state is actually in tension with sovereignty, since the use of force against individuals actually undermines their ability to govern themselves.

Classical liberalism has already identified the 'sovereign' capacity of individuals to govern their own lives. This idea can only become historical, dynamic and relational by locating it within a changing world in which the use of force to settle conflicts of interest becomes increasingly counterproductive. Of course as long as social conflicts are so deep-rooted and divisive that institutions claiming a monopoly of legitimate force are needed to sort them out, states remain in business. But identifying sovereignty with the imposition of order through force (and all the paradoxes that that generates), renders the concept impossibly problematic.

If we are to define it coherently, we have to detach sovereignty from the state. Statist sovereignty is absurd. It can only be (provisionally) justified if it contributes to the creation of (poststatal) communities in which the sovereignty of individuals as relational and autonomous beings takes root. If this is a 'utopian' vision, it is one which is rooted in the contradictory realities of the liberal state. For the modern state is premised upon what I have called elsewhere (Hoffman, 1988: 158–9) 'subversive abstractions' which embody a conflict between an emancipatory form and despotic content.

These subversive abstractions also inform the notion of an international 'anarchy' composed of sovereign states all of which are (in a legal sense) free and equal. It is true that the egalitarian sovereignty of states coexists with a deepening material inequality between them. But if it is naive to take egalitarian statism at face value, it is also wrong to ignore its emancipatory potential. Rosenberg, for example, argues that the abstract equality of modern states has no implications for concrete 'material' practice, just as he denies that the egalitarianism of universal suffrage can pose any kind of challenge to the class hierarchies of capitalism (1994: 89). Yet on both counts he fails to see that it is precisely the tension between the egalitarian form and despotic content within the liberal sovereign state which invites and stimulates emancipatory argument.

Rosenberg argues that even if all the world's governments were political democracies, and the UN constituted a world assembly wielding executive authority through majority voting, this would do nothing for a more egalitarian global development (1994: 89). Yet the notion of a democratic government, which Rosenberg assumes is unproblematic, already implies a notion of sovereignty which is in tension with the hierarchical institutions of the state. A reformed UN in which member states could exercise majoritarian control would inevitably produce (and have been produced by) powerful pressures for *material* change.

The point is that because liberal statist egalitarianism is abstract, it is fluid, unstable and contradictory. It is out of the tensions and contentions which this egalitarianism generates, that the possibility of a poststatist sovereignty arises. In making a case for detaching sovereignty from the state in the spirit of a 'utopian realism', we need to point to the way in which a poststatist concept of sovereignty is struggling to emerge from the contradictory logic of the liberal state.

References

Bartelson, J. (1995) *A Genealogy of Sovereignty*. Cambridge: Cambridge University Press.
Biersteker, T. J. and Weber, C. (eds) (1996) *State Sovereignty as Social Construct*. Cambridge: Cambridge University Press.
Bull, H. (1977) *The Anarchical Society*. Basingstoke: Macmillan.
Clastres, P. (1977) *Society against the State*. New York: Urizen.
D'Entreves, A. (1967) *The Notion of the State*. Oxford: Clarendon Press.
Easton, D. (1953) *The Political System*. New York: Alfred Knopf.
Easton, D. (1981) 'The Political System Besieged by the State', *Political Theory*, **9**, 303–25.
Forsyth, M. (1987) 'State', in D. Miller *et al.* (eds) *The Blackwell Encyclopedia of Political Thought*. Oxford: Blackwell.
Gallie, W. (1955) 'Essentially Contested Concepts', *Proceedings of the Aristotelian Society*, **56**, 167–98.
Harding, S. (1990) 'Feminism, Science and the Anti-Enlightenment Critique', in L. Nicholson (ed.) *Feminism/Postmodernism*. New York and London: Routledge.
Hinsley, F. (1986) *Sovereignty*. Cambridge: Cambridge University Press.
Hoffman, J. (1988) *State, Power and Democracy*. Brighton: Harvester.
Hoffman, J. (1995) *Beyond the State*. Cambridge: Polity.

Hollis, M. and Smith, S. (1990) *Explaining and Understanding International Relations*. Oxford: Clarendon Press.

James, A. (1986) *Sovereign Statehood*. London: Allen and Unwin.

Mair, L. (1962) *Primitive Government*. Harmondsworth: Penguin.

Murphy, A. (1996) 'The Sovereign State System as Political-Territorial Ideal', in T. J. Biersteker and C. Weber (eds) *State Sovereignty as Social Construct*. Cambridge: Cambridge University Press.

Nettl, P. (1967–8) 'The State as Conceptual Variable', *World Politics*, **20**, 559–92.

Newman, M. (1996) *Democracy, Sovereignty and the European Union*. London: Hurst.

Nicholson, M. and Reynolds, P. (1967) 'General Systems, the International System, and the Eastonian Analysis', *Political Studies*, **15**, 12–31.

Nicholson, P. (1984) 'Politics and Force', in A. Leftwich (ed.) *What is Politics?* Oxford: Blackwell.

Onuf, N. (1991) 'Sovereignty: Outline of a Conceptual History', *Alternatives*, **16**, 425–46.

Parekh, B. (1990) 'When Will the State Wither Away?', *Alternatives*, **15**, 247–62.

Roberts, S. (1979) *Order and Dispute*. Harmondsworth: Penguin.

Rosenberg, J. (1994) *The Empire of Civil Society*. London: Verso.

Taylor, P. (1991) 'British Sovereignty and the European Community: What is at Risk?', *Millennium*, **20**, 73–80.

Taylor, T. (ed.) (1978) *Approaches and Theory in International Relations*. Harlow: Longman.

Weber, C. (1995) *Simulating Sovereignty*. Cambridge: Cambridge University Press.

Wight, M. (1966) 'Why Is There No International Theory', in M. Wight and H. Butterfield (eds) *Diplomatic Investigations*. London: Allen and Unwin.

CHAPTER 2

What Has Happened to the Sovereignty of Parliament?

R. L. BORTHWICK

The sovereignty of Parliament has fallen on hard times. In the late nineteenth century it was put on a pedestal by Dicey and others who regarded it as the 'secret source of strength' of the British constitution. A century later commentators are less kind. One has described it as 'the last refuge of the constitutional scoundrel' (Lewis, *International Herald Tribune*, 1 November 1995), while another has suggested it is 'something reassuring to suck when things look bad, the mental equivalent of a boiled sweet' (Marr, 1996: 111). The task of this chapter is to explore how and why this change has occurred.

The doctrine of the sovereignty of Parliament has acquired an almost mythical status in Britain. For students of politics and the parliamentary system it is traditionally held as one of the central explanatory planks of the British constitution; perhaps the key to that constitution. For judges and lawyers it is no less important: for them it is central in defining the relationship between Parliament and the courts. In effect there are two versions of the sovereignty of Parliament. In the broad sense it is almost a substitute for the British constitution. In the narrow sense it governs the relationship between judges and Parliament.

For Dicey there were two central parts to the idea of the sovereignty of Parliament. First, that Parliament (by which he meant monarch, Lords and Commons) 'has, under the English constitution, the right to make or unmake any law whatever' and secondly 'that no person or body is recognized by the law of England as having a right to override or set aside the legislation of Parliament' (Dicey, 1959: 39–40). In essence, Dicey was asserting that Parliament was sovereign in the sense that it could legislate on any topic it wished and that there was no higher authority that could be appealed to. Implicit in the notion was that no Parliament could bind its successors.

Since Dicey first articulated these views (though, of course, the ideas themselves go back much further than Dicey), there has been considerable debate about both the status and the content of the doctrine. Its status is unclear because no source can be given for the idea. Is it, therefore, simply part of the common law inheritance? If so, it clearly has a special status; it is not something which can be amended by statute law in the way that other bits of common law can be superseded.

As Jennings pointed out, '[sovereignty] is a word of quasi-theological origin which may easily lead us into difficulties' (1959: 147). Despite his warning it would be fair to say that the difficulties have not been avoided. Part of the lack of clarity arises from the central ambiguity of the concept of sovereignty. The term straddles two related issues: first the idea of the sovereign state in international relations and secondly the idea that within that state Parliament is the supreme source of authority.

The idea of the sovereign state has a long and distinguished ancestry deriving from the ideas of Bodin and Hobbes via Bentham down to Austin. Central to this tradition is the notion of an identifiable person or body to whom we pay habitual obedience and who has the ability to enforce their commands and to make the ultimate decisions. It follows from this view that there must be in every political system an ultimate source of authority; in the case of Britain, that is Parliament. The theory has a superficial attractiveness: it appears to offer a clear and decisive answer to the question of where power ultimately lies and to provide a definite source for decisions within the territorial area of the British state (and indeed beyond in the heyday of empire).

An alternative view of the organization of the state seeks to deny the need for a single sovereign body. Some federal systems like the USA are founded on the attempt to escape from the constraints, or dangers, of sovereign power. In the American example there is a fundamental law, the Constitution, which is superior to ordinary law. In this system the legislature is not sovereign both in the sense that the Constitution goes to great lengths to separate and balance the powers of the different branches of government but also in the particular sense that legislation is subject to review by the judicial branch, ultimately in the Supreme Court. This power, as is well known, is not explicitly set out in the American Constitution but has been accepted ever since Chief Justice Marshall asserted it in the case of *Marbury v. Madison* in 1803.

Nothing could be further from the British/English tradition, in which the judges have been encouraged to think in terms of the sovereignty of Parliament. Indeed one of the most important aspects of that doctrine is its role in defining the relationship between Parliament and the judiciary. For several centuries judges have accepted that Parliament is the rightful source of the law and that it is not their role to challenge Parliament's legislative supremacy.

The purpose of the rest of this chapter is to examine the challenges which the sovereignty of Parliament has faced and continues to face. Some of these are political: the rise of the executive branch and the role of groups, for example. Some are political and legal, notably the impact of Britain's membership of the European Communities/Union and the consequences that flow from the passage of the European Communities Act 1972. Some challenges are more narrowly legal, particularly the growing confidence of the judiciary and what has been perceived as a challenge from that quarter to traditional notions of parliamentary supremacy. Finally, there are possible developments which, if they come to pass, will have an impact on the position of Parliament. Among these are the growing demands for the use of the referendum, the introduction of a written constitution and the incorporation of a bill of rights into British law.

Not all of these challenges are of equal weight, but their combined impact is sufficient to raise questions about the continued utility of the concept of the sovereignty of Parliament.

The challenge from the executive

Even as Dicey was polishing his observations on the nature of parliamentary sovereignty, political factors were working to make Parliament subservient to the executive rather than the other way round. Outwardly nothing changed: legislation duly passed by the Commons, Lords and sanctified by the Royal Assent remained the supreme source of legal authority in the land. The reality was, however, that the growth of disciplined parties following the 1867 Reform Act, together with the extension of the franchise culminating in universal adult suffrage by 1928, meant that decisions about government, having passed from the monarch to Parliament, now moved on to the electorate. To that extent political sovereignty no longer belonged to Parliament but to the people.

On lesser questions, concerning, for example, the shape and content of legislation, the effective sovereign power was no longer Parliament's but belonged to the executive. Governments were able to act in a cohesive way because they were backed by a disciplined party in the House of Commons. They were able to get their way over the outputs of the system because they combined that discipline with control of the timetable of the Commons. By 1902 this control had been cemented in the Balfour reforms of that year, which guaranteed the government of the day the lion's share of parliamentary time in return for recognition of the rights of the Opposition and backbenchers. From then on there could be no question that the executive controlled the Commons, and thus notions of parliamentary sovereignty, whatever their legal accuracy, were not much use for describing the distribution of political power.

Government domination of the system was reinforced by the reduction in the powers of the House of Lords. The 1911 Parliament Act made clear that the Lords could in future delay, but not ultimately prevent, the wishes of the Commons (in effect the government) from prevailing. Thus one of the checks in the system was weakened. Of Dicey's trinity of Commons, Lords and monarch, the decisive voice belonged to the Commons. What was also clear was that while the voice might belong to the Commons, the words spoken would most often be those of the government of the day.

In an age when popular election confers legitimacy, it is hard to resist the argument that the only popularly elected part of national government should be dominant. Equally hard to resist is the argument that effective direction of government business demands a disciplined party. Certainly for much of the twentieth century the House of Commons has been an arena dominated by governments formed from a single party. Notwithstanding periods of coalition government and shorter periods of minority government, the prevailing model has been of single-party government able to enact most of its legislative programme. That model has been reinforced by the development of the doctrine of the mandate, whereby the proposals of that government are deemed to have been authorized by the electorate if they were in the winning party's manifesto.

With single-party governments effectively in control of the House of Commons, the idea of the sovereignty of Parliament became something of a fiction. The laws that passed owed much more to the wishes of the cabinet than to the views of Parliament. Perhaps the high point of this system was reached in the period 1945–70, when governments rarely had serious trouble from the House of Commons over their legislation.

According to Norton, MPs became more difficult after 1970 (Norton, 1980). The Labour government of 1974–9, admittedly in a minority for part of its life, had considerable difficulties with Parliament. The Thatcher governments which followed it had fewer problems, but that was due in part to the larger majorities which they enjoyed. Even Thatcher with a majority in excess of 100 could be defeated on a Shops Bill and forced to backtrack on other items by pressure from the backbenches. The Major governments after 1990, and especially after 1992, had considerable problems with Parliament, that process being exacerbated by the gradual erosion of its majority in the four years after 1992.

At its height, executive domination of Parliament was evident not just in the content of legislation. It affected the whole way in which things were done. Reform of parliamentary procedure, for example, was

largely determined by the government: changes were made which
suited them, and changes which might have made their life more
difficult were resisted, usually successfully. Thus, for a very long time,
there was little or no provision of facilities for MPs: such things as office
space and support staff were judged unnecessary, and MPs even had to
pay their own postage costs. Similarly there was no great belief in the
need for detailed scrutiny of executive action. A few committees existed
in the Commons: Public Accounts, Estimates and so on, but little
detailed examination of the work of government took place outside
these few committees. The argument advanced by government, and
accepted by many on the backbenches, was that scrutiny was best
carried out on the floor of the House through such devices as Question
Time and debates.

It is understandable that governments should subscribe to such views
and that Opposition frontbenches should share them. The broad lines of
these views remain in place though there have been changes: changes of
personnel which mean that backbenchers are less amenable to
leadership; in facilities (accommodation, staff and resources); and in
structures, notably the expansion of the select committee system in the
Commons in 1979.

But there are still limits: suggestions, for example, that the legislative
process might be improved by evidence-taking sessions at the start of
the committee stage of legislation have mostly not been accepted. It
remains true also that Parliament can offer little by way of a career
structure. For the most part, the career aims of MPs remain centred on
the executive: to become a minister is the best prospect of exercising
influence.

Executive dominance over Parliament extends beyond the activities
of prime minister and government. A consequence of the growth of
government in the twentieth century has been an increase in delegated
or subordinate legislation. This type of legislation has presented
particular difficulties for Parliament and has raised further questions
about its ability to control matters.

In the interwar period some members of the judiciary, most famously
Lord Chief Justice Hewart in *The New Despotism*, became much exercised
about this growing power. Other observers were more relaxed. Mount
remarks that Jennings writing at almost the same time as Hewart saw
little danger: 'For Jennings, these [bureaucratic] growths were benign,
and, within the limits of good sense, to be encouraged to grow further,
as part of the "modernizing" of the British Constitution' (Mount, 1992:
67). Whichever view is taken, there is not much doubt that much of this
type of law-making is effectively in the hands of civil servants with a
very limited degree of parliamentary control.

The traditional means for Parliament to exercise more general control over the civil service has been through the doctrine of ministerial responsibility. Over the years this doctrine has been discussed and its effectiveness much questioned. Whatever limited effect it has had is now in further doubt as increasingly civil service activities are conducted in semiautonomous agencies under the Next Steps programme. Parliament's ability to extract information about such activities has inevitably been diminished.

To the extent that party discipline has become less reliable towards the century's end, it is possible to speak of some resurgence in Parliament as a decision-making body. At the same time Parliament's public reputation is at a low ebb. Respect for it and its members is low. However, to form a fuller picture of the part played by Parliament, it is necessary to move beyond its relations with the executive.

The challenge from Europe

Of all the threats to the supremacy of Parliament none is more serious than the challenge presented by the United Kingdom's membership of the European Communities and now the European Union. Other challenges, for example from a powerful executive, did not in the end alter the legal basis on which Parliament operated. They affected the political reality but not the formal, legal position. With membership of the Community this is a position much harder to maintain. Since joining the European Economic Community (EEC) on 1 January 1973 something fundamental has happened to the sovereignty of Parliament.

Britain's accession to the EEC was effected by passage of the European Communities Act 1972. Under this Act, the UK acceded to the Treaty of Rome and accepted the obligations of membership of the Communities. Section 2 of the European Communities Act laid down that 'parliamentary statutes, "both past and future", take effect subject to Community law' (Peele, 1995: 36). In other words, it was explicitly accepted by the Westminster parliament that from now on Community law was superior to UK law. It was some time, however, before the full implications of this change sank in.

In part this was because there were, during the 1972 Act's passage through Parliament, disingenuous statements to the effect that the sovereignty of Parliament was unaffected by the passage of the Act and by Britain's entry into the Community. In a very limited sense the claim that sovereignty was unaffected could be justified in that the UK parliament could in principle change its mind. Part of the doctrine of the sovereignty of parliament had always been that no parliament could bind its successors and so it was open in theory for a later parliament to take Britain out of the Community. Short of that, however, it is hard to see how it could be argued that the sovereignty of Parliament was unaffected by the 1972 Act.

Nevertheless the desire to reassure Parliament and public that nothing fundamental was being changed by entry to the Community ran very deeply. Indeed, it perhaps still does: during the debates on the legislation enacting the Maastricht Treaty twenty years later, John Major was at pains to reassure the House of Commons that the sovereignty of Parliament was unaffected by anything in the treaty (*House of Commons Debates* 12 May 1992, col. 493; see also MacCormick, 1993: 1).

Yet it was clear that Community law would in future take precedence over national law. If it did not, it was hard to see in what sense one could speak of this being a community/union rather than merely an intergovernmental agreement. In that respect membership of the Community entailed much greater obligations than, say, Britain's membership of the North Atlantic Treaty Organization (NATO) or the International Monetary Fund (IMF). Membership of international organizations like those could certainly be argued to involve some loss of national sovereignty, in the sense that a state's freedom to do as it wishes is inevitably restricted. However, such organizations have a much narrower focus and lack much of the apparatus of government associated with the EC/EU, especially a constitutional court with what proved to be extensive jurisdiction.

Laws proposed by the European Commission are subject to the approval of the Council of Ministers. But then they take effect: directly, if made as regulations or indirectly, via implementation by the member states, if made as directives. In that context the right of veto possessed by member states could be said to be some protection. In so far as that right of veto has been weakened under the Single European Act and is likely to be further diminished as qualified majority voting becomes more extensively used, the protections for nation-states are weakened.

That weakness is exacerbated in the case of the British parliament by the difficulty which Westminster has had in adapting its procedures to the demands of Community membership. It has proved very difficult for MPs to exercise any effective voice in legislative proposals coming from Brussels. Even if the proposals can be debated in a timely manner, there is no guarantee that opinions expressed at Westminster will carry any weight in meetings of European ministers. Even if British ministers are persuaded by Parliament, they may well be outvoted in meetings of the Council of Ministers.

The superiority of European law over British law has gradually become more and more apparent. Initially, much of this was glossed over. The role of the European Court of Justice in relation to national courts is explicit in the Treaty of Rome:

Under Article 177 of the Treaty of Rome, if a legal dispute reaches the House of Lords (the final court of appeal in the British system), there *must* be a reference (a formal request for a ruling) to the Court of the European Community (ECJ), which has the task of harmonizing laws within the member states. (Peele, 1995: 36)

In the case of lower courts such a reference is optional.

For some time after Britain's accession, conflicts seemed to be muted. In recent years however the conflicts have become much more apparent. In part this is because, as Peele suggests, British courts have shifted from relying on the 1972 European Communities Act to relying 'on the structure of the Community and the priority of its treaties for their reasoning' (Peele, 1995: 36). In part it is probably due to a greater self-confidence within the European Court which has emerged more and more as the main instrument for asserting the superiority of Community law over national law. Some credit should be given to successive British governments for their willingness to accept the rulings of the European Court because the court's enforcement mechanisms in the absence of national compliance with its rulings are somewhat unclear.

In some areas new European law has simply taken precedence. As a result member states are governed in an increasing part of their law by rules made in Brussels. For example, in a whole range of cases involving such issues as the retirement age for women; the rules surrounding maternity leave; prescription charges for men over 60 and the levying of VAT, Britain now finds itself governed by rules made in Brussels and interpreted by a Court in Luxembourg.

In other areas it seems the power is negative in the sense that British ministers now find themselves arguing that things cannot be done at Westminster because of European rules. For example, in March 1996 a transport minister opposed legislation to ban 'bull-bars' on the grounds that the government would be prevented from imposing such a ban because of European competition rules (*The Times*, 30 March 1996). A similar argument had been used earlier in various other road traffic matters such as seat-belts on coaches. In effect then it appears in such areas legal competence has been ceded to Brussels.

It has also become clear beyond any doubt that laws passed prior to Britain's accession to the Community can in effect be annulled if they conflict with European rules. This was the implication of the decision in the *Do-It-All* case in which the 1950 Shops Act was in effect overturned (Wade, 1991: 3–4). Such a decision was always likely at some point, given the wording of Section 2 of the European Communities Act.

Perhaps the most striking and unambiguous demonstration of the new realities of legislative power has been in relation to the UK parliament's Merchant Shipping Act of 1988. This Act was designed to deal with the problem of Spanish fishermen registering as British in order to take advantage of the UK's quotas under the European Fisheries policy. The aim of the Act was to prevent non-British nationals registering their vessels as British. The disadvantaged Spanish fishermen took legal action alleging that the Act infringed their rights under European law. The case, which has become known as the *Factortame* case, was dealt with first by the European Court of Justice in 1990 in an interim judgment when the matter was referred to it by the House of Lords.

The claimants sought in effect two things: the suspension of the 1988 Act and interim compensation for the losses they incurred as a result of its passage, pending a final decision in the case. When the case reached the House of Lords as the highest court of appeal, the Law Lords decided that, in accordance with the traditional doctrine of the sovereignty of Parliament, they had no power to set aside an Act of Parliament by issuing an interim injunction restraining the Secretary of State for Transport from complying with the Act. At the same time 'the House of Lords referred to the European Court of Justice the question of whether there was an "overriding principle of Community law" that required national courts to secure effective interim protection for the applicants' rights in Community law' (Bradley, 1994: 96).

In its 1990 judgment the European Court told the Lords that in order to achieve compliance with Community law, it must disallow the 1988 Merchant Shipping Act by restraining the Secretary of State from complying with it. 'Any legal rule or judicial practice which might withhold from the national court the power to ensure the full effect of community rules was contrary to Community law. Thus, any rule of national law that prevented a court from granting interim relief had to be set aside by that court' (Bradley, 1994: 96–7).

In effect the House of Lords was told that it had been wrong to believe that it was prevented from disallowing, even temporarily, an Act of Parliament. The traditional view that the courts cannot question what Parliament has decided has been described by one observer as simplistic and no longer appropriate in a situation where domestic law must give way to Community law (Wade, 1991: 2).

There could be no clearer evidence that the doctrine of parliamentary sovereignty, as traditionally understood by the judiciary in the UK, had been seriously eroded. A British court was compelled to exercise what Americans would recognize as judicial review, albeit at the behest of a higher European authority.

The judgment established a number of things: first, that an Act of the UK parliament could be overruled by the European Court of Justice; secondly, that courts must grant interim relief if compliance with European law demanded that; and thirdly, what the European Court in effect said was that the 1972 European Communities Act, under which the UK agreed to accept the supremacy of Community law, must take precedence over the 1988 Merchant Shipping Act. This interpretation means that the traditional element of parliamentary sovereignty that no parliament can bind its successors is now much less certain.

Thus the House of Lords was left with little option but to reverse itself which it duly did despite the political protests which greeted the European Court's judgment. As Wade has observed:

> Factortame shows how international law, in the shape of treaty obligations, may help to overthrow the dogmas of constitutional law, and how smoothly the courts may discard fundamental doctrine without appearing to notice. (Wade, 1991: 4)

The protests which greeted the 1990 judgment were to be repeated in 1995 and 1996 when the case again made headlines as the European Court ruled that the British government must compensate the Spanish fishermen for the losses sustained during the period in which they had been prevented from fishing under the 1988 Act. The sense of outrage which this verdict early in 1996 generated was considerable. Yet in a sense it was entirely consistent with the earlier judgment. Nevertheless, in the highly charged Euro-sceptical atmosphere of the mid 1990s it was sufficient to provoke demands that the British government ignore the ruling of the European Court.

This requirement that Britain compensate the Spanish fishermen was seen in some quarters as one more piece of evidence that the European Court was becoming the main engine of greater European integration and an important instrument in the development of a European superstate. 'The European Court of Justice is the real force acting on what has been referred to as the ratchet of European centralization and the creation of full political union' (I. Duncan Smith, The Times, 12 March 1996). What particularly worried the critics was the absence of any kind of formal constitution for Europe other than the major treaties. Students of American history are familiar with the way in which a court was able to claim for itself successfully the power to decide what a constitution meant and whether laws both national and state were compatible with it.

However, it is hard to avoid the conclusion that Factortame is a logical outcome of the decision in 1972 to join the European Community. That decision was further cemented by the passage of the Single European Act and the adoption of the Maastricht Treaty. Many British MPs are only belatedly catching up with the fact that passage of the European Communities Act of 1972 means that 'Acts of Parliament are now subject to a higher law and to that extent they now rank as second-tier legislation' (Wade, 1991: 3).

The challenge from the courts

There have been growing claims in recent years that the courts in Britain are prepared to be much more assertive in relation to other branches of government than has traditionally been the case. As we have seen, the traditional position of the courts in relation to Parliament has been defined by a strict interpretation of parliamentary sovereignty: it is not their right to challenge laws properly passed by Parliament. They might however legitimately challenge the actions of officials if they were, in the court's view, exceeding the powers granted them under statute.

Over the past twenty years there has been a considerable growth in the applications for and the granting of judicial review. Among many examples is the House of Lords overruling the decision of the Home Secretary to ignore the rules approved by Parliament for criminal injuries compensation. Apart from the cases where the courts find ministers and others to have exceeded their powers under statute, there have been in recent years a number of well-publicized disputes between ministers and judges in such areas as sentencing policy.

These disputes, though important, do not represent a challenge to parliamentary sovereignty, but they are partly responsible for the sense that there is a growing rivalry between the courts and other branches of government. Certainly headlines such as 'Speaker warns courts on powers' (*The Times*, 22 July 1993) and 'Labour law chief attacks judges' supremacy claim' (*The Times*, 16 October 1995) give the impression that Parliament's supremacy is under challenge. Such headlines reflect a concern that the courts may be straying into areas that have traditionally been regarded as the prerogative of Parliament. The first of these headlines was prompted by the legal challenge to the Maastricht Treaty which seemed to some to be in danger of running counter to a traditional separation of roles which was enshrined in the bill of rights at the end of the seventeenth century. In the event the judges dismissed the attempt to block the implementation of the Maastricht Treaty. Although that particular challenge disappeared, it served to draw attention to the fact that one of the features which limits parliamentary sovereignty in practice is the royal prerogative. Under this, ministers are able to exercise powers over such things as declaring war and signing treaties which are not subject to parliamentary approval. However, the argument among the defenders of Parliament was that it was up to the latter to attempt to control the prerogative, and Parliament should not look to the judges to help them do this.

There have been more general worries among some parliamentarians that the judiciary were becoming too assertive. In 1995 the Shadow Lord Chancellor, Lord Irvine, suggested that some members of the judiciary were supporting a new interpretation of the constitution which represented a challenge to the traditional notions of parliamentary sovereignty. Such judges, he suggested, 'say that Parliament and judges share sovereignty and are co-equal in their respective spheres' (*The Times*, 16 October 1995). Although he proclaimed his faith in parliamentary sovereignty, it was not entirely clear why Lord Irvine had such faith in the doctrine's ability to deal with the problems which had come before the courts. It has been argued that part of the explanation for the growing assertiveness of the judiciary has been the inability of Parliament to operate effectively as a protector of the citizen or as a real check to the exercise of ministerial powers. There is no doubt that to some extent judges have seen themselves exercising a degree of independence of which Parliament is incapable. Of course, members of the judiciary deny that their aim is to challenge the authority of Parliament.

Some have argued that the power of the judges to challenge Parliament would be greatly enhanced if the UK were to incorporate the European Convention on Human Rights into British law and to that topic we now turn.

The European Convention on Human Rights and a written constitution

Although the UK signed the European Declaration of Human Rights as long ago as 1951, it has resisted incorporating the Convention into British law. This means that British citizens may take their grievances to the European Court of Human Rights in Strasbourg but that action under the Convention is not possible in the British courts.

Despite this, there has been no shortage of cases from Britain finding their way to Strasbourg, and British governments have, in a number of them, come in for criticism from the European Court of Human Rights. Adverse decisions of that court do not have full legal force; in that respect they are different in status from judgments of the European Court of Justice. However, in practice, British governments have not wanted to be seen to be flouting too often the judgment of the court, and a good many have been complied with.

Such a state of affairs leads to two reactions. The first is that in practice, if not in constitutional theory, Parliament's authority is affected by the verdicts of the European Court of Human Rights. Secondly, adverse judgments from the court add to the sense of resentment felt in some quarters about the steady encroachment into British life of European rulings. The fact that the rulings are not technically binding matters little if they are likely to be adhered to. In that respect such

judgments merely confirm the suspicions of those who see a growing
European threat to the freedom of manoeuvre of the British parliament.
The extent of that concern was evident in early 1996 when, it was
reported, the Lord Chancellor was planning to lobby other European
countries for limits to be put on the court, particularly by ensuring that
it pays 'full regard to the decisions by democratic legislatures and
differing legal traditions' (*The Times*, 9 April 1996).

One question which has been much discussed is whether the
European Convention should be added to British law, to form in effect a
new bill of rights. Discussion of such incorporation is part of a wider
debate about the desirability of a bill of rights and perhaps a written
constitution. Leaving aside the issue of whether such a move would be
desirable, there are questions as to whether it is possible under the
traditional norms of parliamentary sovereignty and what the effect on
Parliament would be if it were to happen.

When the doctrine of the sovereignty of Parliament held sway, it was
widely believed that it would be either impossible or meaningless to
add something like a bill of rights to the British statute book. Such a
document would have no special status: it would therefore be possible
for any subsequent parliament to amend it or abolish it. To put matters
in another way, there was no mechanism for entrenching such a
guarantee of rights in the British system. By extension the same
argument made it impossible for a written constitution to be given a
special status in a system dominated by parliamentary sovereignty.

Such a view may still be correct, but to the extent that confidence in
parliamentary sovereignty has been weakened, it is perhaps no longer
the end of the story. Two lines of approach have been raised. The first is
to ask whether it would be possible to incorporate the European
Convention into British law by means of a piece of legislation
comparable to the European Communities Act of 1972. Wade has raised
the question of whether recent interpretations of that Act (notably in
the *Factortame* case) provide any parallels. He admits however that the
argument is weaker in this case than it is in relation to membership of
the European Communities (Wade, 1991: 4). Others have argued that it
might be possible to enact a bill of rights that took precedence over past
law but that it would be more difficult to ensure that it took precedence
over later law. Nevertheless there are signs that even without
incorporation, the courts are beginning to pay attention to the
Convention (Bradley, 1994: 101).

An extension of this principle would be one possible way of adding a
bill of rights to UK law. This is what one authority has called the
'Interpretation Act' route. Under this approach, judges would be
required to take the text of a document such as the European
Convention into account when framing their judgments. Stronger

versions of incorporation would provide for a bill of rights which overrode existing legislation, while an even stronger version would give it precedence over subsequent legislation (Bradley, 1994: 102–3). The unanswered question is whether it would be possible to prevent subsequent legislation overriding such a bill. Devices like approval by referendum might serve to make such overriding more difficult.

There is a much greater willingness than was once the case to consider the idea of some written guarantees of fundamental rights as part of the UK system of government. However, that still leaves the problem of specifying the content of such guarantees and raises the inevitable concern that it may lead to greater power for judges. Certainly American experience would suggest that that is an inevitable outcome. That prospect worries even some of those who are sympathetic to the idea of a bill of rights.

The challenge from the referendum

Part of the doctrine of parliamentary sovereignty is that it is Parliament which decides on issues of public policy in Britain. That principle is challenged by the idea that on some issues the electorate themselves should decide through a referendum. Supporters of the referendum point to the fact that there have been three examples in the UK in the past 25 years: in Northern Ireland on the border in 1973, across the whole UK in 1975 on continuing membership of the EC and in Scotland and Wales in 1979 on devolution.

The status of the referendum in British constitutional theory is unclear. They have been held on a small number of occasions and yet they are still often described as contrary to our constitution. Opponents argue that Parliament is the proper place for matters to be decided. The growth in demands for referendums reflects the conjunction of a number of factors. The first is the declining status of Parliament: for some the verdict of Parliament is no longer sufficiently legitimate. Those reservations have coincided with the emergence of a number of constitutional issues, particularly those potentially involving loss of powers for the Westminster parliament, either to the European Union or to devolved assemblies within the UK.

Demands for referendums on various aspects of Britain's relations with Europe have persisted for some time. In 1993 efforts to secure a referendum on the Maastricht Treaty were unsuccessful but left proponents of the referendum arguing that the British electorate had been denied what had been available to their Danish and French counterparts. Subsequently there were loud demands for a referendum on a single European currency. At the time of writing it looks as though

these may bear fruit, in part because the referendum represents a way
for a divided Conservative Party to cope with the issue. The case for
such a referendum is strong, especially as it is impossible for the
electorate to express their view on the matter through a general
election.

On other issues too there is the possibility of a referendum being
used as a way of eliciting the electorate's opinion. Referendums on
reform of the electoral system and on Scottish and Welsh devolution
have been promised by the Labour Party. Clearly there are potential
difficulties in a situation without clear rules as to how referendums are
generated. Advocates of capital punishment have long been dissatisfied
with the verdict of Parliament and no doubt, there are numerous other
candidates for similar treatment.

Whatever the suitability of particular topics, the idea of letting voters
decide major constitutional issues will not go away. A political party
established to fight a general election on the issue may have the
potential to do damage to other parties. It is by no means clear that
MPs are still regarded as the most appropriate people to decide such
major issues. As an editorial in *The Economist* put it:

> It is simply not true that the sovereignty of Parliament is any longer the
> foundation of Britain's constitution. Parliamentary sovereignty, an idea
> rooted in 19th-century notions of representative government, has long
> been obsolete. (23 March 1996)

Conclusion

It will be apparent by now that the sovereignty of Parliament has a
strange status in British constitutional theory. On the one hand it is
claimed as one of the central props of the constitution, perhaps *the*
central idea underpinning it; on the other, it is argued by many that it
no longer exists.

The challenges which the idea has had to face have been
considerable. Executive domination of Parliament is so familiar a feature
of the British system that it is hard to imagine the system operating in
any other way. Yet in the late twentieth century the ineffectiveness of
Parliament has again become an issue. The standing of Parliament, as
highlighted by inquiries such as Nolan's, is not high. Many of its own
members have been highly critical of it. Its ability to discover what the
executive is doing, as revealed by the Scott Report, is not impressive.
Against such a background, for Parliament to claim that it is sovereign
strains credibility.

More tangible as a challenge has been Britain's membership of the

European Union. It is clear that that has meant parliamentary supremacy is much diminished. The role of European institutions, especially the Court of Justice, has had a major impact on Parliament's ability to decide what laws apply within the UK. It is an unresolved question whether, *de facto*, the European Court of Human Rights is heading in the same direction of supplanting Parliament's authority.

Demands for greater use of the referendum reflect the diminished status of Parliament. If these demands are conceded, and in some instances the case for doing so is strong, that will do little to enhance the supremacy of Parliament. Other changes too may have an impact on the practical application of the doctrine, for example moves towards devolution, the possible addition of a bill of rights and even of a written constitution.

So as we approach the century's end, the ghost of Dicey seems hardly likely to frighten anyone. Lip-service is still paid to the sovereignty of Parliament but it is hard to see what substance there is to it any longer. It may still have a little life in its narrow sense as guide to the judiciary, but even in that guise it has been badly dented by European developments. In its wider political sense, it is increasingly difficult to give the concept much substantive content.

References

Bradley, A. W. (1994) 'The Sovereignty of Parliament − in Perpetuity?', in J. Jowell and D. Oliver (eds) *The Changing Constitution*, 3rd edn. Oxford: Oxford University Press.

Dicey, A. V. (1959) *Introduction to the Study of the Law of the Constitution*, 10th edn 1959; 1st edn 1885. London: Macmillan.

Jennings, Sir W. I. (1959) *The Law and the Constitution*, 5th edn 1959; 1st edn 1933. London: University of London Press.

MacCormick, N. (1993) 'Beyond the Sovereign State', *The Modern Law Review*, **56**, 1−18.

Marr, A. (1996) *Ruling Britannia*. Harmondsworth: Penguin.

Mount, F. (1992) *The British Constitution Now*. London: Heinemann.

Norton, P. (1980) 'The Changing Face of the British House of Commons in the 1970s', *Legislative Studies Quarterly*, **5**, 333−57.

Peele, G. (1995) *Governing the UK*, 3rd edn. Oxford: Blackwell.

Wade, H. W. R. (1991) 'What Has Happened to the Sovereignty of Parliament?', *The Law Quarterly Review*, **107**, 1−4.

Sovereignty and the European Union: Eroded, Enhanced, Fragmented

PHILIP LYNCH

Sovereignty is central to the debates about European integration currently under way within and between the nation-states of Western Europe. Yet in political analysis the term is contested, and in popular discourse often seems more likely to confuse than inform. Surveying its multiple uses before the creation of the European Union (EU),[1] Benn argued that 'there would seem to be a strong case for giving up so Protean a word' (Benn, 1955: 122).

A cursory examination of the British debate on 'Europe' shows it has developed still more, often contradictory, connotations. Thatcher takes a maximalist line on sovereignty, but has variously equated it with the legislative supremacy of Parliament; the independent policy-making capacity of the state or executive; the expression of democratic consent through election or referendum, and with nationhood and self-governance. Thompson quotes an unnamed colleague of Thatcher on her 'no' to membership of the Exchange Rate Mechanism (ERM) in 1985: 'she stood out on grounds of sovereignty, a concept she had read about somewhere but could never tell you where' (Thompson, 1996: 62). In contrast to Thatcher, Howe claims that 'sovereignty is not virginity, something you either have or you don't; a nation can add to its own strength ... by distributing a part of its sovereignty to a wider and more authoritative entity' (Howe, 1990: 679, 688).

Responding to Benn's critique of sovereignty, Stankiewicz claimed that

> the most significant developments that are likely to come out of the sovereignty concept in the future will be related to its ability to make classifications of political behaviour meaningful. Too much effort in the past has been spent on proving or disproving the concept and not enough on studying its potentialities as a tool of analysis. (1969: 298)

This chapter examines the concept of sovereignty in European integration theory, noting the different perspectives offered by statecentric and multilevel governance models, and assessing the impact of the EU on state sovereignty. It argues that only by viewing sovereignty as a multidimensional concept, and using it as a tool of political analysis in conjunction with concepts such as power, autonomy and legitimacy, can the complex relationship between European integration and sovereignty be fully understood.

Dimensions of sovereignty

Classic accounts of sovereignty tend to refer to the absolute authority of the state within a given territory, unrestrained by law, and its monopoly of legitimate force. But this raises further questions about the practical and normative limits to the exercise of sovereignty; the location of sovereignty; and the relationship between sovereignty and society (Camilleri and Falk, 1992: 18). Given the normative and empirical difficulties of establishing a single authoritative and verifiable definition, it is more productive to recognize different facets of sovereignty − state, constitutional and popular − in which European integration has had complex effects, and relate these to legitimacy, power and autonomy.

The *state dimension* locates sovereignty within the era of the modern state and of nationalism. It can be further subdivided: state sovereignty has a territorial element, defining the physical limits of sovereign power and legitimacy; a functional element, concerning the limits of the state's economic, social and administrative role; and an external element, the recognition that the sovereign authority within the state has exclusive rights of jurisdiction over its citizens, and that states have equal standing under international law. State sovereignty is also connected to nationhood through the doctrine of national self-determination (the fusion of 'nation' and 'people' in the nation-building process, and the right of nations to sovereign statehood), and its symbolic importance within civic nationalism.

The *constitutional dimension* addresses the location of sovereign power within the polity and its constitutional standing. The doctrine of the supremacy of Parliament is a cornerstone of the British constitution. For Dicey, parliamentary sovereignty is 'the dominant characteristic of our constitution', establishing that Parliament has 'the right to make or unmake any law whatever; and further that no person or body is recognized by the law of England as having a right to override or set aside the legislation of Parliament' (Dicey, 1982: xviii). In turn, no parliament can bind its successors. However, the gap between the theory of parliamentary sovereignty and political reality is considerable, and notions of executive autonomy often prove more useful.

The *popular dimension* of sovereignty focuses on the relationship between state and society, exploring the conceptual links between sovereign power, democracy, legitimacy and individual rights. Popular sovereignty implies that the authority of the state derives from the consent of the political community.

Absolutist understandings of sovereignty are valid in legal theory (though this too is problematic, see MacCormick, 1993), but of limited efficacy for the political analysis of European integration. The subdivision of sovereignty into state, constitutional and popular dimensions helps unravel the variety of ways in which the EU has affected these areas, but further clarification on the nature of sovereignty, particularly in relation to other concepts, is still required. Held usefully distinguishes between *de jure* sovereignty (the supreme legal authority to take decisions) and *de facto* sovereignty (the practical exercise of sovereign authority) (Held, 1989). Analysis of the exercise and effectiveness of sovereignty is also aided by reference to autonomy, a state's capacity to achieve its desired results and control its destiny (Wallace, 1986: 368–9). This locates the sovereignty implications of the EU in a wider political, economic and security context, noting the constraints on state action arising from globalization and 'informal integration' (Wallace, 1994: 53–5). The global economy (multinational companies, the power of international finance markets), technological change (nuclear weapons, global communications), global or regional dilemmas which cross national borders (migration, terrorism, ecological problems) all limit the autonomy and the *de facto* sovereignty of the nation-state (Camilleri and Falk, 1992).

European integration and sovereignty

Disputes over the nature and desirability of state sovereignty, plus the implications of European integration for its various guises, have been prevalent in studies of the EU. Federalists eagerly anticipated the demise of the nation-state and the transfer of its sovereign authority to a European polity. Neofunctionalist theories predicted the erosion of state sovereignty as functions were transferred to more efficient supranational bodies through a technocratic process of 'spillover'. In contrast, neorealist or intergovernmentalist accounts stressed the resilience of the nation-state. Here, national governments are accorded dominant actor status, defending their sovereignty and national interests in areas of 'high politics'.

Since the launch of the Single European Market (SEM) project in the mid-1980s, studies of European integration have moved away from the sterile debate between neofunctionalists and intergovernmentalists. The EU does not comfortably fit traditional models of state development or international organization. It has not developed into a fully fledged federal state (although it has some state-like attributes, its core institutions are weak and have only limited autonomy), but neither is it simply an intergovernmental organization made up of autonomous states. Instead the EU is 'part framework for a continuous process of multilateral bargaining among state governments, part apex of a pattern of multi-level governance which has significantly weakened the centrality of the state' (Wallace, 1996: 451).

Community law: eroding sovereignty?

Community law has greater sovereignty implications than do general principles of international law. Weiler claims that the development of doctrines of direct effect, supremacy and implied powers, amount to a 'constitutionalization' of the EU's legal structure (Weiler, 1991, 1996). European Court of Justice (ECJ) judicial activism has 'constitutionalized' the treaties and fashioned federal-type relationships between the European Community (EC) and its member states by exercising judicial review, using national courts to confirm the supremacy of Community law, and extending the EC's policy competences. In the 1963 case *Van Gend en Loos*, the Court stated that:

> the Community constitutes a new legal order of international law for the benefit of which the states have limited their sovereign rights, albeit within limited fields, and the subjects of which comprise not only Member States but also their nationals.[2]

This formula was subsequently extended by the court, so that by 1986, the ECJ was defining the EC as a community based on the rule of law, with the treaty its constitutional charter.[3]

Community law has a number of attributes which have affected the state, constitutional and popular dimensions of sovereignty. It is integrated into the legal systems of the member states and has primacy: in cases of conflict, Community law takes priority over national law. Treaty provisions and regulations are directly applicable in all member states, their legal effects occurring automatically, without the need for further legislative action at national level. Under the principle of direct effect, provisions of Community law which confer rights or impose obligations on individuals are recognized and enforced by national courts. The ECJ has extended this principle and has taken a strict line on breaches of obligation. National courts are obliged to apply fully Community law and overturn any provision of national law which conflicts with it, whether the national law was made prior or subsequent to the Community rule. National courts are also, on occasion, obliged to seek a preliminary ruling from the Court of Justice on questions of interpretation of Community law. The ECJ itself determines which norms come within the sphere of Community law, using this *Kompetenz-Kompetenz* to develop, extend and expand Community competence, notably on individual and social rights (Weiler, 1991). In addition to EC legislation and ECJ jurisprudence, 'soft law' — rules of conduct which guide the actions of states, institutions and individuals but which are not legally enforceable — also shapes EC governance (Bulmer, 1994: 367–8).

Community law and the member states

In Britain, the supremacy of Community law was illustrated in the *Factortame* case which overturned an Act of Parliament, parts of which were found to be contrary to Community law. The 1988 Merchant Shipping Act sought to prevent non-British citizens registering their boats as British in order to qualify for the United Kingdom's Common Fisheries Policy quota. A number of Spanish fishermen duly challenged the Act under Community law and applied for interim relief (the suspension of the new rules pending a final verdict). The House of Lords, aware that the doctrine of parliamentary sovereignty cautioned it against suspending the application of an Act of Parliament, referred to the Court of Justice for a preliminary ruling.[4] In 1990 the ECJ ruled that to comply with Community law, the Act had to be 'disapplied' and interim relief granted (Pollard and Ross, 1994: 397–406). The government passed an Order in Council reversing the offending sections of the 1988 Act.

The 'disapplication' of an Act of Parliament provoked Euro-sceptic hostility, yet the outcome was not unexpected. Thus, Lord Bridge noted that the overriding of national legislation and granting of interim relief in protection of rights under Community law, was a reaffirmation of the supremacy of Community law rather than a 'novel attack' on parliamentary sovereignty (Pollard and Ross, 1994: 404–5).[5] The European Communities Act 1972 gave present and future Community law its legal force and required UK courts to defer to it. Although the Act avoided an explicit statement of the supremacy of Community law, it denied effectiveness to national legislation which conflicts with it (Lasok and Bridge, 1994: 359–62).

The supremacy of Community law is not, however, limitless. In 1979, Lord Denning stated that

if the time should come when our Parliament deliberately passes an Act –
with the intention of repudiating the Treaty or any provision of it – or
intentionally of acting inconsistently with it – and says so in express terms
– then I should have thought that it would be the duty of our courts to
follow the statute of our Parliament ... Unless there is such an intentional
and express repudiation of the Treaty, it is our duty to give priority to the
Treaty. (Quoted in Collins, 1990: 33)[6]

Denning's view that deliberate repudiations of Community law should
be treated differently from inadvertent incompatibility won widespread
support. Although the 1972 Act saw Parliament bind its successors by
giving legal force to future Community legislation, it did not prevent a
future parliament from repealing the European Communities Act.
Parliamentary sovereignty is not defunct, but depends on political will
for its fullest expression. Ultimately, the relationship between
Community and national law cannot be fully appreciated in legal
theory, but must take account of political power and interests. Although
the treaties do not contain a secession clause, a future UK parliament
could repeal the European Communities Act and leave the EU, though
the practical problems of doing so should not be underestimated.

A number of recent ECJ rulings against the British government – on
pensions, rights for part-time workers, compensation for Spanish
fishermen, and the Working Time Directive – have further illustrated
the erosion of national sovereignty and state autonomy. At the Inter-
Governmental Conference (IGC), the Major government has demanded
constraints on the court's powers, including limits to the retrospective
effects of ECJ judgments and the damages a state may be forced to pay,
plus rapid amendment of legislation interpreted by the court in ways
contrary to the Council's intentions.[7]

Concerns about the status of the EU were prominent in France and
Germany during the ratification of the Maastricht Treaty (properly the
Treaty on European Union). In France, the treaty was referred to the
Constitutional Council for a ruling on the constitutional meaning of
state sovereignty. The 1789 Declaration of the Rights of Man states
that 'sovereignty resides in the nation' while the 1958 constitution
declares that 'national sovereignty belongs to the people who exercise
it by their representatives and by referendum'. The council rejected
absolutist notions of sovereignty and set aside a complex distinction
between unconstitutional 'transfers of sovereignty' and constitutional
'limitations of sovereignty' by ruling that France could transfer
competences to the EU (Stone, 1993: 73–4). It found the Maastricht
Treaty 'not contrary' to the constitution, but a new heading had to be
added to the constitution authorizing EMU and the participation of
non-nationals in municipal elections.

The German Federal Constitutional Court also found the Maastricht Treaty compatible with the national constitution. The Basic Law obliges Germany to participate in the development of the EU (defined as a 'community of states'), and the *Bundestag* and *Bundesrat* supported the constitutional amendments required to ratify the treaty. In the *Brunner* case, the court discussed the constitutional implications of the treaty, and although finding it compatible with the Basic Law, this was not a ringing endorsement. The court was concerned about the EU's democratic deficit, declaring that as further legislative authority was transferred to the EU, so the role of the European Parliament (EP) should be strengthened. But given the legislative weakness of the EP, the judges at Karlsruhe implied that substantial competences should remain in the national domain and subject to legitimization by the *Bundestag*. Crucially, the court stated that it would have the last word on the constitutionality of future EU actions, raising the prospect of clashes with the ECJ (Ress, 1994: 56–69).[8]

Community law and individual rights

The EU has direct links to nationals of member states through Citizenship of the Union, direct elections to the EP and Community law, which applies to individuals as well as institutions. In *Van Gend en Loos*, the ECJ stated that 'independently of the legislation of Member States, Community law ... not only imposes obligations on individuals but is also intended to confer upon them rights which become part of their legal heritage' (quoted in Weiler, 1996: 521). Given direct effect and supremacy, rights conferred by Community law can trump national legislation and must be fully and uniformly applied. In *Francovich*, the ECJ ruled that states are liable for damages caused to individuals by breaches of Community law for which they are responsible, further protecting individual rights.[9]

Community legislation and ECJ rulings have spelled out that the EU is not just concerned with economic co-operation, but aims to improve living and working conditions and promote social cohesion. However, the conferring of rights (e.g. freedom of movement) has been an incremental process and remains incomplete. Action has tended to address the rights of workers as economic actors. EU social policy now embraces a range of topics, but competence often remains at national level or is shared with the EU. A coherent EU welfare regime is unlikely given national differences and the variable geometry procedures of the Social Protocol and EMU. However, Liebfried contends that the EU's social dimension has limited state sovereignty (ECJ decisions limit the state's formal authority to take independent social policy decisions), while economic interdependence and pressures on welfare spending have constrained the autonomy of national welfare systems (Liebfried, 1994).

The EU has played an important role in tackling sex discrimination, enhancing the rights of migrant workers, and strengthening health and safety regulations. Article F.2 of the Maastricht Treaty confirms that fundamental rights protected by the European Convention on Human Rights are to be respected as general principles of Community law. The Court of Justice has also treated fundamental rights as a key element of the general principles of law it upholds (Wincott, 1994). But in a 1996 opinion the ECJ ruled that accession of the EU itself to the convention could only be achieved through treaty revision.[10]

The Maastricht Treaty's provisions for a Citizenship of the Union are an important (but limited) move by the EU towards political rights and away from a concentration on individuals' economic or social status (Meehan, 1993; Jessun D'Oliveira, 1995). Articles 8–8d grant a number of rights: freedom of movement and residence; the right of EU citizens residing in a member state of which they are not a national to vote and stand as a candidate in municipal and European parliament elections (but not national elections), under the same conditions as nationals of that state; diplomatic protection in a third country by the diplomatic or consular authorities of any member state, and the right to petition the EP and apply to the EU Ombudsman. This codified rights of free movement and nondiscrimination, some of which were already in place, but Article 8e states that further rights may be added. The treaty does not specify any citizenship duties.

These provisions loosened the conceptual links between citizenship and the sovereign nation-state, notably by giving voting rights to nonnationals. However, Citizenship of the Union still relies on the conceptual framework of the nation-state and does not replace national citizenship. Only nationals of member states can become citizens of the Union and enjoy rights thereof. A treaty declaration confirms that decisions on nationality remain the sole prerogative of member states, who continue to operate different nationality laws. Non-nationals with 'denizen' status (i.e. permanent residents with economic and social rights, but not political rights or full citizenship) are therefore not entitled to the rights enjoyed by citizens of the Union.

Policy in the EU: exercising and extending sovereignty?

The supremacy of Community law has clearly eroded the *de jure* sovereignty of member states. However, a reduction of a state's policy-making authority may simultaneously extend policy-making capacity (the ability to achieve policy goals). European nation-states have responded to the loss of autonomy resulting from globalization by 'pooling' their individual sovereignties, allowing them to achieve together more than they could alone.

Milward contends that postwar European integration has meant 'the European rescue of the nation-state' rather than its demise; 'the nation-state became more powerful after 1945 in Western Europe than it had been before' (Milward and Sørensen, 1994: 4). Some initiatives remained primarily national (e.g. the state's welfare role), but governments recognized that some policy goals (industrial restructuring, agricultural production and trade expansion) could be best advanced by pooling sovereignty in a European framework. States make only limited surrenders of sovereignty, doing so for narrowly defined purposes, and preserve a balance of power which favours national governments by requiring unanimity for 'sovereignty-related reforms' and working through intergovernmental institutions rather than granting open-ended authority to supranational bodies (Moravcsik, 1991: 25–7).

National governments pursue domestic policy objectives through European integration, though what constitutes the 'national interest' is contested. Moravcsik's 'liberal intergovernmentalism' recognizes that states are not unitary actors, but that policy emerges from bargaining between a range of actors – ministers, national bureaucracies, MPs from the governing party and interest groups (Moravcsik, 1991, 1994). He argues that co-operation in the EU redistributes domestic political influence in ways that strengthen the executive. EU policy-making offers the executive greater scope for policy initiative; alters institutional arrangements (weakening parliaments); gives the executive access to information unavailable to other domestic actors; and provides additional ideological justification for its policies (Moravcsik, 1994: 4–15). As only the executive is directly involved in EU negotiations, ministers can 'cut slack' during interstate bargaining, loosening the constraints imposed by domestic pressures.

The Single European Market

Moravcsik argues that national governments played the leading role in negotiating the Single European Act (SEA); that the SEA was made possible by a convergence of domestic policy preferences in the three largest member states; that it reflected lowest common denominator bargains, and that 'minimalist' institutional reforms confirmed the desire of major states to maintain sovereignty (Moravcsik, 1991).

Statecentric explanations of EU policy-making have been challenged by studies noting the complexity of EU decision-making and the plurality of factors affecting European integration. These draw on methods used in political science or public policy rather than international relations theory, depicting EU decision-making as a multilayered process which involves a range of actors whose influence varies across policy sectors (Marks *et al.*, 1996). This multilevel governance approach accepts that nation-states and national executives are the most important actors, but argues that decision-making competencies are shared rather than monopolized by the executive. Statecentric models contend that the state is strengthened and executive autonomy enhanced in the EU, whereas multilevel governance argues that they are eroded as subnational and supranational institutions have authority of their own.

For this 'new institutionalist' perspective, institutions matter: although institutional structures, procedures and norms are not the determinants of political behaviour, they do shape its pattern (Bulmer, 1994: 355–7). The extension of Qualified Majority Voting (QMV) and decline of the exercise of the national veto under the Luxembourg compromise have eroded *de jure* sovereignty and contributed to a change in the culture of EU negotiations which stresses coalition-building rather than resort to national vetoes. Whether a legislative proposal is subject to QMV or unanimity thus shapes interstate and interinstitutional bargaining. The treaty basis of a measure is significant, determining whether an issue is subject to QMV or the jurisdiction of the ECJ.

The European Commission has been credited with a policy leadership role and 'considerable influence over policy outcomes', particularly in the Single European Market (Nugent, 1995: 620). The commission was an important actor in the SEM project given Cockfield's 1985 White Paper *Completing the Internal Market*; its adoption of principles of mutual recognition and minimum harmonization, and Delors' linking of SEM success to EMU and the social dimension, plus its agenda-setting role and location at the hub of policy networks in technology and energy policy (Ross, 1995; Wincott, 1995: 603–6). However, the commission is hampered by structural shortcomings, is susceptible to changes in public opinion, and relies on national bureaucracies for policy implementation.

The EU has expanded its regulatory role, applying uniform rules in the single market and strengthening competition policy. States delegate sovereignty to ensure compliance with credible SEM rules, while the European Commission sees regulation as a way to expand its powers without sustaining great political or economic costs (Majone, 1994). Curbs on state aid limit executive autonomy, but the drive towards liberalization may also be used by states to export domestic policy objectives (Kassim and Menon, 1996: 5–8). British Conservatives have found it difficult to balance their neoliberal support for the SEM with their desire to protect sovereignty and executive autonomy.

'Policy networks' models contend that relationships between interested actors in policy networks shape policy at an early stage (Richardson, 1996). While national governments play a key role in 'history-making decisions' (treaty amendments, European Council decisions), they are less well placed to control 'policy-setting' decisions taken at a systemic level, where EU institutions may be influential, or 'policy-shaping' decisions at a subsystemic level, where policy networks are active (Peterson, 1995: 71–6). The extent to which actors depend on each other for resources (technical expertise, political influence), and the nature of the network (tightly integrated policy communities or looser issue networks) are significant variables at this level.

EU regional policy and regionalism

The growth of regionalism, a trend encouraged by the EU, has important implications for the sovereignty and territorial integrity of West European nation-states. In regions with a strong sense of identity, local elites dissatisfied by centralized decision-making and 'top-down' regional policies have sought greater political and economic autonomy. With the decline of the interventionist state, local policy 'entrepreneurs' turned to local public–private-sector co-operation, inward investment and cross-regional partnerships to promote economic growth and specialization.

In many cases, the central state itself has given subnational government a greater role. Again a variety of factors may account for this: ethnic nationalism; claims of economic efficiency or democracy; pressure from sectional or regional interests, and EU action. Belgium has become a federal state, the powers of the Spanish autonomous communities have been increased, as has the administrative role of subnational government in France and Italy. Subnational government is weak in the UK: there is no regional tier of government, the Conservative government opposes legislative devolution and has eroded the autonomy of local government.[11]

The EU has also encouraged regionalism and subnational mobilization (Marks, 1993). Reforms of the Structural Funds in 1988 doubled the aid available to its poorer regions. The European Commission has stressed the principle of partnership, actively involving subnational government in making and implementing EU regional policy. It has also encouraged cross-regional political and economic collaboration. In turn, subnational government has been 'Europeanized': regional lobbying and information offices have been set up in Brussels, reflecting the EU's increased role in areas directly affecting regional and local authorities (economic development, environment, transport etc.). The Maastricht Treaty established the Committee of the Regions, and confirmed that ministers from subnational governments may attend relevant sessions of the Council of Ministers when delegated to do so by national governments. Finally, the principle of subsidiarity was included (but inadequately defined) in the treaty. Article 3b states that the Community should act only when objectives cannot be better achieved at a lower level, while the treaty preamble talks of decisions being taken 'as close as possible to the people'.

Of Europe's regions, the German Länder have had most influence. They successfully lobbied for references to subsidiarity in the Maastricht Treaty and for the creation of the Committee of the Regions, mobilizing other regions to support these goals. The Länder have also clawed back some of the powers lost to the federal government as EU competences expanded. Article 23 of the Basic Law was altered to give the *Bundesrat* veto powers over future transfers of sovereignty to the EU. They argued that EU decision-making should not be viewed as traditional foreign policy but as 'European domestic policy' affecting the distribution of power within member states, and in which subnational government should therefore be involved (Jeffery, 1996).

The European Commission, subnational government and central governments are all involved in EU decision-making and policy implementation, though the latter continue to play the leading role. Expectations of an emerging 'Europe of the Regions' are unrealistic. Differences in the constitutional status, political influence and economic prosperity of Europe's regions are considerable. National governments continue to predominate in EU decision-making, and regional elites often have to rely on them to pursue their interests. Resources available to subnational governments (their constitutional status or access to the Council of Ministers) are shaped by decisions made by the centre. The Committee of the Regions is denied any real influence by limited powers, structural problems and disputes between regional and local government representatives. Finally, the 1992 Edinburgh Council declaration stated that subsidiarity did not imply a redistribution of competences within member states.

Economic and Monetary Union

EMU re-emerged on the Community agenda in the late 1980s, culminating in the Maastricht Treaty's provisions for the creation of a single currency by 1999 for those states meeting the convergence criteria. No single factor can adequately account for the move towards EMU. Dyson characterizes the EMU policy process as having a 'hollow core', a dynamic process without a single policy-brokering centre (Dyson, 1994: 329–32). National governments played a critical role in shaping the final agreement and the Bundesbank's influence over German policy was particularly significant. External factors (German unification, the power of the foreign exchange markets), a convergence of national interests and economic policies (commitments to low inflation and fixed exchange rates) and European Commission activism were all necessary but not sufficient factors.

National governments will forfeit economic sovereignty in a number of ways *en route* to and within 'irreversible' EMU. States looking to qualify for EMU find their national economic policies governed by the requirements of the convergence criteria (on the budget deficit, public debt, inflation and interest rates, plus ERM membership), and must make their national central banks independent of government control. The Maastricht Treaty does however allow the European Council some flexibility in deciding which states meet the criteria. On joining EMU, states cede monetary sovereignty to the European System of Central Banks (ESCB), headed by an independent European Central Bank (ECB) which is constitutionally bound to maintain price stability and has authority over exchange rate policy, interest rates and the reserve supply. National currencies will be replaced by a single currency (the Euro) at permanently fixed rates. States will be prevented from maintaining high debt levels and will not be bailed out by the ECB or national banks, reducing their ability to manage asymmetric shocks.

Despite this erosion of formal monetary sovereignty, states may collectively, and individually for all but Germany, increase their influence and relative autonomy through EMU. France sees EMU as a way to increase its voice in monetary policy as German dominance of the ERM had limited its economic autonomy, particularly when German unification and resulting high interest rates prolonged the French recession. Despite ECB independence, French elites believe their interests are more likely to be heard under EMU (with French representation in the ESCB and European Council) than in an ERM in which the Deutschmark is the anchor currency, and the Bundesbank makes the key decisions. As the ERM allowed states to achieve their goals of price and exchange rate stability by ceding monetary sovereignty, so the EMU convergence criteria have been used by governments in Italy, Spain and Belgium to legitimize unpopular cuts in public spending, and insulate the executive from domestic pressures. But by exploiting EMU in this way, France and Germany fuelled domestic anti-EU sentiment which may in turn hinder future EU activity. The British government faced a similar outcome when its strategy of using ERM membership to entrench economic discipline ended in ignominious exit and domestic hostility which effectively closed off the ERM as a policy option.

Leading up to Maastricht, Britain and Denmark were particularly fearful of the sovereignty implications of EMU, and both ultimately won opt-outs from Stage III. The British opt-out allows Parliament to exercise its sovereignty by deciding whether or not to sign up for EMU. A referendum to endorse any decision to adopt the single currency also seems likely. Major claims that the opt-out allows Britain to influence EU decisions on EMU, while giving the government time to assess the economic and political implications of membership and nonmembership (Major, 1996). But he is also 'wary of ... its serious political and constitutional implications' (*Hansard*, vol. 255, col. 1068, 1 March 1995). Joining EMU will diminish monetary sovereignty, but staying outside the EMU hard core would see Britain lose further influence over the economic and monetary decisions which affect it. Though Major opposes participation in a new style ERM linking the currencies of non-EMU states to the Euro, the EU's plans for a 'stability pact' place additional pressure on the government to maintain budgetary discipline and avoid devaluation.

The intergovernmental pillars

The EU's Common Foreign and Security Policy (CFSP) and Justice and Home Affairs intergovernmental 'pillars' aim to provide co-ordinated action on common problems of security and migration, while preserving national sovereignty. The pillars extended existing intergovernmental machinery for consultation and co-operation in which unanimity is the norm and supranational institutions have only a minimal role. But the arrangements are not purely intergovernmental. Under CFSP, decisions may be taken by Qualified Majority Voting (QMV) once joint action has been agreed, provided member states agree beforehand by unanimity on the areas to which QMV will apply. In the third pillar, similarly tortuous provisions for the use of QMV exist, and Article K.9 allows some decisions to be taken under the EC pillar procedures if all states agree. However, these have yet to be fully utilized, and the intergovernmental procedures have been blamed for policy short-comings (Monar, 1996: 1030–5).

Co-operation in foreign, defence and immigration policy may yet have major sovereignty implications. Article J.4 of the Maastricht Treaty talks of 'the eventual framing of a common defence policy, which might in time lead to a common defence'. Police co-operation under the Europol Convention has real and symbolic implications for state sovereignty. National differences on Justice and Home Affairs issues persist. Seven members of the Schengen group removed their internal frontiers in 1995, though Britain continues to block EU progress on the removal of internal frontiers. Whereas Britain appears determined to protect national sovereignty, Germany has tried to 'export' the migration issue out of the domestic arena to the EU in order to tackle a common problem more effectively, legitimize policy decisions and insulate the executive from domestic pressures (Henson and Malhan, 1995: 128–30).

EU democracy: sovereignty frustrated?

Many policies formerly under the exclusive jurisdiction of the sovereign state now fall, in whole or in part, within the remit of EU decision-making. Yet this transfer of decision-making authority from national governments, accountable to parliaments and their electorates, has not been matched by an equivalent extension of EU legitimacy or democracy. As the EU has taken on more powers, an increasing democracy and legitimacy deficit has become apparent, fracturing the link between the people and the sovereign authority, eroding popular sovereignty.

Though its legislative role is limited, increased powers for the European Parliament are insufficient to bestow significantly greater legitimacy upon the EU in the eyes of many citizens. The nation-state remains the focal point for identity, legitimacy and popular sovereignty. Territorial boundaries remain important: representative politics is primarily conducted at national level, and popular sovereignty is equated with the consent of the people as nation.

The erosion of state sovereignty and national autonomy has not been matched by an equivalent erosion of national identity. Neither has the development of the EU been matched by that of a European civic or cultural identity. The enthusiasm for integration felt by many political and economic elites has not trickled down to the peoples of Europe. As expressions of popular sovereignty, the 1992 Danish and French referendums illustrated public distrust of and distaste for the technocratic 'Monnet method' of integration, plus a gulf between the cultural attachments of electorates and elites.

National, regional and European identities are not mutually exclusive. In Germany and Italy, EU membership is bound up with the state identity, and membership has been crucial for the modernization of the Union's peripheral states. Regionalist parties view European integration as an opportunity rather than a threat to their identity. Resistance to 'ever closer union' has been strongest in two states where sovereignty is central to nationhood: in Britain, where parliamentary sovereignty is, for Conservatives at least, a defining feature of English identity; and Denmark, where sovereign statehood is bound up with cultural nationalism (Hedetoft, 1994; Laffan, 1996: 86–7).

To overcome its legitimacy problems, the EU should not seek to replace national identities with a European identity. A stronger sense of European identity may emerge, though, within a framework of multiple identities, in which nations or regions are the focus of ethnic and cultural identities, while a reformed EU (with a shared 'political space' and expanded Citizenship of the Union) fosters a civic identity alongside those rooted in the nation-state (Tassin, 1992: 187–90; Laffan, 1996: 98–9). European identity should not – probably cannot – be constructed around ethnic myths: traditional routes to nation- and state-building do not offer a road map for the EU (Smith, 1992).

Given the continued importance of the nation-state as political community and reservoir of legitimate authority, the EU should protect states' rights while developing stronger direct links with European citizens. States wary of further integration ought not to be forced into binding political or economic union if doing so overrides the sovereign will of the people as expressed in elections or referendums. The extension of QMV might increase policy efficiency, but exacerbate legitimacy problems by overriding the interests of governments with clear democratic mandates. A variable geometry scenario may then appear to be optimal; but determining which are core policies binding on all member states and from which areas states may opt out, may prove problematic.

Conclusions: can less equal more?

Treating sovereignty in an absolutist or zero-sum manner precludes effective analysis of the complex impact of European integration on the state and society. A pluralistic approach, treating sovereignty as a multidimensional concept, is more fruitful but the term still needs to be analysed in conjunction with concepts such as power, legitimacy and, particularly, autonomy. *De jure* sovereignty – the formal independence of the state as sovereign power from any higher authority – has been eroded by the supremacy of Community law and the extension of QMV and Community competence. European integration also has repercussions for the constitutional dimension of sovereignty, that is the location of sovereign authority within the nation-state. In some respects, executive autonomy has been enhanced by the dominant role national governments play in shaping major EU decisions. But the SEM, EU regional policy and EMU constrain executive autonomy and grant supranational institutions extra functions and allow other domestic actors access to the EU's multilevel policy-making process. Individual and popular sovereignty have been extended by Citizenship of the Union and legislation affecting individual rights, but fragmented by the EU's democracy and legitimacy deficit.

As well as losing formal sovereignty within the EU, West European nation-states have had their autonomy (capacity to achieve policy goals and exercise sovereign power) diminished by globalization. But in the context of shrinking capacity for effective action, transferring or 'pooling' formal sovereignty in the EU has enhanced autonomy and effective sovereignty. Less can equal more. By ceding *de jure* sovereignty to the EU, states can gain executive autonomy in the domestic arena, more effectively manage economic and security interdependence, and achieve beneficial economic results which may otherwise remain beyond their reach. Furthermore, the loss of *de jure* sovereignty is not irreversible: if the political will to withdraw from the EU (or, more problematically, EMU) is strong enough, national courts and other member states would be hard pressed to resist legitimate demands.

The Protean nature of the concept of sovereignty, decried by Benn more than 40 years ago, has been added to by European integration. For the purposes of political analysis only a limited rescue of the concept appears possible, based on an unpacking of its multiple connotations and awareness that concepts such as autonomy may prove more useful. Despite the erosion of state sovereignty and autonomy, national governments remain central actors in the EU, and national identities show few signs of decline. Nation-states can no longer be viewed as the impermeable 'billiard balls' of realist international relations theory: EU policy-making is a multilevel process involving a variety of actors and institutions, while aspects of national politics have been 'Europeanized'.

Making sense of sovereignty in popular political discourse is more problematic given its frequent misuse. Sovereignty has emerged as a new fault-line in British party politics in recent years, with Euro-sceptic Conservatives urging a vigorous defence of the constitution and nation-state. Labour's attachment to parliamentary sovereignty has waned since it embraced legislative devolution and a more pro-European stance, but the party remains wedded to the 'Europe of nation states' model (Nugent, 1996). The symbolic importance of sovereignty in British politics and the UK's 'semidetachment' from the EU (its different values and interests, failure to fully utilize EU procedures, and its minority position in opposition to further integration) mean that sovereignty will continue to be central to British debates (Bulmer, 1992). Unless effective analysis of the sovereignty implications of scenarios such as further integration, variable geometry and withdrawal permeates these debates, voters will continue to find it difficult to exercise popular sovereignty on the crucial issue of Britain's role in the EU.

Notes

1. The chapter generally refers to the European Union, except where references are specific to the Community pillar. I use the phrase 'Community law' as the jurisdiction of the Court of Justice is almost exclusively limited to the Community pillar.
2. Case 26/62 *Algemene Transport-en Expeditie Onderneming van Gend en Loos NV v. Nederlandse administratie der belastingen* [1963] ECR 1. In subsequent reworkings of this statement, the ECJ dropped the reference to international law.
3. Case 294/83 *Parti ecologiste 'Les Verts' v. European Parliament* [1986] ECR 1339.
4. *Factortame Ltd v. Secretary of State for Transport* [1989] 2 All ER 692, HL.
5. *Factortame Ltd v. Secretary of State for Transport (No 2)* [1991] 1 All ER 70, HL.
6. Case 129/79 *Macarthys Ltd v. Wendy Smith* [1980] ECR 1275.
7. British Memorandum on the Court of Justice, 28 August 1996.
8. 'The German Constitutional Court will examine whether legal acts of the European institutions and organs are within the limits of the competencies granted to them or whether they exceed those limits.' *Bundesverfassungsgericht (BVerfG)*, 12 October 1993 − 2 BvR 2134/92 and 2159/92: 439.
9. Cases C-6,9/90 *Francovich and Bonifaci v. Republic of Italy* [1991] ECR I-5357.
10. Opinion 2/94, 28 March 1996. Alleged violations of the convention are heard by the European Court of Human Rights in Strasbourg. This is separate from the EU and should not be confused with the ECJ. The UK has not incorporated the convention into domestic law.
11. Special circumstances apply in Northern Ireland. In *A New Framework for Agreement* (HMSO, 1995), the British and Irish governments proposed the creation of a North/South institution which would discuss relevant EU matters, develop an agreed approach for the whole island, and implement and manage some executive matters (Paras 24–34). The Labour Party supports a Scottish parliament with legislative and limited tax-raising powers and a weaker Welsh assembly, though the creation of these depends on referendums.

References

Benn, S. (1955) 'The Uses of "Sovereignty"', *Political Studies*, **3**, 109–22.

Bulmer, S. (1992) 'Britain and European Integration: Of Sovereignty, Slow Adaptation, and Semi-Detachment', in S. George (ed.) *Britain and the European Community: The Politics of Semi-Detachment*. Oxford: Clarendon Press.

Bulmer, S. (1994) 'The Governance of the European Union: A New Institutionalist Approach', *Journal of Public Policy*, **13**, 351–80.

Camilleri, J. and Falk, J. (1992) *The End of Sovereignty? The Politics of a Shrinking and Fragmented World*. Aldershot: Edward Elgar.

Collins, L. (1990) *European Community Law in the United Kingdom*, 4th edn. London: Butterworths.

Dicey, A. V. (1982, 1st edn 1885) *Introduction to the Study of the Law of the Constitution*. Indianapolis: Liberty Classics.

Dyson, K. (1994) *Elusive Union: The Process of Economic and Monetary Union in Europe*. London: Longman.

Hedetoft, U. (1994) 'The State of Sovereignty in Europe: Political Concept or Cultural Self-Image', in S. Zetterholm (ed.) *National Cultures and European Integration*. Oxford: Berg.

Held, D. (1989) *Political Theory and the Modern State*. Cambridge: Polity.

Henson, P. and Malhan, N. (1995) 'Endeavours to Export a Migration Crisis: Policy Making and Europeanisation in the German Migration Dilemma', *German Politics*, **4**, 128–44.

Howe, G. (1990) 'Sovereignty and Interdependence: Britain's Place in the World', *International Affairs*, **66**, 675–95.

Jeffery, C. (1996) 'Towards a "Third Level" in Europe? The German Länder in the European Union', *Political Studies*, **44**, 253–66.

Jessun D'Oliveira, H. (1995) 'Union Citizenship: Pie in the Sky?', in A. Rosas and E. Antola (eds) *A Citizens' Europe: In Search of a New Order*. London: Sage.

Kassim, H. and Menon, A. (1996) 'The European Union and State Autonomy', in H. Kassim and A. Menon (eds) *The European Union and National Industrial Policy*. London: Routledge.

Laffan, B. (1996) 'The Politics of Identity and Political Order in Europe', *Journal of Common Market Studies*, **34**, 81–102.

Lasok, D. and Bridge, J. W. (1994) *Law and Institutions of the European Communities*, 6th edn. London: Butterworths.

Liebfried, S. (1994) 'The Social Dimension of the European Union: En Route to a Positively Joint Sovereignty', *Journal of European Social Policy*, **4**, 239–62.

MacCormick, N. (1993) 'Beyond the Sovereign State', *Modern Law Review*, **56**, 1–18.

Majone, G. (1994) 'The Rise of the Regulatory State in Europe', *West European Politics*, **17**, 77–101.

Major, J. (1996) 'We Must Not Allow EMU to Be Fudged', *The Times*, 5 October.

Marks, G. (1993) 'Structural Policy and Multilevel Governance in the EC', in A. Cafruny and G. Rosenthal (eds) *The State of the European Community*, vol. II, *The Maastricht Debates and Beyond*. Boulder, CO: Lynne Rienner.

Marks, G., Hooghe, L. and Blank, K. (1996) 'European Integration from the 1980s: State-Centric v. Multi-Level Governance', *Journal of Common Market Studies*, **34**, 341–78.

Meehan, E. (1993) *Citizenship and the European Community*. London: Sage.

Milward, A. and Sørensen, V. (1994) 'Interdependence or Integration? A National Choice', in F. Lynch et al. *The Frontier of National Sovereignty*. London: Routledge.

Monar, J. (1996) 'European Union Justice and Home Affairs: The Deficits and Reform Possibilities of a Policy Area of Major Concern to European Citizens', in I. Hampsher-Monk and J. Stanyer (eds) *Contemporary Political Studies, 1996*, vol. II. Belfast: Political Studies Association.

Moravcsik, A. (1991) 'Negotiating the Single European Act: National Interests and Conventional Statecraft in the European Community', *International Organization*, **45**, 19–56.

Moravcsik, A. (1993) 'Preferences and Power in the European Community: A Liberal Intergovernmentalist Approach', *Journal of Common Market Studies*, **31**, 473–524.

Moravcsik, A. (1994) 'Why the European Community Strengthens the State: Domestic Politics and International Cooperation', *Centre for European Studies Working Paper Series No. 52*. Cambridge, MA: Harvard University Press.

Nugent, N. (1995) 'The Leadership Capacity of the European Commission', *Journal of European Public Policy*, **2**, 603–23.

Nugent, N. (1996) 'Sovereignty and Britain's Membership of the European Union', *Public Policy and Administration*, **11**, 3–18.

Peterson, J. (1995) 'Decision-Making in the European Union: Towards a Framework for Analysis', *Journal of European Public Policy*, **2**, 69–93.

Pollard, D. and Ross, M. (1994) *European Community Law: Text and Materials*. London: Butterworths.

Ress, G. (1994) 'The Constitution and the Maastricht Treaty: Between Co-operation and Conflict', *German Politics*, **3**, 47–74.

Richardson, J. (1996) 'Actor-Based Models of National and EU Policy-Making', in H. Kassim and A. Menon (eds) *The European Union and National Industrial Policy*. London: Routledge.

Ross, G. (1995) *Jacques Delors and European Integration*. Cambridge: Polity.

Smith, A. (1992) 'National Identity and the Idea of European Unity', *International Affairs*, **68**, 55–76.

Stankiewicz, W. J. (1969) 'The Validity of the Concept of Sovereignty', in W. J. Stankiewicz (ed.) *In Defense of Sovereignty*. New York: Oxford University Press.

Stone, A. (1993) 'Ratifying Maastricht: France Debates European Union', *French Politics and Society*, **11**, 70–88.

Tassin, E. (1992) 'Europe: A Political Community?', in C. Mouffe (ed.) *Dimensions of Radical Democracy: Pluralism, Citizenship and Community*. London: Verso.

Thompson, H. (1996) *The British Conservative Government and the Exchange Rate Mechanism*. London: Cassell.

Wallace, W. (1986) 'What Price Independence? Sovereignty and Interdependence in British Politics', *International Affairs*, **62**, 367–89.

Wallace, W. (1994) 'Rescue or Retreat? The Nation State in Western Europe, 1945–93', *Political Studies*, **42**, special issue, 52–76.

Wallace, W. (1996) 'Government without Statehood: The Unstable Equilibrium', in H. Wallace and W. Wallace (eds) *Policy-Making in the European Union*. Oxford: Oxford University Press.

Weiler, J. H. H. (1991) 'The Transformation of Europe', *Yale Law Journal*, **100**, 2403–83.

Weiler, J. H. H. (1996) 'European Neo-Constitutionalism: In Search of Foundations for the European Constitutional Order', *Political Studies*, **44**, special issue, 517–33.

Wincott, D. (1994) 'Human Rights, Democracy and the Role of the Court of Justice in European Integration', *Democratization*, **1**, 251–71.

Wincott, D. (1995) 'Institutional Interaction and European Integration: Towards an Everyday Critique of Liberal Intergovernmentalism', *Journal of Common Market Studies*, **33**, 597–609.

The Search for Peace and a Political Settlement in Northern Ireland: Sovereignty, Self-determination and Consent

STEPHEN HOPKINS

Introduction

It is a commonplace that the Northern Ireland problem is best characterized in terms of the struggle between two competing national allegiances or identities (Boyle, 1991). The overwhelming majority of the people in Northern Ireland, though not all, classify themselves as belonging to one or other of the two main antagonistic communities. These communities may be described as Protestant, unionist or British, and Catholic, nationalist or Irish, though which term is used can say something significant about where the observer locates the primary source of conflict (Hadfield, 1989; 1992). As we shall discover, such descriptions are not unproblematic, going as they do to the heart of the conflict, which is about national identity and state sovereignty. The territory has been, and remains, subject to contested claims of sovereignty.

This chapter follows Whyte (1990; 1988), McGarry and O'Leary (1995; 1990) and O'Leary and McGarry (1993) in distinguishing between explanations of the conflict in Northern Ireland that emphasize primarily endogenous or exogenous causes. Analytically distinct they may be, but in the practical world of conflict resolution, internal and external explanations are not easily separable. From the Anglo-Irish Agreement of 1985, through to the Frameworks Documents of 1995 and beyond, the British and Irish states appear now to recognize that 'the current conflict does not simply, or even primarily, stem from causes endogenous to Northern Ireland, important though these are' (O'Leary and Arthur, 1990: 6).

This chapter will provide a brief synopsis of the historical background to the contested understanding of sovereignty in the context of political developments in Northern Ireland, and between the British and Irish states (Ward, 1993). This will enable a preliminary analysis of the contemporary and evolving political and peace processes in Northern Ireland. Attention will be focused upon the developing positions of the crucial protagonists. The evolution of the use of concepts such as 'national self-determination', 'consent' and the notion of 'veto' or 'guarantee' will be critically assessed with reference to the Joint Declaration of the British and Irish governments (15 December 1993), and the Frameworks Documents (February 1995). A final section will speculate on the limits of the recent 'peace process' and the continuing relevance of fundamentally irreconcilable conceptions of sovereignty in the Northern Ireland polity.

Facing two ways: neither wholly British nor wholly Irish

Neither Britain nor Ireland has proved able to construct a lasting set of political institutions (a sovereign authority) that can command the common allegiance of the deeply divided people on the island. As far as issues of nationality, constitutional authority and religion are concerned, the historical failure to win the majority of people in Northern Ireland to a common *identity* has left society divided, segmented, with communities embittered and alienated. The controversy over the third Home Rule Bill in 1912–14 underlined competing visions of sovereignty and self-determination. Republicans and nationalists, although they disagreed about the degree of independence from Britain that 'the Irish nation' should seek, argued that 'this nation (should be) granted the entire territory of Ireland for its state boundaries, in accordance with the principle of national self-determination' (McGarry and O'Leary, 1995: 25).

The Government of Ireland Act of 1920 was never introduced in the South, as it was overtaken by the Anglo-Irish Treaty that brought the republican 'War of Independence' to a close, and gave dominion status (a self-governing territory within the British empire) to the Irish Free State. Thus, Ireland was divided and governed by 'a combination of two constitutional structures: a Dominion in the South and a Home Rule Parliament in the North which was in theory subordinate to Westminster' (Boyle, 1991: 74). Neither traditional republicanism nor traditional Irish unionism had received all that they desired from this settlement.

Republican Ireland fought a ferocious civil war which ended in defeat for the anti-treaty militant wing of Sinn Féin (Hopkinson, 1988; Foster, 1989: 502–15). Unionists had opposed home rule for all of Ireland, but Craig (who became the Prime Minister of Northern Ireland) accepted the Government of Ireland Act, thereby effectively abandoning Protestants and unionists in the South.

O'Leary and Arthur (1990: 10) argue:

> Ulster unionist leaders knew that home rule would provide them with an effective bulwark against both the untrustworthy intentions of London governments, and the claims of the Irish Free State (intent on achieving complete independence from Britain and on the political unification of the island of Ireland).

The precariousness of the unionist position led to Ulster unionism focusing almost entirely upon the maintenance of Protestant communal solidarity; any efforts made to win the consent of Northern Ireland's Catholic population to the new devolved parliament at Stormont took second place to the perceived danger of allowing 'disloyal' elements to undermine the regime's *raison d'être*.

This parliament and executive formed a 'semi-state' based upon the Westminster model of parliamentary sovereignty and majoritarianism. This may have been workable in the long term had there been a much smaller Catholic minority than the one-third of the population in Northern Ireland who, largely, displayed allegiance to the newly created Free State parliament.

There has been a structural split in Northern Ireland's Catholic population. Some have displayed what Crick (1988: 114) would call 'virtual' consent to the sovereign authority at Stormont or Westminster, either through engaging in political activity within these institutions, or through indifference and apathy. At the same time, this group often retains an aspiration towards a united Ireland or an identification with the Republic of Ireland. On the other hand, another group of Catholics is willing to display its refusal to consent (either actively or passively) to the constitution in Northern Ireland, by engaging in open rebellion (O'Connor, 1993; Phoenix, 1994).

Fianna Fáil, the remnants of the defeated anti-treaty Republicans, established the Free State constitution in 1937 which laid legal claim to the territory of Northern Ireland and appeared to confirm a Catholic ethos as integral to the southern state. This helped to confirm the Ulster Unionist Party (UUP) in its defensive strategy of hegemonic control.[1] The attempt by unionists to justify this control during the Stormont years ignores the obvious fact that 'the attitude of many Catholics to the state (Northern Ireland) was as much the product of their treatment by it as it was of Nationalist ideology' (Patterson, 1996a: 8).

After the Second World War, British governments continued to view 'hegemonic control [by the UUP], provided its uglier manifestations were not too visible, [as] preferable ... to the known historical costs of direct intervention and management of Irish affairs' (O'Leary and McGarry, 1993: 144). In response to the declaration of an Irish republic in the South in 1949, the Ireland Act was passed at Westminster, affirming that Northern Ireland remained part of His Majesty's dominions and that its status could only change with the consent of the parliament of Northern Ireland.[2]

The formal constitutional position appeared to be given a greater sense of stability through the passage of the Ireland Act, but the 1960s saw the start of several interrelated processes of fundamental change in social and political life in Northern Ireland which led by 1972 to the collapse of unionist hegemony. This resulted in the most serious communal violence in Northern Ireland since the 1920s, exposing critical divisions within the unionist constituency, and breathing new life into the ailing tradition of physical force republicanism. The difficulties associated with the attempt by Prime Minister O'Neill to reform UUP rule after 1963, the growth of Catholic demands for equal civil rights within the Northern Ireland state (Purdie, 1990; Munck, 1992), and the evolution of British and Irish state strategies for 'managing' incipient change in Northern Ireland, have all been well documented elsewhere (O'Leary and Arthur, 1990: 32–40; O'Leary and McGarry, 1993: 153–80; Arthur, 1996a: 11–19).

What is important to note here is that whilst issues of formal sovereignty were not directly addressed by many of the protagonists in the initial phase of these developments, nevertheless it gradually became clear, to most if not all, that the *form of government* that had prevailed in Northern Ireland could not continue indefinitely. As Arthur (1996a: 12) recognizes, the crisis of 1968–72 was different to those that had periodically beset the Northern Ireland polity previously:

> It was not simply a conflict between Unionism and the enemy within. It was to become just as much a fundamental debate within the Unionist family about (a) what type of Unionism was relevant for the late twentieth century; (b) what its relationship was to be with the sovereign powers at Westminster; and ultimately (c) the very identity of the Union.

Arguably, these questions have remained unanswered. For nationalists in Northern Ireland the reform of the Stormont regime became confused with concepts of consent, legitimacy and identity. Was Northern Ireland to be viewed as a 'failed political entity' because of Stormont's inability or unwillingness to respond quickly or fully enough to civil rights demands? Was Irish unity on the agenda? It had become patently clear that 'the issue was not solely one of the formal mechanisms of government or of civil rights; it was also about the status of Northern Ireland' (Hadfield, 1992: 8). Morrow (1996: 21) concurs, arguing that the question of political stability and communal relations in Northern Ireland had become 'a struggle about the sources and nature of political legitimacy'.

British intervention and Anglo-Irish relations

For much of the period from the mid-1920s until the mid-1960s the question of sovereignty had been shelved. After the situation in Northern Ireland deteriorated to the point where it was clear that intervention by the 'sovereign power' was unavoidable, Britain still hoped to return the province to local control. 'British policy-makers between 1968 and 1972, by their indecision and willingness to sustain Stormont, albeit in a reformed mode, showed they were not prepared to contemplate the integration option [of Northern Ireland into the United Kingdom]' (O'Leary and Arthur, 1990: 40). Like Lloyd George before them, policy-makers were not prepared to contemplate coercing unionists into a united Ireland against their will.

After 1972, and the decision to prorogue the Stormont parliament and transfer executive power back to Westminster, the British government sought cross-community support in Northern Ireland for a power-sharing (rather than majoritarian) devolved government.[3] Aside from the short-lived Sunningdale experiment in 1973–4 (Rose, 1976; Oliver, 1982), this prize has proved elusive, and direct rule from London, through the Secretary of State and the Northern Ireland Office, has been the norm. In terms of the effects on representative accountability and participation, Hadfield (1992: 6) is surely right to argue that 'the salient features of direct rule ... [are] at best disquieting and at worst deplorable'.

British policy was conducted as if London could act as a 'neutral arbiter' between the antagonistic communities (O'Leary and Arthur, 1990: 41–2; O'Leary and McGarry, 1993: 183–5). The failure to engineer power-sharing devolution, and the related fact that crucial protagonists (both unionist and nationalist) in Northern Ireland refused to acknowledge the 'benevolent neutrality' of the British, meant that during the early 1980s a shift of potentially huge significance occurred: 'British arbitration would eventually be replaced by a limited form of *joint* arbitration by Britain and the Republic of Ireland through the institutions of the Anglo-Irish Agreement' (O'Leary and McGarry, 1993: 185). From 1972 on, through the various constitutional initiatives (the Border Poll, Sunningdale, Constitutional Convention of 1975, the Atkins talks in 1979–80, the Northern Ireland Assembly and Prior's 'rolling devolution' between 1982 and 1986, the Anglo-Irish Agreement (AIA),[4] and the Brooke–Mayhew talks in 1990–2),[5] Morrow identifies three key elements of British policy: willingness to maintain British sovereignty (for as long as the majority uphold it), an 'Irish dimension', and power-sharing devolved government within Northern Ireland.

Crick recognized at an early stage that, if the choice is restricted to a united Ireland or the unity of the present United Kingdom, then this rests on 'a traditional but now very suspect and self-deluding view of the sovereign state' (1982: 231). Although the AIA was denounced by both unionists and republicans as a surrender of legitimate claims to sovereignty in Northern Ireland, it could be read as an undertaking *by both governments* that the 'constitutional guarantee', as it had been reiterated in the 1973 Northern Ireland Constitution Act, would be upheld.[6] At the same time it recognized 'new forms of government or of inter-government relations [that] reflect the fact, not change the fact, that Northern Ireland faces two ways' (Crick, 1982: 231).

From the Sunningdale agreement of 1973 through to the Downing Street Declaration in 1993, the British and Irish governments (of whatever stripe) have been committed to the principle of explicit or active consent for constitutional change to the *de facto* status of Northern Ireland. However, as Crick (1988: 115) points out, in the AIA, and also again in the Joint Declaration of 1993 and the Frameworks Documents of 1995, the British government has been willing to impose the form of government in Northern Ireland (whether it be through the intergovernmental conference or through the proposal for cross-border institutions with executive powers), and it has been willing to confront unionist hostility and protest at these measures. O'Leary (1987a: 14) argues persuasively that the AIA 'signifies the formal end of Unionist supremacy within Northern Ireland: Unionism without an Ulster Unionist veto on the structure of the union or policy-making within the union'.

Unionists argued strongly after 1985 that although the AIA may have retained the formal constitutional guarantee, it had in fact changed the constitutional status of the province by stealth. They pointed to the continued existence of Articles 2 and 3 in the Irish constitution, and the fact that in several court cases, the legal system in the Republic had underlined the belief that the reintegration of the national territory remained a 'constitutional imperative' and confirmed unionist fears that the AIA did not represent a formal or legal abandonment of the Republic's territorial claim. Although unionists retained the formal protection of the 'constitutional guarantee', as embodied in the Northern Ireland Constitution Act of 1973, after 1985 they have been politically on the defensive. British sovereignty did not end with the AIA, and there was no commitment to share sovereignty with the Irish Republic, as some of the siren voices alleged at the time. Nevertheless the exercise of British sovereignty has been substantially modified. Moreover, this modification has generally been in the direction least favourable to unionist perceptions of their interests.

The recognition of an important role for the so-called 'Irish dimension' had been included in the original Government of Ireland Act, and the 1973 Constitution Act (Section 12) and Sunningdale Agreement had provided for a Council of Ireland (consisting of a

Council of Ministers made up from seven representatives of the new Northern Ireland Executive and seven from the Republic's government, as well as a Consultative Assembly). However, the intergovernmental conference established by the AIA gave the 'Irish dimension' an institutionalized presence within Northern Ireland, irrespective of unionist opinion. This has been widely, and correctly, viewed as responding to the agenda set by the leader of the Social Democratic and Labour Party (SDLP), John Hume (Rolston, 1987).

When militant republicanism reached a high point, after the 1981 hunger strikes, the New Ireland Forum (of 'constitutional nationalist' parties in Ireland, North and South) took a first step towards persuading the major political forces in the Republic to engage seriously with the problems facing Northern Ireland's nationalists, rather than hiding behind the irredentist rhetoric of the past.[7] The British government was prepared to move in a similar direction, albeit after initially rejecting the Forum's proposals, and bolster the position of the SDLP, even at the expense of enraging unionist opinion. This should be seen as proof of both the failure of previous efforts to end direct rule solely by British arbitration, and of the tremendous anxiety induced by the growth of Sinn Féin as an electoral force.

The 'Irish dimension' has proven a fundamental sticking point in all recent discussions about how to move towards power-sharing devolution. For unionists, the problem was that the 'Irish dimension' of the AIA 'invites Ulster politicians to take a ticket on a constitutional mystery tour without an end in sight' (Cox, 1993: 32). For 'constitutional nationalists', there was no incentive to bargain away the gains made through the AIA; the SDLP could not realistically be expected to settle for power-sharing within Northern Ireland, with an 'Irish dimension' of much-reduced saliency. As Cox has astutely pointed out, the governments did not produce a clear enough constitutional framework within which the parties in Northern Ireland would have to work. It was the ambivalence of the AIA, rather than its perceived favouritism to one side or the other, that helped to produce stalemate.

> In other words, much − though not ... all − of the blame for the constitutional impasse ... really rests with the two sovereign governments in their desire, each for its own reasons, to keep their constitutional options open. (Cox, 1993: 32)

From the Downing Street Declaration to the Frameworks Documents

Whilst the Brooke–Mayhew talks laboured on towards their unsatisfactory conclusion in November 1992, the paramilitaries on both sides of the sectarian divide appeared to have the upper hand. Amidst the 'everyday', 'ordinary' violence, there were several bombings and assassinations that aroused particular public revulsion: the IRA bomb in Warrington that killed two young boys; the IRA bomb at a fish shop on the Shankill Road, and the murderous reaction of loyalist paramilitaries at Greysteel (Bew and Gillespie, 1996). It seemed as though Northern Ireland had reached the nadir. The communities were frightened and polarized, their political representatives at loggerheads, and the governments to which they looked for support seemed inured to the depressing cycle of killing. October 1993 was the worst month for deaths by political violence in Northern Ireland since the mid-1970s.

However, despite this bleak picture, several of the main protagonists had continued working on strategies to overcome the impasse. Hume and Adams had held a series of meetings as far back as 1988. These discussions ended with disagreement over the critical question of the British government's strategic or political interest in remaining the sovereign power in Northern Ireland. The Sinn Féin view was that Britain retained its selfish interests, whereas the Social Democratic Labour Party (SDLP) position was that Britain was essentially neutral. They also argued over the best way to implement 'national self-determination' and over the related issue of the consent of the unionist population, or as Sinn Féin presented it, the unionist 'veto'. Nonetheless, the seeds were sown for future political contacts. Hume and Adams took up their dialogue again in early 1993.[8]

Hume's main argument was that the division of the people on the island of Ireland was more significant than the division of the territory, and that the British government would legislate for Irish unity, if a mandate was forthcoming from a majority of the people in Northern Ireland. In these circumstances, the IRA's campaign of violence was in fact making this objective less probable. Adams was impressed that the SDLP had shown little interest from the early 1980s in 'partitionist internal diversions', i.e. devolved government within Northern Ireland, and gradually Sinn Féin became more interested in developing a new mass movement on an all-Ireland basis, 'open to everyone committed to the principle and objective of Irish national self-determination' (Patterson, 1989: 189, citing Adams, 1989). However, the way in which this right to self-determination should be exercised, and in particular the question of the right of the majority *within* Northern Ireland to withhold consent, remains the kernel of the differences between the strands of Irish nationalist opinion.

Meanwhile, the British and Irish governments continued to meet under the auspices of the regular intergovernmental conferences of the AIA. Even after the breakdown of interparty talks, bilateral discussions were maintained. Hume reported the substance of his discussions with

Adams to the Dublin government of Albert Reynolds (an unprece-
dented Fianna Fáil–Labour coalition), and the latter decided to run with
the 'Irish Peace Initiative' (as the Hume–Adams document was known to
nationalists). From late summer through the autumn of 1993, whilst the
level of violence was at its height, the British and Irish governments
attempted to reach a position that would contain the potential for an
IRA ceasefire, but could also assuage unionist fears of a sell-out by
London.

Consideration of the contested issue of sovereignty has played a
large part in the differences and tension that emerged between the
British and Irish governments. After the Downing Street Declaration
was finalized, there was a great deal of optimism, although it quickly
became apparent 'it [was] a piece of tortuous syntax that defies textual
exegesis' (Arthur, 1994: 219). For Sir David Goodall, who had been
involved in drafting the Anglo-Irish Agreement, the declaration was a
diplomatic masterpiece. 'It was neither a formal agreement nor a treaty
setting the framework for a comprehensive constitutional settlement. It
was a political statement of attitude and intent directed primarily at the
IRA. The two heads of government have carefully shelved all the
difficult longer term issues ... in order to make a bid for an IRA
ceasefire' (cited in Arthur, 1994: 219).

Paragraph 4 of the declaration was perhaps the clearest example of
the ambivalence at the heart of the document. Major affirmed that the
British government 'will uphold the democratic wish of a greater
number of the people of Northern Ireland on the issue of whether they
prefer to support the Union or a sovereign united Ireland'. He reiterated
the view that the British government had no 'selfish strategic or
economic interest in Northern Ireland'. Some of the language used here
was first mooted in the early discussions between the SDLP and Sinn
Féin, but from the republican perspective there were crucial differences
between the declaration and the 'Irish Peace Initiative' (O'Brien, 1995:
286–324). It was the clause dealing with self-determination where the
sleight of hand in the document was most obvious:

> The British government agree that it is for the people of the island of
> Ireland alone, by agreement between the two parts respectively, to
> exercise their right to self-determination on the basis of consent, freely and
> concurrently given, North and South, to bring about a united Ireland, if
> that is their wish. (From Paragraph 4 of the Declaration)

Writing in the *Guardian* (17 December 1993), Cole picked up on
Paragraph 4. He argued that 'self-determination' and 'consent' were
really synonyms, and that the

modern Irish problem has always been about ... which of those units (Northern Ireland or the whole island) is *entitled* to self-determination ... In lands with divided national loyalties, self-determination is not a mere United Nations legalism, but a recognition that governments, who like to pose as 'sovereign powers', can never permanently prevail against an unwilling people. That dictum slices both ways in Ireland ... It is this which makes Paragraph 4 futile. Correction: it will not be futile if the IRA leadership uses it as an occasion for calling off violence.

This necessarily ambiguous sentence fell far short of the Republican movement's central ideological goal of 'national self-determination', and was at the heart of its unwillingness to endorse the declaration.

The Downing Street Declaration thus remained unpalatable to the republicans. The special conference of Sinn Féin at Letterkenny in July 1994 that paved the way for an IRA ceasefire announced the following month, also made it plain that republicans could not accept 'the unionist veto' or 'the absence of a British commitment to "persuade" unionists that ... they can have any Ireland they like as long as it's united' (Wilson, 1994a: 5). The Republican movement had not undergone 'an ideological conversion'. As Wilson argues, 'it was opening up tactically to *alternatives* to the "armed struggle", not strategically *abandoning* it'. According to a 'broad republican perspective', the declaration used a discourse that had acquired a 'nationalist shadow', but the substance remained 'very much unionist. The veto of unionism is to stay firmly in position. Once that is established, all that is novel in the declaration — such as references to "self-determination" — becomes secondary or irrelevant' (McIntyre, 1994: 17).[9]

Whilst the initial reaction to the declaration from republicans may have been 'almost entirely rejectionist' (O'Brien, 1995: 302), nonetheless they could hope to retain a critical influence in the 'emerging nationalist consensus'. Sinn Féin has argued that the British must become active 'persuaders' of the unionist community, but the Major government has insisted that it will not 'predetermine' the outcome of negotiations, stating that the adoption of such a position would amount to a restriction on the free exercise of self-determination by the people of Northern Ireland. Despite the misgivings of many in the Republican movement, an open-ended IRA ceasefire eventually resulted from 'the consolidation of nationalist unity around Hume–Adams–Reynolds' (O'Brien, 1995: 320).

What the Republican movement wished to see was a commitment by both governments to a political dynamic that would lead to 'transitional arrangements' within a clear-cut timeframe. Whilst the Frameworks Documents of February 1995 could be interpreted from this perspective, and unionist anger suggested that they also saw them in this light, the lack of momentum came as a severe disappointment for Sinn Féin. The republican strategy was imperilled at a relatively early stage by the collapse of the Reynolds government in November 1994, and its replacement by a Fine Gael, Labour, Democratic Left administration, led by Bruton, and less supportive of traditional nationalist aspirations (Duignan, 1995).

The Irish government had, in Article 5 of the declaration, explicitly recognized that

> it would be wrong to attempt to impose a united Ireland, in the absence of the freely given consent of a majority of the people of Northern Ireland. ... [t]he democratic right of self-determination by the people of Ireland as a whole must be achieved and exercised with and subject to the agreement and consent of a majority of the people of Northern Ireland.

Furthermore, in Article 7, Reynolds committed the Irish government,

> in the event of an overall settlement ... as part of a balanced constitutional accommodation, [to] put forward and support proposals for change in the Irish Constitution which would fully reflect the principle of consent in Northern Ireland.

Unionists were relatively comforted by these sections, even if they remained sceptical about the 'pan-nationalist' agenda that Dublin appeared to favour.

With the ceasefire of the Combined Loyalist Military Command, there did seem the opportunity for a peace that could allow the paramilitary organizations on both sides to engage in solely political activity, and for a start to be made on all-party negotiation on Northern Ireland's future. Given the IRA's resumption of violence in February 1996, this now seems to be a matter for speculation. Yet, it should come as no surprise that the road towards such talks would raise obstacles. In part, at least, because of the ambiguities contained within the Downing Street Declaration, representatives on both sides of the communal divide (both 'constitutional' politicians and erstwhile defenders of political violence) have been able to claim to their supporters that they have won (or, are winning; or, can win in the future) significant concessions. As Wilson (1994b: 5) succinctly put it:

> the Provos have stopped because they think that, for the first time since 1921, the union is 'on the table', whereas the loyalists have stopped because they think that, for the first time since 1925, nationalism has recognised the legitimacy of the northern state. Somebody, somewhere, is heading for a rude awakening.

The two governments, despite differences regarding the pace and direction of the tactics to be pursued after the ceasefires, were both committed to work on an updated joint document. The 'shared understanding between the British and Irish governments to assist discussion and negotiation involving the Northern Ireland parties' (the subtitle of the joint framework document) provides the most up-to-date expression of recent thinking by British and Irish elites regarding the constitutional future of Northern Ireland.

The document builds upon the Downing Street Declaration, taking the 'guiding principles of self-determination, the consent of the governed, exclusively democratic and peaceful means, and full respect and protection for the rights and identities of both traditions' as the benchmark for interparty discussion (Summary from Paragraph 10). The three-stranded approach is maintained (Paras 12–13), and the constitutional doctrine of both the British and Irish states is subject to critical analysis (Paras 14–21). Recognizing 'the absence of consensus and depth of divisions' the two governments aim to enhance and codify traditional constitutional doctrines, in order to win the 'fullest attainable measure of consent across both traditions in Ireland'. Practically, the British government commits itself to exercise its jurisdiction 'with rigorous impartiality on behalf of all the people of Northern Ireland, in a way which does not prejudice their freedom to determine Northern Ireland's constitutional status'. The British government is ready to incorporate this flexible approach to its sovereignty over Northern Ireland, either by amendment to the 1920 Government of Ireland Act, or with its replacement by appropriate new legislation (Para. 20). For its part, the Irish government will support the introduction of constitutional change such that

> the Irish Constitution will fully reflect the principle of consent in Northern Ireland and demonstrably be such that no territorial claim of right to jurisdiction over Northern Ireland contrary to the will of a majority of its people is asserted. (Para. 21)

The crucial point to be made with reference to the issue of sovereignty is that the two governments have agreed to abide by the majority decision of the people in Northern Ireland, and to guarantee minority rights. Whether these guarantees of minority rights (or 'parity of esteem' in the jargon of the document) will be sufficient to induce the political parties in Northern Ireland to engage seriously in working towards a new accommodation remains unclear, but the prospects do not look favourable, at least in the short term.

Conclusion

The proposals of the Frameworks Documents do *not* provide for joint authority by the British and Irish governments over Northern Ireland. Nonetheless they do mean a further deepening of the close British–Irish interstate co-operation, and the further development of agreed principles for understanding the Northern Ireland problem that began in the early 1980s. Whilst this represents a significant degree of progress with respect to the formal position of contested sovereignty, it has not been achieved without disagreement. It also remains the case that this interstate co-operation has not *directly* tackled the fundamental issue of formally contested sovereignty. Both the British and Irish states have agreed that they will modify their constitutional claim to the territory of Northern Ireland, in order to make such claims compatible with the principle of the consent of the majority of the people in Northern Ireland, whether they wish to be governed under the sovereignty of the United Kingdom, or by a united Ireland.

However, whilst it is undoubtedly a significant step forward for the two sovereign governments to agree to amend their respective constitutions in accordance with these principles, the parties and the communities in Northern Ireland also need to forge a common commitment to the concepts of self-determination, consent, sovereignty and minority rights. The attitude of several of the major protagonists in Northern Ireland remains ambivalent, or indeed, downright hostile, to the two governments' agreed approach. At present, the talks that began in Northern Ireland in June 1996 (Arthur, 1996b; Bew and Gillespie, 1996) are not satisfactory in this regard, for several reasons. First, they do not comprise all of the main protagonists, with Sinn Féin disallowed from taking its place (or, in the eyes of some commentators, disqualifying itself) at the table as a result of the IRA's decision to end its ceasefire in February 1996. Second, the talks have not moved beyond procedural items, and there appears the distinct danger that a substantive agenda will not be forthcoming in the near future. Third, and of most concern for the long-term prospects for a peaceful political settlement, it is by no means clear that either the majority of Northern Ireland's population or its political representatives are interested or willing to make the leap of faith required for far-reaching compromises on long-cherished goals.

Whilst observers always need to remain mindful of the rhetorical belligerence of politicians, jockeying for bargaining positions, nonetheless it is also incumbent upon commentators to recognize uncompromising extremism, and not to wish it out of existence. In the context of Northern Irish political life, there is little evidence to suggest that many unionists are willing to contemplate the sort of role for the Irish Republic envisaged in the joint Framework Document's sections on North–South relations.[10] Similarly, there is little to support the view that republicans have fully and unambiguously accepted the understanding of self-determination and consent contained in the Frameworks Documents (and the Downing Street Declaration and AIA before them). Over the course of the past decade or more, the British and Irish governments have worked closely together. Yet, they have not attempted to solve their fundamental differences over sovereignty. It is hard to see how they could without imposing an unwanted outcome on one section or other of the Northern Ireland population. As Bruton said of the Frameworks Documents:

> it aims at a balance between aspirations that are, if put within a traditional, absolutist and territorial matrix, basically irreconcilable ... It is the beginning of work towards a wholly new form of expression of traditional aspirations, focusing on individuals and communities rather than on territory. By expressing aspirations in this new way, we hope that the two otherwise irreconcilable sets of aspirations can, in fact, be reconciled. (Cited in Bew and Gillespie, 1996: 85)

Governments may have been able to change, and build up trust, but the communities within Northern Ireland, for understandable reasons, are finding this process of modifying aspirations a hugely problematic undertaking.

Notes

1. The articles of the 1937 Constitution that have caused, and continue to cause particular Unionist alarm are 2 & 3:

   Art.2: The national territory consists of the whole island of Ireland, its islands and the territorial seas.
   Art.3: Pending the re-integration of the national territory and without prejudice to the right of Parliament and Government established by this Constitution to exercise jurisdiction over the whole of that territory, the laws enacted by that Parliament shall have the like area and extent of application as the laws of Saorstat Eireann (Irish Free State) and the like extra-territorial effect.

   For further discussion of the 1937 Constitution see Hunter, 1982: 23–6; O'Leary and Arthur, 1990: 21–3 and Dunphy, 1995: 205–10.
2. The critical import of the Ireland Act is cited by O'Leary and McGarry (1993: 145):

   Northern Ireland remains part of His Majesty's dominions and of the United Kingdom and it is hereby affirmed that in no event will

Northern Ireland or any part of thereof cease to be part of His Majesty's dominions and of the United Kingdom without the consent of the parliament of Northern Ireland.

3. For further details of the proroguing of Stormont, and the Northern Ireland Constitution Act of 1973, see Hadfield, 1992; Oliver, 1982; Morrow, 1996; O'Leary and McGarry, 1993: 193–7.

4. On the AIA, see: O'Leary and McGarry, 1993; O'Leary, 1987a, 1987b, 1989; Crick, 1988; FitzGerald, 1993; Arthur, 1993a; Hadden and Boyle, 1989; Aughey, 1989.

5. On the Brooke–Mayhew talks and the British and Irish general elections of 1992, see O'Leary and McGarry, 1993: 312–22; Arthur, 1990, 1992, 1993b; Wilford, 1992; Cox, 1993.

6. With the abolition of the Stormont parliament, the provision of the 1949 Ireland Act was effectively replaced by the 'constitutional guarantee' in the Northern Ireland Act, 1973 (see footnote 2 above).

7. For further discussion of the New Ireland Forum, see Rolston, 1987; Boyle and Hadden, 1984, 1985. It is instructive to compare the debates held under the auspices of the New Ireland Forum, and those that were initiated by the Reynolds government in October 1994, the Forum for Peace and Reconciliation (see *Paths to a Political Settlement in Ireland:* Policy Papers submitted to the Forum, 1995).

8. For details of the Hume–Adams dialogue and the various joint statements they released, see Bew and Gillespie, 1993: 210, 297–8; 1996; Patterson, 1989: 179–93; Arthur, 1994: 224–7; Mallie and McKittrick, 1996; Duignan, 1995; Rowan, 1995.

9. McIntyre (1994: 17) went on to argue that 'the declaration is a device designed to exonerate the British state, running with the logic that the conflict is internal and does not really concern sovereignty ... How realistic is it, then, for anyone to expect the IRA to call a halt to its campaign, when the *raison d'être* of it – the denial of national self-determination on the pretext of the unionist veto – has not been remotely addressed?' This passage illustrates the difficulties that the Republican movement had in accepting the declaration, the internal problem of winning the ceasefire, and the probability, since demonstrated, that any ceasefire would be of a fragile nature.

10. See Bew and Gillespie, 1996: 87 for a discussion of this basic unwillingness to compromise: 'Most unionists gave power-sharing as a preferred option, but only 12% opted for power-sharing plus an Irish dimension. Both governments would hope for a shift.'

In a recent interview (*New Statesman,* 1 November 1996: 19), David Trimble, leader of the UUP, appears to reject the whole basis for the Anglo-Irish intergovernmental approach: ' "Anglo-Irishry" ... the idea that you can construct some sort of constitutional halfway house between Northern Ireland being part of the UK, or being part of a united Ireland ... This is one of the issues on which I am hard. But all Unionists regard this as a zero-sum issue, because that is what it is.'

References

Adams, G. (1989) *A Pathway to Peace*. Cork and Dublin: Mercier.

Arthur, P. (1990) 'Negotiating the Northern Ireland Problem: Track One or Track Two Diplomacy?', *Government and Opposition*, **25**(4), 403–18.

Arthur, P. (1992) 'The Brooke Initiative', *Irish Political Studies*, **7**, 111–15.

Arthur, P. (1993a) 'The Anglo-Irish Agreement: A Device for Territorial Management?', in D. Keogh and M. Haltzel (eds) *Northern Ireland and the Politics of Reconciliation*. Washington DC: Woodrow Wilson Center Press; Cambridge: Cambridge University Press.

Arthur, P. (1993b) 'The Mayhew Talks 1992', *Irish Political Studies*, **8**, 138–43.

Arthur, P. (1994) 'The Anglo-Irish Joint Declaration: Towards A Lasting Peace?', *Government and Opposition*, **29**(2), 218–30.

Arthur, P. (1995) 'Some Thoughts on Transition: A Comparative View of the Peace Processes in South Africa and Northern Ireland', *Government and Opposition*, **30**(1), 48–59.

Arthur, P. (1996a) 'Northern Ireland 1968–1972', in A. Aughey and D. Morrow (eds) *Northern Ireland Politics*. London and New York: Longman.

Arthur, P. (1996b) 'Time, Territory, Tradition and the Anglo-Irish "Peace" Process', *Government and Opposition* **31**(4), 426–40.

Aughey, A. (1989) *Under Siege: Ulster Unionism and the Anglo-Irish Agreement*. London: Hurst; New York: St. Martin's Press.

Bew, P. (1994) *Ideology and the Irish Question: Ulster Unionism and Irish Nationalism, 1912–1916*. Oxford: Clarendon Press.

Bew, P. and Gillespie, G. (1993) *Northern Ireland: A Chronology of the Troubles, 1968–1993*. Dublin: Gill & Macmillan.

Bew, P. and Gillespie, G. (1996) *The Northern Ireland Peace Process, 1993–1996: A Chronology*. London: Serif.

Boyle, K. (1991) 'Northern Ireland: Allegiances and Identities', in B. Crick (ed.) *National Identities: The Constitution of the United Kingdom*. Oxford: Blackwell.

Boyle, K. and Hadden, T. (1984) 'How to Read the New Ireland Forum Report', *Political Quarterly*, **55**(4), 402–17.

Boyle, K. and Hadden, T. (1985) *Ireland: A Positive Proposal*. Harmondsworth: Penguin.

Boyle, K. and Hadden, T. (1995) 'The Peace Process in Northern Ireland', *International Affairs*, **71**(2), 269–83.

Cox, W. H. (1993) 'The Northern Ireland Talks', *Politics Review*, **3**(2), 28–32.

Crick, B. (1982) 'The Sovereignty of Parliament and the Irish Question', in D. Rea (ed.) *Political Co-operation in Divided Societies: A Series of Papers Relevant to the Conflict in Northern Ireland*. Dublin: Gill & Macmillan.

Crick, B. (1988) 'The Concept of Consent and the Agreement', in C. Townshend (ed.) *Consensus in Ireland: Approaches and Recessions*. Oxford: Clarendon Press.

Duignan, S. (1995) *One Spin on the Merry-Go-Round*. Dublin: Blackwater Press.

Dunphy, R. (1995) *The Making of Fianna Fáil Power in Ireland, 1923–1948*. Oxford: Clarendon Press.

FitzGerald, G. (1993) 'The Origins and Rationale of the Anglo-Irish Agreement of 1985', in D. Keogh and M. Haltzel (eds) *Northern Ireland and the Politics of*

Reconciliation. Washington DC: Woodrow Wilson Center Press; Cambridge: Cambridge University Press.

Flackes, W. D. and Elliott, S. (1994) *Northern Ireland: A Political Directory, 1968-1993*. Belfast: Blackstaff Press.

Foster, R. F. (1989) *Modern Ireland, 1600-1972*. Harmondsworth: Penguin.

Hadden, T. and Boyle, K. (1989) *The Anglo–Irish Agreement: Commentary, Text and Review*. London: Sweet & Maxwell; London: Edwin Higel.

Hadfield, B. (1989) *The Constitution of Northern Ireland*. Belfast: SLS.

Hadfield, B. (ed.) (1992) *Northern Ireland: Politics & The Constitution*. Buckingham: Open University Press.

Hopkinson, M. (1988) *Green Against Green: The Irish Civil War*. Dublin: Gill & Macmillan.

Hunter, J. (1982) 'An Analysis of the Conflict in Northern Ireland', in D. Rea (ed.) *Political Co-operation in Divided Societies: A Series of Papers Relevant to the Conflict in Northern Ireland*. Dublin: Gill & Macmillan.

Lijphart, A. (1996) 'The Framework Document on Northern Ireland and the Theory of Power-Sharing', *Government and Opposition*, 31(3), 267–74.

Mallie, E. and McKittrick, D. (1996) *The Fight for Peace: The Secret Story Behind the Irish Peace Process*. London: Heinemann.

McGarry, J. and O'Leary, B. (eds) (1990) *The Future of Northern Ireland*. Oxford: Clarendon Press.

McGarry, J. and O'Leary, B. (1995) *Explaining Northern Ireland: Broken Images*. Oxford, and Cambridge, MA: Blackwell.

McIntyre, A. (1994) 'Not Worth the Paper', *Fortnight*, no. 325.

McKittrick, D. (1996) *The Nervous Peace*. Belfast: Blackstaff Press.

Morrow, D. (1996) 'Northern Ireland 1972–1995', in A. Aughey and D. Morrow (eds) *Northern Ireland Politics*. London and New York: Longman.

Munck, R. (1992) 'The Making of the Troubles in Northern Ireland', *Journal of Contemporary History*, 27(2), 211–29.

O'Brien, B. (1995) *The Long War: The IRA and Sinn Féin from Armed Struggle to Peace Talks*. Dublin: O'Brien Press.

O'Connor, F. (1993) *In Search of a State: Catholics in Northern Ireland*. Belfast: Blackstaff Press.

O'Leary, B. (1987a) 'The Anglo-Irish Agreement: Meanings, Explanations, Results and a Defence', in P. Teague (ed.) *Beyond the Rhetoric: Politics, the Economy and Social Policy in Northern Ireland*. London: Lawrence and Wishart.

O'Leary, B. (1987b) 'The Anglo-Irish Agreement: Statecraft or Folly?', *West European Politics*, 10(1), 5–32.

O'Leary, B. (1989) 'The Limits to Coercive Consociationalism in Northern Ireland', *Political Studies*, 37(4), 562–88.

O'Leary, B. and Arthur, P. (1990) 'Introduction: Northern Ireland as a Site of State- and Nation-Building Failures', in J. McGarry and B. O'Leary (eds) *The Future of Northern Ireland*. Oxford: Clarendon Press.

O'Leary, B. and McGarry, J. (1993) *The Politics of Antagonism: Understanding Northern Ireland*. London and Atlantic Heights, NJ: Athlone Press.

Oliver, J. (1982) 'The Evolution of Constitutional Policy in Northern Ireland Over the Past 15 Years', in D. Rea (ed.) *Political Co-operation in Divided*

Societies: A Series of Papers Relevant to the Conflict in Northern Ireland. Dublin: Gill & Macmillan.

Palley, C. (1972) 'The Evolution, Disintegration and Possible Reconstruction of the Northern Ireland Constitution', *Anglo-American Law Review*, 1(3), 462–75.

Paths to a Political Settlement in Ireland. (Policy Papers submitted to the Forum for Peace and Reconciliation) (1995). Belfast: Blackstaff Press.

Patterson, H. (1989) *The Politics of Illusion: Republicanism and Socialism in Modern Ireland.* London: Hutchinson Radius.

Patterson, H. (1996a) 'Northern Ireland 1921–1968', in A. Aughey and D. Morrow (eds) *Northern Ireland Politics.* London and New York: Longman.

Patterson, H. (1996b) 'Nationalism', in A. Aughey and D. Morrow (eds) *Northern Ireland Politics.* London and New York: Longman.

Patterson, H. (1996c) 'Misunderstanding TUAS', *Times Change: Quarterly Political and Cultural Review*, **8**, 32–3.

Phoenix, E. (1994) *Northern Nationalism: Nationalist Politics, Partition and the Catholic Minority in Northern Ireland, 1890–1940.* Belfast: Ulster Historical Foundation.

Purdie, B. (1990) *Politics in the Streets: The Origins of the Civil Rights Movement in Northern Ireland.* Belfast: Blackstaff Press.

Rolston, B. (1987) 'Alienation or Political Awareness? The Battle for the Hearts and Minds of Northern Nationalists', in P. Teague (ed.) *Beyond the Rhetoric: Politics, the Economy and Social Policy in Northern Ireland.* London: Lawrence and Wishart.

Rose, R. (1976) *Northern Ireland: A Time of Choice.* London: Macmillan.

Rowan, B. (1995) *Behind the Lines: The Story of the IRA and Loyalist Ceasefires.* Belfast: Blackstaff Press.

Ward, A. (1993) 'A Constitutional Background to the Northern Ireland Crisis', in D. Keogh and M. Haltzel (eds) *Northern Ireland and the Politics of Reconciliation.* Washington DC: Woodrow Wilson Center Press; Cambridge: Cambridge University Press.

Whyte, J. (1988) 'Interpretations of the Northern Ireland Problem', in C. Townshend (ed.) *Consensus in Ireland: Approaches and Recessions.* Oxford: Clarendon Press.

Whyte, J. (1990) *Interpreting Northern Ireland.* Oxford: Clarendon Press.

Wilford, R. (1992) 'The 1992 Westminster Election in Northern Ireland', *Irish Political Studies*, **7**, 105–10.

Wilson, R. (1994a) 'Echoing Footsteps', *Fortnight*, no. **324**.

Wilson, R. (1994b) 'New Times, Old Words', *Fortnight*, no. **333**.

Coping with Diversity: Sovereignty in a Divided Society

J. E. SPENCE AND DAVID WELSH[1]

South Africa's transition from a racial oligarchy, in which untrammelled sovereignty was vested in a parliament controlled by representatives of the white minority, to a liberal democratic system, in which the constitution is sovereign, has rightly been acclaimed as a remarkable political achievement. Few analysts believed that it was likely or possible, at least not without major violence, perhaps a full-scale civil war.

The emergence of South Africa as a democratic state raises two questions which lie at the heart of the analysis developed here. How effective will the new state be in tackling the diversity of a divided society, and what implications does the dramatic transition from racial oligarchy to liberal democratic state have for the concept of sovereignty?

The period of the Union

From the inception of the modern South African state in 1910 to the abandonment of apartheid in the early 1990s, neither the issue of coping with diversity nor the question of sovereignty had posed particularly serious problems to successive governments. In terms of the South Africa Act of 1909 – which served as the Union's constitution until it was replaced by a republican form in 1961 – South Africa was a dominion of the (British) Commonwealth. The Balfour Declaration of 1926, its formal legal incorporation into the Statute of Westminster (1931) and the Status of the Union Act (1936) appeared to have settled the vexed question of sovereignty. In effect, the Balfour Declaration gave formal recognition to the principle of sovereign equality for all members of the British Commonwealth and the right to pursue an independent foreign policy for each dominion. Thus, while in 1914

Britain had declared war on behalf of South Africa, in 1939 the decision to fight Nazi Germany and its allies was made in the Union's role as an independent sovereign state.

Indeed, throughout the interwar period and for some years thereafter South Africa's right to conduct its own affairs — whether internal or external — was rarely, if ever, challenged by external actors. South Africa was therefore a beneficiary of the traditional doctrine — dating back to the Treaty of Westphalia (1648) — that the state was the sole source of law, authority and — most important — order within its territorial jurisdiction. By the same token, South Africa enjoyed the benefits deriving from the sanctity and legal protection of domestic jurisdiction, the separation of foreign and domestic policy, and the reciprocal obligation of nonintervention. This legal status, the theoretical construct of the prevailing system of international law, was reinforced in practice by the high status South Africa enjoyed in diplomatic discourse and day-to-day interaction with its fellow members of international society. Hence South Africa was regarded as a committed and conscientious member of the League of Nations and the British Commonwealth; a faithful and efficient ally in peace and war; a valued trading partner; and as the Cold War got under way, a strategic bastion for the defence of the West.

This favourable position in the society of states was to change profoundly after the Second World War. Indeed the roots of this change can be traced back to the Treaty of Versailles and the emphasis placed on the principle of national self-determination as the basis for the post-1919 world order. It is worth noting in this context that this principle was the source of the plea of an African National Congress (ANC) delegation for recognition of the claims of the unenfranchised black majority in South Africa's political system.

The inroads made into the traditional doctrine of sovereignty after 1945 forced the Nationalist government (elected in 1948) into a defensive mode in the conduct of its foreign policy, precisely because the right the government claimed to conduct its internal affairs unchallenged clashed fundamentally with the norms that came to dominate international discourse in the postwar period. The Western allies were determined to restructure the shattered economic and political systems of Axis powers in their own democratic image. Following the belated discovery of the horrors of the Holocaust, the definition of a new legal standard embracing 'crimes against humanity' represented a major break with the doctrine of domestic jurisdiction and nonintervention — the traditional hallmarks of sovereignty.

The question of sovereignty was also central to the constitutional crisis of the 1950s when the National Party (NP) government had considerable difficulty in removing 'coloured' male voters from the

Cape's common voting roll. The NP's determination to ensure that the sovereign parliament represented only whites was taken a step further in 1959 when the vestigial separate representation accorded to Africans in 1936 was terminated.

The problem of apartheid

Apartheid's rationale rested on the belief that Africans could enjoy political rights only in their 'homelands', the ring of fragmented blocs of territory that represented the shrunken remnants of lands to which Africans could historically lay claim. In the earlier phase of apartheid, no thought was given to the possibility that these ethnic homelands might evolve into sovereign states.

Dr Verwoerd (Prime Minister from 1958 to 1966) reformulated the policy to permit the possibility of eventual 'sovereign independence' for individual homelands. In succeeding years four such homelands were granted nominal independence. The sovereignty that Transkei, Venda, Ciskei and Bophuthatswana received, however, was illusory. None was recognized internationally and in reality, their status as economic hostages to South Africa remained unchanged. As an exercise in the division of sovereignty by partition or 'ethnic self-determination', the homelands policy was a calamitous failure. The enthusiasm with which ordinary citizens of the homelands accepted 'reintegration' into South Africa as part of the democratic transformation showed how alienating the policy had been.

International law had traditionally asserted that a state's claim to sovereignty protected it against criticism or intervention, and the principle of domestic jurisdiction had been written into the Charter of the UN (Article 2:7). However, as South Africa found to its cost, this provided scant protection as the issue of 'human rights' came to dominate the agenda of the UN's General Assembly and a whole host of other international organizations. Third World majorities in these organizations were insistent that colonialism and racism could no longer enjoy the protection of domestic jurisdiction, and to that end the UN approved a series of Declarations and Covenants affirming the sanctity of human rights and legitimizing resolutions for protecting them.[2]

South African sovereignty was effectively challenged, and indeed undermined by these UN Declarations and Covenants in so far as collective acts of states, repeated by and acquiesced in in sufficient numbers with sufficient frequency, eventually attain the status of law (Higgins, 1963). Moreover the dozens of resolutions passed by the UN condemning apartheid were legally justified on the grounds that human rights have long since ... passed into that realm which is of legitimate interest ... [that] ... specific resolutions directed at individual states ... [are] ... a legitimate method of bringing pressure upon a state and yet not falling foul of the prohibition against interference in article 2:7, the domestic jurisdiction clause of the UN Charter. (Higgins, 1984: 35–6)

Thus South Africa fell foul of a new value system which embraced anticolonialism; the right of national self-determination; racial equality within and between states; and the right of intervention when these norms were transgressed by a particular state. Indeed, South Africa was often perceived as a microcosm of the global predicament facing the Third World: a rich white minority oppressing an unenfranchised, deprived black majority.

In defending its claim to be master in its own house, South Africa initially rested its case on the alleged inviolability of the principle of domestic jurisdiction. Time after time in the 1950s, Louw, South Africa's Foreign Minister, berated his critics for observing double standards; *tu quoque* accusations were levelled at countries as diverse as Sweden (for its treatment of the Lapps!) and India, because of its caste system. Yet South Africa in the eyes of many was a unique case simply because it alone in the international society enshrined racial discrimination in legal statute. Thereafter, as the Bantustan policy got under way in the 1960s, the government's defence was based on the principle of 'separate but equal', claiming that the homelands satisfied ethnic claims for self-determination. But this argument was rejected. The belief — widely held at the UN and the Organization for African Unity (OAU) — was that these homelands did not fit the legal definition of self-determination required for the recognition of independent states. Self-determination was now commonly defined in racial terms and deemed only applicable in a colonial context.

Related to this problem is the question of the unit to which it is deemed appropriate to apply the principle. According to Higgins, 'self-determination refers to the right of the majority within a generally accepted political unit to the exercise of power' (1963: 104). This definition has been widely accepted for three reasons: (1) the unit has to be 'generally acceptable', otherwise there is the obvious danger of fragmentation of the international system — in other words, a line (literally) has to be drawn somewhere; (2) without some clearly understood means for determining who is eligible for self-determination, conflict across state boundaries would be encouraged; (3) the great majority of new states had demonstrated a willingness to accept the frontiers inherited from their colonial masters. In this context we should note the 'solemn declaration' in 1964 of the Cairo Conference of African Heads of State that 'all Member States pledge themselves to respect the borders existing on their achievement of national independence' (Cervenka, 1969: 94).

Given this definition, the arguments advanced against recognition of the homelands included the following: first, that they were not generally accepted political units, but rather the artificial creation of the South African government. Secondly, the claim was advanced that the 'unit' in question was the Republic itself and the 'majority' in question was the African population as a whole. Thirdly, that nothing should be done to dismember the South African state as this 'majority' could be expected to achieve self-determination in due course. Thus here we see the clear connection between self-determination conceived in racial terms and the principle of majority rule as a requirement for self-determination. After the Second World War, as Emerson remarks, 'ethnic identity is essentially irrelevant, the decisive, indeed, ordinarily, the sole consideration being the existence of a political entity in the guise of a colonial territory' (1971: 463).

From the point of view of the OAU and the UN, South Africa was therefore a 'colonial situation' in which a white regime was illegally exercising power over a dispossessed black majority. Thus for the Republic's critics, the homelands did not fit the orthodox definition of self-determination, and their hopes for admission to the UN and the OAU proved unfounded. The homelands policy was visibly in tatters, and other major elements of the apartheid policy, like influx control (the 'pass laws' which sought to limit the entry of Africans into towns) were palpably failing. The rise of powerful black trade unions, and the regrouping of internal opposition after 1976–7, also made it clear to the leaders of the apartheid state that significant policy modifications were required.

At the constitutional level, a shoring up of white power was attempted by means of the so-called Tricameral Parliament that was introduced in 1983. This bizarre constitutional creature was the product of six years of debate within the NP which sought to co-opt the coloured and Indian minorities by extending to them the franchise for the election of separate chambers of parliament. It was done in such a way as to combine the semblance of power-sharing with the reality of overall white control. Even this form of sham-consociationalism proved too much for the extreme right-wingers of the NP. Treurnicht's objection to the proposed Tricameral Constitution obliquely raised the issue of sovereignty. He complained that an NP information officer had claimed that there could only be one government in a single country, otherwise 'coloured and Indian ministers ... will co-rule over me and all white, etc. etc. and this is a completely unacceptable idea' (cited by Ries and Dommisse, 1982: 110). Treurnicht and 21 of his supporters were drummed out of the NP caucus and later established the Conservative Party.

Not only did most coloured and Indian voters boycott the elections for the Tricameral Parliament, but even the most moderate and pliant African leaders were outraged by their exclusion. Alienation would reach new heights, as the turbulent period in 1985 showed. Powerful new internal organizations like the United Democratic Front (later widened into the Mass Democratic Movement) arose and the noose of international isolation tightened. Although not generally apparent at the time, these developments were the death-knell of the apartheid order. The power-holders would have to recognize that diversity could not be accommodated by intensified repression or constitutional subterfuges: it would require the extension of full citizenship rights to all South Africans, the abolition of racial discrimination, and the negotiation of a democratic constitution. Only with the acceptance of these preconditions was it possible to cope with diversity in a constitutional and political way.

Negotiating a new constitution

As the ANC soon recognized after its unbanning in February 1990 and the inception of 'talks-about-talks' thereafter, it was not dealing with a defeated enemy. Constitutional negotiations got under way in December 1991 at the Convention for a Democratic South Africa (CODESA). CODESA got off to a resounding start with the general acceptance of a Declaration of Intent that specified in broad outline the elements of a liberal democratic constitution. Early in 1992, however, it was apparent that the principal parties, the ANC, the NP and Inkatha Freedom Party were far apart from one another, not only on fundamental constitutional issues but also on the vital issue of how a final constitution was to be negotiated. As far as the ANC was concerned, CODESA could never be a substitute for a democratically elected constituent assembly that would draft a constitution. The NP, on the other hand, maintained that the ANC's proposed constitution-making procedure put the political cart before the constitutional horse, meaning that this procedure could sweep aside issues that had still to be negotiated. In simple terms, the NP feared that the constituent assembly route might result in an overwhelming ANC majority able to ride roughshod over minority concerns. Inkatha's objections stemmed from the same cause. By now it had realized that its support was largely confined to KwaZulu-Natal; nationally its political significance would be much diminished.

Apart from the fundamental differences over the mode of constitution-making, substantive constitutional differences were also apparent at CODESA. The NP proposed a complex form of executive power-sharing, involving a troika-style presidency and an upper house loaded in favour of minorities. Both proposals were vigorously opposed by the ANC, which favoured a majoritarian democracy that was unitary and made little or no allowance for the salience of ethnicity or regionalism.

In its first attempt to flesh out the broad principles of the Freedom Charter of 1955 (and accepted as policy by the ANC in 1956), the ANC's Constitutional Guidelines of 1988 went so far as to propose the outlawing of racist, ethnic, fascist and regional parties. As the Freedom Charter had done, the Guidelines did accept the multicultural character of South Africa. They envisaged a unitary state but conceded a degree of decentralization for administrative purposes. However, throughout the constitutional negotiations (most of which it boycotted) Inkatha has demanded a much greater degree of decentralization and an extension of provincial autonomy for KwaZulu-Natal. It has also demanded full constitutional protection for the Zulu monarch and the *amakhosi* (traditional leaders), who constitute an important source of support in Inkatha's strongholds among the rural peasantry.

Given South Africa's political and constitutional tradition of a Westminster-type system (though, of course, without democracy and the protection of civil rights) and a parliament that was sovereign in all but limited respects, it was an important advance in the constitutional negotiations that all participating parties readily accepted the principle of constitutionalism. In the final draft, agreed to in May 1996, clause 2 reads: 'This Constitution is the supreme Law of the Republic; law or conduct inconsistent with it is invalid, and the duties imposed by it must be performed' (Final Constitution, 1996).

The constitution also contains several references to the diversity of the society. For example, the preamble contains the clause that 'South Africa belongs to all who live in it, united in our diversity.' The bill of rights in chapter 2 provides (clause 30) that everyone has the right to use the language and to participate in the cultural life of their choice, but that no one exercising these rights may do so in a manner inconsistent with any provision of the bill of rights. Clause 31 extends protection, subject to the same limitation, to cultural, religious or linguistic communities.

Clause 6 recognizes no fewer than eleven official languages, all of which must enjoy 'parity of esteem' and equitable treatment. This clause, however, concedes that for practical reasons, national and provincial governments may use particular official languages for the purposes of government provided that they do not use only one. In addition to the official languages, clause 6 requires that the state take 'practical and positive measures to elevate the status and advance the use' of indigenous languages that have historically been neglected or downgraded. Provision is made for a Pan South African Language Board whose task it is to promote and create conditions for the development and use of official languages, other nonofficial indigenous languages (Khoi, Nama and San), and sign language. The Board must also ensure respect for other nonindigenous languages commonly used by (in practice) small communities.

The constitution-makers may well have created a Babel's Tower of linguistic communities in their apparent liberality. In the critical area of education, however, this liberality may, in certain respects, be curtailed. Clause 29 (2) provides that everyone has the right to receive education in the official language of their choice in public educational institutions 'where that education is reasonably practicable'. In giving effect to this right, the state must consider all reasonable educational alternatives, including single-medium institutions, taking into account three criteria: equity, practicality, and the need to redress the result of past racially discriminatory law and practice.

In practice these limitations suggest that the claims of parents to have single-medium schools for their children, have to be weighed against the criteria noted above, a possibility that has set alarm bells ringing among Afrikaans organizations who, in this respect and many others (such as the sharp reduction in the amount of time allocated to Afrikaans broadcasting by the South African Broadcasting Corporation TV), detect a concerted drive on the part of the ANC-led government to limit the use of Afrikaans in official and semi-official contexts. Their fears extend to the five Afrikaans-medium universities whose language exclusivity is under threat since an inability to use Afrikaans prevents many African students from attending. It is highly likely that before long, only two of the existing Afrikaans-medium universities will remain as such.

The final constitution contains a further provision that purports to cope with diversity. Clause 185 provides for the establishment of a Commission for the Promotion and Protection of the Rights of Cultural, Religious and Linguistic Communities. According to President Mandela, this Commission will ensure

> that our people of South Africa as a whole have an additional instrument in their hands to enable them to avoid the emergence of any situation in which ethnic and other tensions might drive us back to apartheid solutions or to an imitation of the cruel example of Bosnia. (Mandela, 1996: 54)

The Commission is to be composed of members who are broadly representative of the main cultural, religious and linguistic communities, as well as the gender composition of South Africa. Apart from the nebulous duty of promoting respect for these communities and developing mutual tolerance among them, it has the power, to be regulated by national legislation, to recommend the establishment or recognition of cultural councils. The powers of these possible councils are not spelled out. The Commission's functions are to be regulated by national legislation, and it may also report on any matters falling within its purview to another statutory body, the Human Rights Commission, for investigation.

The lukewarm reception accorded to this clause by Afrikaans cultural organizations stems from the lack of any real power vested in the Commission. The Commission, which has not yet been appointed, may be a faint echo of the Cultural Councils of Belgium, but it, and the cultural councils whose creation it may recommend, will almost certainly be a far cry from any significant degree of 'corporate federalism' or the 'segmental autonomy' of consociational theory. It is hard to resist the conclusion that the clause, a much-diluted version of the NP's original proposal, was agreed to by the ANC largely for symbolic purposes or, as Giliomee puts it, as 'bait thrown to Afrikaners to keep them "sweet"' (cited in *Rapport*, Johannesburg, 29 September 1996).

Other formal constitutional provisions relating indirectly to diversity and the question of sovereignty are symbolic ones: the flag and the national anthem. A flag that was entirely new and neutral (in the sense that neither its design nor colours bore any perceivable connection to a particular party) was widely welcomed in 1994 and, even though it was deemed 'provisional', it has been retained. A 'dual' national anthem was agreed to, in terms of which both *Nkosi Sikelel' iAfrika* ('God bless Africa') and *Die Stem van Suid-Afrika* ('The voice of South Africa') were sung on formal occasions and at international sporting events. The final constitution, however, empowers the President to determine the anthem by proclamation. In due course *Die Stem* is likely to be dropped.

As the quotation from President Mandela shows, fear of ethnic and racial conflict remain. 'Nonracialism' remains a distant, perhaps, chimerical ideal. 'Nation-building' may also prove elusive, if it implies creating an overarching sense of primary loyalty to an abstract concept. The experience of other divided societies, frankly, does not lend much encouragement to optimistic views on either of these counts. The interim constitution, in terms of which the country will be governed until 1999 (when the final constitution will come into force) was notable for the Government of National Unity (GNU) which was essentially an attempt to cope with diversity by means of a constitutionally required coalition of the principal parties. Its basic feature was that parties which won 10 per cent of the national vote in the election of April 1994 were entitled to a proportionate allocation of cabinet portfolios, and parties winning 20 per cent or more of the vote were entitled to an executive deputy presidency. The cabinet is to function

in a manner which gives consideration to the consensus-seeking spirit underlying the concept of a government of national unity as well as the need for effective government. (Clause 89:2, Interim constitution, 1993)

The evidence suggests that, apart from the occasional well-publicized spats between Mandela and de Klerk, the consensus-seeking spirit was respected at least for the first eighteen months or so of the GNU's existence. Thereafter, the NP and Inkatha ministers were increasingly marginalized until, in May 1996, de Klerk withdrew the NP. Ostensibly his reason for doing so was because the ANC had declined to consider the NP's proposal that the GNU principle be carried over into the final constitution. It is likely that the more pressing reason was the increasing dissatisfaction among NP backbenchers with the invidious and ambiguous position of being simultaneously a party of government and of opposition. Inkatha, on the other hand, decided to remain in the GNU, despite a lukewarm attitude to the principle and allegations that ANC ministers took little or no notice of Inkatha's views.

Democracy and the diffusion of power

The NP's withdrawal from the GNU may lead one to conclude that the attempt to forge national unity by the ANC government has been a failure. This view overlooks the crucial role played by the GNU in lowering the stakes of the founding election of April 1994. The realistic possibility that the NP would retain some influence in the executive after the election was a source of reassurance to white voters that facilitated what was otherwise a fundamental shift of power. An election fought on a 'winner-take-all' basis might well have led to disaster (Welsh, 1997).

While the GNU may not necessarily have been the most appropriate mechanism for this purpose, there is abundant evidence from divided societies that consensus-building instruments of a formal or informal kind are necessary if democratic polities are to be sustained. 'Grand coalitions' have commonly served this purpose, though the successful ones have resulted from political agreements or pacts, rather than constitutional requirements.

Two important facts should be recalled in discussing South Africa's diversity and how to cope with it. First, that voting went largely along 'racial' lines in both the national elections of April 1994, and the local government elections of November 1995 and May 1996. This pattern seems most unlikely to change in the foreseeable future. Secondly, the margin between the winning party's share of the vote in 1994 (the ANC won over 62 per cent) and the next biggest party (the NP with over 20 per cent) is said to be the biggest in the democratic world.

There is no legitimate constitutional device that can attenuate, or mitigate the consequences of these facts. Single-party dominance is South Africa's likely trajectory, with all the attendant dangers of political sclerosis, arrogance and the blurring of the dividing line between party and state. 'Tyranny of the majority', underpinned by continued 'racial' voting, undermines any credible notion of democracy – as it did in the subsystem of Northern Ireland or in Sri Lanka. South Africa's final constitution provides essentially for 'winner-take-all' outcomes (notwithstanding an electoral system that will be based 'in general' on proportional representation). Adversarial politics in this institutional context could hardly provide a better recipe for eroding democracy and alienating minorities.

Many students of South Africa have advocated federation as a means of coping with diversity. Possibly the fragmenting of sovereignty and the diffusion of power would be more supportive of democracy. Neither the interim nor the final constitution provides for a genuinely federal system, although the provinces will be important links in the administrative chain for implementing policies determined by national government. Although it is prudent not to insist upon clear-cut distinctions between federal and unitary systems, South Africa's constitutions lean strongly towards the unitary system, even if they have federal fig leaves.

Only minor areas of exclusive legislative competence are vested in the provinces, and their taxing powers are severely limited. Far more significant powers (including primary and secondary education, health, housing and welfare services) are to be exercised by the national and provincial legislatures, but all are subject to powerful overrides available to the central government.

It has been the question of how unitary or federal South Africa should be that is at the heart of the long-standing dispute between Inkatha and the ANC. Inkatha's constitutional proposals for a highly decentralized federal relationship between KwaZulu-Natal and the rest of South Africa were substantially embodied in a draft adopted by the KwaZulu-Natal Legislative Assembly on 15 March 1996. The document envisages KwaZulu-Natal as a self-governing province with a constitutional monarch (in the form of the Zulu king) and its own coat of arms, flag, anthem and other symbols, as well as its own bill of rights and constitutional court. It claims extensive exclusive provincial powers and virtually unrestricted taxing powers.

As anticipated, the draft constitution was rejected by the Constitutional Court. For the time being, at any rate, the document is useful principally as an indication of the width of the gulf between Inkatha and the ANC in relation to constitutional thinking. Clearly this has a bearing on the issue of diversity since it is that section of the Zulu population (largely rural) which supports Inkatha (amounting to perhaps 50 per cent) which are mobilized on an ethnic basis. Inkatha's major goal is to retain political control of KwaZulu-Natal which it won by the narrowest of margins in 1994, and to extend provincial powers so as to ward off what it perceives to be creeping ANC hegemony.

Inkatha's demands, which verge on being of a confederal character, have alarmed the ANC and confirmed its worst suspicions that stronger federalism could even pave the way to the break-up of the country. In particular it has opposed Inkatha's demand for control of the provincial police. This is a reaction to the role of the KwaZulu (homeland) police in the apartheid years when, in the eyes of the ANC's internal surrogates, it was little more than Inkatha's private army.

If Inkatha's demands are unlikely to get very far in the foreseeable future, the same is true of the white right wing's demand for an exclusive ethnic enclave called a *volkstaat*. On the eve of the elections in 1994, General Viljoen (a popular right-wing leader of the Freedom Front and retired chief of the South African army) decided that violent counter-revolution was not a viable strategy, and instead opted to pursue the Front's goals by constitutional means. In this way the danger posed by the right wing was largely neutralized (Welsh, 1995). Mandela and the ANC, in appreciation, created a constitutional opening for the Freedom Front by agreeing to include in the interim constitution a principle which recognized the right of the South African people as a whole to self-determination. Such recognition did not preclude

> constitutional provision for a notion of the right to self-determination by any community sharing a common cultural and language heritage, whether in a territorial entity within the Republic or in any other recognised way. (Constitutional Principle 34 (1), Interim Constitution, 1993)

It was further stipulated that the final constitution could give expression to any particular form of self-determination 'provided there is substantial proven support within the community concerned for such a form of self-determination'. A further agreement enabled the establishment of a Volkstaat Council, whose task it was to make concrete proposals.

The Freedom Front, alas, was unable to prove that it had substantial support among Afrikaners during the elections, nor were the right-wingers, who have always been a fragmented category, capable of reaching agreement on the location of a putative *volkstaat*. What lent an air of unreality to all the discussions among right-wingers and the deliberations of the Volkstaat Council was the virtual certainty that the ANC would never agree to the establishment of a racially exclusive enclave – however well Mandela and Viljoen got on together, and however much gratitude the ANC owed Viljoen.

In May 1995 the Volkstaat Council produced a report that recommended a *volkstaat* in which a majority of the inhabitants were Afrikaners (First Interim Report, 1995: 31–3). The proposals fell on deaf ears. After further lengthy internal discussions, the Freedom Front announced yet further proposals in August 1996. These envisaged an area in the Northern Cape between the Orange River and the West Coast as an Afrikaner *volkstaat* and two other areas in the Bushveld and in the Pretoria/Centurion area which could be developed as areas of 'regional autonomy' (*streekoutonomie*). Further proposals envisaged cultural councils, including local-level Afrikaner Councils that are to be co-ordinated by a national Afrikaner Council. This package is to be negotiated with the ANC.

The proposals are envisaged as a long-term project. Eventually, it is hoped, between 600,000 and 1 million Afrikaners would be attracted to the *volkstaat*. No forced removals of non-Afrikaners are contemplated (they would in any case be unconstitutional) and neither are any extraconstitutional actions. In its statement the Freedom Front says:

> the Afrikaners, as a minority people, in a plural multiethnic state, have the right to a continued existence and to resist swamping and assimilation. It [the Freedom Front] believes that this can best be achieved by means of the different forms of self-determination which are provided for in the Constitution. (*Rapport*, 1 September 1996)

The *volkstaat* proposals are unlikely to be received with much sympathy by the ANC.

In reviewing the extent of South Africa's diversity and the attempts to cope with it, it will have been apparent that it is premature to pronounce on the success or otherwise of these efforts. The 'rainbow nation' remains an ideal that is yet to be realized. The scant success that 'nation-building' has achieved elsewhere in Africa may incline one to pessimism, though it is at least an advantage that none of the potential candidates for a secessionist movement appears to have nearly enough political resources to succeed.

With the partial exception of a segment of the Zulu, none of the other African ethno-linguistic groups has evinced much interest in mobilizing on an ethnic basis. Since none is a majority, and population dispersal has been extensive, the prospects for such ethnic mobilization may be slender. Notwithstanding these qualifications, South Africa's diversity and sovereignty exists in a volatile, even turbulent, society whose future political configurations cannot be predicted. It is doubtful whether the current set of political institutions will be equal to the task of coping without substantial modifications.

A normative concept of sovereignty

The inauguration of South Africa's first democratically elected government on 10 May 1994 was rightly interpreted as signalling the re-entry of the 'new' state into the international community. The South African government's sovereign right to 'constitutional independence' was now regarded as legitimate in a way which was not the case during the apartheid era. Apart from formal recognition by a host of states which had refused to accept Pretoria's claim to sovereignty in the past, there were a variety of symbolic moments signifying the reincorporation of South Africa into the Commonwealth, the OAU and the General Assembly of the UN. In this respect, the new South Africa met the normative criteria of sovereignty – responsibility and accountability – which in the view of one influential school of thought must now be given their full weight in any meaningful definition of sovereignty in the post-Cold War period (Deng *et al.*, 1996: xvii–xxviii).

In this context these criteria advanced in the Deng study are worth citing at length:

> The normative principles of sovereignty, responsibility and accountability have internal and external dimensions. The internal dimension has to do with the degree to which the government is responsive to the needs of its people, is accountable to the body politic, and is therefore legitimate. The international dimension has to do with the co-operation of sovereign states in helping or checking one another when a fellow state loses or refuses to use its capacity to provide protection and assistance for its citizens. (Deng *et al.*, 1996: xvii–xxviii)

These criteria apply neatly to South Africa as presently constituted, entitling the government to claim that its sovereignty is both responsible and accountable, and fully validated by the international community. Furthermore, sovereignty, defined in this innovative mode, raises important questions about how the new South Africa might exercise its sovereign responsibilities in both a regional and continental setting.

Wider responsibilities

Policy-makers in Pretoria have emphasized their government's willingness to help promote regional integration in the immediate hinterland of Southern Africa and at the same time play a constructive role in the task of rejuvenating a continent which has been battered by civil war, underdevelopment and inadequate and corrupt government. But the African environment in which South Africa has to operate is unpropitious: the immediate region is characterized by a high degree of uneven development and the progress of regional integration is likely to be slow and haphazard.

What is crucial for success in this context is the prior establishment of a security regime to cope with transnational threats — drug and arms smuggling, environmental degradation and enforced migration — against which the individual sovereign state — whether in Europe or Africa — cannot cope unaided by its neighbours. The Southern African region is a long way from establishing supranational institutions of the kind that exist in the European Union, and the states of the region can be expected to guard their sovereignty jealously in efforts to accommodate each other's interests and aspirations. Indeed, the pattern of co-operation is likely to be intergovernmental and — on the EU model — structural form will only follow the substance of co-operation. A prior condition for this is an acceleration of transnational transactions involving the movement of capital, goods and services which will ultimately impel governments to recognize the need for regulation, to establish a 'level playing field' and, by definition, create institutions with responsibility for rule-making. South Africa, as the dominant state in the region, will have to exercise its authority and influence with sensitivity and skill if it is not to antagonize its poorer neighbours.

As for the wider constitutional context, the spectacle of state collapse, for example in Liberia, the Sudan, Zaire and Somalia, has called into question the validity and relevance of sovereignty as traditionally defined. In these circumstances it could be argued that the international community has a duty to intervene, not simply to provide humanitarian assistance but to engage effectively in the business of peace-keeping and, if necessary, peace-making involving the use of force to disarm warring factions. The elaboration of this doctrine provides both incentives and constraints for the Mandela government and, indeed, all African states. On the one hand, it has a profound interest in helping to stabilize — by peace-keeping and peace-making efforts — a continent which has lost the capacity to govern effectively. On the other hand, the same constraints that inhibit intervention by Western powers — whether in Bosnia or Rwanda — apply in South Africa's case: the need for a clear and specific mandate, the availability of resources, and the prospect of an effective 'exit strategy'. There is too the traditional commitment of the OAU to noninterference in the domestic affairs of member states to be reckoned with. There is evidence however that this aspect of orthodox sovereignty is now under serious review, especially in states where law and order has completely broken down. Thus the Secretary General of the OAU, Salim Ahmed Salim, has argued that:

> if the OAU ... is to play the lead role in any African conflict, it should be enabled to intervene swiftly, otherwise it cannot be ensured that whoever (apart from African regional organisations) acts will do so in accordance with African interests. The basis for 'intervention' may be clearer when there is a total breakdown of law and order ... and where, with the attendant human suffering, a spill-over effect is experienced within the neighbouring countries ... However, pre-emptive involvement should also be permitted even in situations where tensions evolve to such a pitch that it becomes apparent that a conflict is in the making. (Cited by Deng et al., 1996: 15)

The Secretary General has argued that the OAU should take the lead in transcending the traditional view of sovereignty, building on the African values of kinship solidarity and the notion that 'every African is his brother's keeper' (cited by Deng et al., 1996: 15). Considering that 'our borders are at best artificial', Salim argues, 'we in Africa need to use our own cultural and social relationships to interpret the principle of non-interference in a way that we are enabled to apply to our advantage in conflict prevention and resolution' (cited by Deng et al., 1996: 15). This view has also received support from Boutros-Ghali, the former UN Secretary General, who argues that:

> A major intellectual requirement of our time is to rethink the question of sovereignty – not to weaken its essence which is crucial to international security and co-operation, but to recognise that it may take more than one form and perform more than one function. This perception could help solve problems both within and among states. And underlying the rights of the individual and the rights of peoples is a dimension of universal sovereignty that resides in all humanity and provides all peoples with legitimate involvement in issues affecting the world as a whole. It is a sense that increasingly finds expression in the gradual expansion of international law. (Cited by Deng et al., 1996: 14)

All that can be said at this stage – especially in view of the vacillating response of the Western and African powers to the Rwandan crisis (1996) – is that South Africa will be extremely cautious about propping up 'failed' states, especially if this involves a long-term commitment to state reconstruction. Attitudes to sovereignty and the legal protection it gives states against intervention are certainly changing, but it is the practical issues which will determine state decision-making with respect to intervention, and South Africa is unlikely to prove an exception to this particular rule.

Yet notwithstanding these constraints, South Africa is committed to devising a constructive and dynamic foreign policy designed to help raise the continent's economic performance and assist in the task of conflict resolution. It is better placed than most African governments to do so by virtue of its human and material resources and — most important — the fact that its sovereignty is now uncontested both at home and abroad. Nor is that sovereignty an empty shell, a legal fiction cloaking an illegitimate, ungovernable regime. Rather it is buttressed by institutions of some substance, paradoxically inherited from the past.

- An institutional framework incorporating a tradition of parliamentary government (admittedly exclusive) and a judicial system which has survived the battering of apartheid. The notion of the rule of law is not, after all, a new exotic foreign import into South African political culture; it has its roots in the country's legal history and has always been vigorously defended when attacked and undermined, as it was during the apartheid years. These institutions are well established; no doubt they will change as time and circumstance dictate, but the new government has happily acknowledged their continuing relevance and legitimacy.
- A commercial legal framework for regulating market transactions that is sorely lacking in, say Eastern Europe and the former Soviet Union. To the overseas trader and investor there is in South Africa a recognizable business centre; e.g. the notion of contract is well understood and there is an efficient legal system for adjudicating disputes in this context.
- An economic infrastructure (telephones work and aircraft fly on time) exists along with human and material resources and elite political groups that have learnt to accommodate one another after years of tough negotiation and compromise.
- A tradition of strong statehood. This is an ambiguous legacy from the past, given the gross abuse of state power and its instruments by the apartheid regime. Yet it is because South Africa's statehood is not fragile that negotiations were encouraged to seek the transformation of state and society within existing boundaries in the hope of avoiding the ethnic fragmentation that has occurred elsewhere. This advantage is important as the state currently does — and will for the foreseeable future — enjoy popular legitimacy.

The new government started, therefore, with the advantage that it did not have to engage in the business of state- and nation-building simultaneously as was the case elsewhere in much of post-independence Africa. The state is very much present in symbolic terms, in its practical reflection through deeply rooted institutions of government and the psychological perception of its citizens. And these advantages give the state a capacity to act if dissent becomes violently obstructive.

South Africa also has a vigorous civil society which emerged through the network of private associations and nongovernmental organizations established in the 1980s. Their numbers have increased in the 1990s to help provide the 'social glue' to hold society together. By themselves the grand institutions of government and public administration can do only so much; for institutional structures to take root and respond to individual needs, the political and social processes which underpin these structures must be vigorous and diverse.

One final caveat: the ANC has inherited the state in an era characterized by the spread of a global culture transcending national boundaries. The chief instruments of this culture − increasing trade and capital flows together with a global communications network − make immense demands on statecraft, the will and capacity to survive and to assert sovereign control of a country's destiny. This is not to say that statecraft as the linchpin of national society is in serious decline. It is simply to assert that statesmanship faces new and important challenges arising from globalization.

In the political context of South Africa, this has required on the part of its present rulers an acknowledgement that the ANC's traditional belief in the virtue and necessity of state control of the commanding heights of the economy has to give way to impersonal constraints emanating from a global marketplace. This constraint has been well defined by Ignatieff: 'the economy in which our needs are now satisfied has become global while the polity in which we try to control the pace and development of these needs remains national' (cited by Hassner, 1993: 55).

How South Africa copes with this dilemma will prove to be the ultimate test of its sovereignty, its capacity to meet the needs of its deprived black majority, and its aspirations to be an international actor of substance in a world in which sovereignty is both asserted and contested in theory and practice.

Notes

1. This is a jointly authored chapter. David Welsh has been responsible for the analysis of South Africa's domestic situation and J. E. Spence for foreign policy developments.
2. For example the Declaration of Human Rights (1948), the Declaration on the Granting of Independence to Colonial Peoples (1966), and the UN-sponsored Convention on the Elimination of All forms of Racial Discrimination (1965).

References

Cervenka, Z. (1969) *The Organisation of African Unity and its Charter*, 2nd edn. London: Hurst.

Deng, F. N. *et al.* (1996) *Sovereignty as Responsibility: Conflict Management in Africa.* Washington DC: Brookings Institution.

Emerson, R. (1971) 'Self Determination', *American Journal of International Law,* **65**(3), 459–75.

Final Constitution (1996) *Constitution of the Republic of South Africa.*

First Interim Report (1995) *First Interim Report of the Volkstaat Council: Broadening Democracy for Stability.* Pretoria: Volkstaat Council.

Friedman, B. (1975) *Smuts: A Reappraisal.* Johannesburg: Hugh Keartland Publishers.

Hassner, P. (1993) 'Beyond Nationalism and Internationalism: Ethnicity and World Order', *Survival,* **35**(2), 49–65.

Higgins, R. (1963) *The Development of International Law through the Political Organs of the United Nations.* London: Royal Institute of International Affairs.

Higgins, R. (1984) 'Intervention and International Law', in H. Bull (ed.) *Intervention in World Politics.* Oxford: Clarendon Press.

Interim Constitution (1993) *Constitution Act of the Republic of South Africa* (Act 200, 1993 amended).

Mandela, N. (1996) Speech to the Houses of Parliament, London, 11 July, *SA Now,* **1**(6), 52–6.

Ries, A. and Dommisse, E. (1982) *Broedertwis.* Cape Town: Tafelburg.

Welsh, D. (1995) 'Right-Wing Terrorism in South Africa', *Terrorism and Political Violence,* **7**(1), 239–64.

Welsh, D. (1997) 'Coalition Government – An Unwilling Marriage?', in B. de Villiers (ed.) *State of the Nation 96/7.* Pretoria: Human Sciences Research Council.

PART 2

THE INTERNATIONAL PERSPECTIVE: POST-SOVEREIGNTY DEVELOPMENTS?

Sovereignty in International Law: A Concept of Eternal Return

ANTHONY CARTY

Introduction

The concept of sovereignty does not, as a rule, trouble international lawyers. From a non-lawyer's perspective perhaps the most important absence of argument surrounds the undertaking of international obligations. A state can, in law, agree to any restriction of its sovereignty, in the sense of independence, provided that it has given its free consent to the restriction. There are supposed to be no limits which lawyers will recognize in terms of the vital interests or national security exigencies of states which could be used to impugn a consent once given.

Thus in the standard case cited, *The Wimbledon*, the interwar Permanent Court of International Justice heard a German argument that the Versailles Treaty which it had signed, with the effect of opening the Kiel Canal to international traffic, had to be suspended in the event of a war, so that Germany could apply the law of neutrality to vessels passing through the canal. The court held against Germany: the conclusion of a treaty is an exercise of and not an abandonment of sovereignty (Court, 1923: 25).

For the international lawyer, then, sovereignty equals independence and consists of the bundle of competences which have not already been transferred through the exercise of independent consent to an international legal order. Such a legal order may signify a regional or international organization, or it may mean simply the material rules of international law, such as additional rules regulating the use of force in armed combat. For the lawyer, sovereignty has come to mean simply that the entity to which the label is attributed has become a full subject of international law. A nonsovereign entity, such as a member of a federation, for example Quebec in Canada, is an entity to which rules of international law do not directly apply. Such an entity could not act directly upon the international legal order and would need a sovereign entity such as Canada to do so for it. However, Canada could easily exercise its sovereignty by agreeing formally that Quebec should have partial or full sovereign independence.

Such a remarkably logical and lucid legal approach to the problem of sovereignty, which has otherwise mystified political theorists for centuries, is based upon an attempted professionalization of our discipline which simply excludes the political dimension. The purpose of this short study will be to attempt to show how this exercise in closure has been undertaken historically in the last 200 years, stressing, by way of conclusion, that the exercise has been unsuccessful and has merely served to trivialize and marginalize the discipline.

Frontiers, resemblances and corporate entities

In the period of transition from the medieval-feudal system of public authority over land and population to the modern absolutist state in the course of the sixteenth and early seventeenth centuries, the focus of the attention of public lawyers was on the terms of submission of subjects to rulers. The tradition that the central legal concept should be *jurisdiction* (of a lord over his vassals in his court) gave way to the more radical notion of the *supreme power* (*potestas suprema*), in effect, in constitutional terms, of an unconstrained executive. This sovereignty made its appearance as a concept in constitutional theory, or in the theory of the state. A fatal development, from the international perspective, was that among public lawyers and political theorists of the state, all interest in justification of the historical legal title to territory which individual states might have, was abandoned. Instead, attention was devoted simply to the capacity of the prince to exercise power over subjects. This had the effect of weakening the international system. If vertical state authority (prince–subjects) depended so completely on power, then horizontal state authority (princes in relation to one another) could only be affected as well. Yet, at the international level, for this power to have sought or found justification would have meant looking to a law of the Holy Roman Empire or of the papacy, as this was the traditional sense given to a higher authority existing above states. The authority of the prince, but only at the national level, was provided with a rationale by political theorists such as Bodin (Willoweit, 1975: 123–6).

Where sovereignty meant separating power from any argument of legitimacy of ruler to ruled, practical lawyers still had to look to some benchmark with which to distinguish the limits of one sovereign authority from another. The concept of frontier came to serve as the means of delimiting the territorial scope of the prince's power (Willoweit, 1975: 275–6). At the same time the concept of territory was defined merely as the area of command of the prince, with a supposedly unquestioning duty of the subject to owe submission to such a prince. However, this territory was only protected by the frontier on a day-to-day basis in peace time. The frontier was not founded on any international principle of legitimacy. The difficulty was that from the sixteenth century until at least the time of the League of Nations, if not the United Nations Charter itself, the territories of princes of Europe did not have a convincing legal foundation.

As a result, there were ever harsher territorial conflicts, as the notion of the need for princely authority in political theory was not matched by an international/European consensus on the basis for territorial title. There had been a sacrifice of political legitimacy at the end of the Middle Ages based on the consent of the population in favour of overwhelming executive power to ensure internal public safety as a matter of constitutional theory. This was understandable in the context of the desire to prevent the repetition of bloody civil wars. However, as a consequence, order was conceived by lawyers in purely internal not international terms (Willoweit, 1975: 306–7, 349–50).

The first attempts of international lawyers to confront this break-up of the European medieval world did not treat the concept of state sovereignty as the central problem in the construction of a new international legal order. Instead, they attempted to retain some version of a medieval scholastic and classical Roman natural law of people in the sense of *lex gentium*. There seems to be agreement between historians of political theory and historians of international law on this matter. In particular, Bartelson, falling within the former category, stresses that the lawyer did not approach international conflict in the sixteenth century in terms of state sovereignty:

> the over-arching legal problem is not how to solve a disagreement between competing sovereigns over the foundation of a legal order, but how to relate concentric circles of *resemblant* laws, ranging from divine law down to natural and positive law. In his effort to work out a coherent relationship between them, Vitoria [the Spanish theologian] relies on a lexicon of legal exampla, in which a wide variety of textual authorities are invoked. (Bartelson, 1995: 128)

Bartelson provides a very illuminating account of the epistemological foundations of this perspective, a retrospective reflexivity, whereby Renaissance knowledge became – thanks to a neoplatonic revival – a knowledge of resemblance between entities whose unity had been shattered (Bartelson, 1995: 108).

As a historian of international law, Jouannet demonstrates the continuity of the medieval legal method throughout the seventeenth and early eighteenth centuries from Grotius to Vattel. All the major legal figures continue some version of the medieval method. The main figures are Grotius himself and those who Jouannet describes as his disciples, Rachel, Zouche, Textor and Bynkershoek (Jouannet, 1993: 141–7). The reason why international law did not become an autonomous discipline in its modern recognizable form is rather surprising. Jouannet notes how none of these jurists conceived of the state or nation, words used interchangeably, as a corporate entity distinct from the person of the government or the prince. The elements which would make up the modern state in international law, that is government, territory and population, remained the property of the prince. He *had* a territory and a population in a patrimonial sense. Such a personalized concept of authority directs attention to individuals and favours the retention of the medieval idea of a common law of human beings applied to the leaders of nations. Grotian-style erudition prevails into the eighteenth century to regulate the affairs of princes, not only in their relations with one another, but also in their domestic and even private affairs.

It is with the Vattelian popularization of Christian Wolff that one arrives at the modern conception of international law where sovereignty as a legal concept comes to play a central part. It relies on the notion of the corporate character of the state. As a legal entity, it has to be separate from both government and governed. It is the state and not the government or prince which is subject to international law. It is and can be subject to international law only if it is sovereign, that is, equally independent of all other states (Jouannet, 1993: 354–88, especially 384 onwards). Jouannet emphasizes that it is essential to the idea of the corporate character of the state that there should be no relations of individuals with one another across state boundaries. All the relations of individuals, for the purpose of international law, are absorbed into the corporate identity of the state, which then has legal relations with other states. In this way it is the sovereign equality of independent states which defines the object and scope of the rules of international law.

The modern state, according to Bartelson, becomes the subject of Descartes' distinction between the immaterial subject and the material reality which it observes, classifies and analyses. Knowledge presupposes a subject, and this subject, for international relations, is the Hobbesian sovereign who is not named but names, not observed but observes, a mystery for whom everything must be transparent. The problem of knowledge is that of security, which is attained through rational control and analysis. Self-understanding is limited to an analysis of the extent of power of the sovereign, measured geopolitically. Other sovereigns are not unknown 'others' in the anthropological sense, but simply 'enemies' – opponents with conflicting interests whose behaviour can and should be calculated.

The purpose of knowledge is now not to re-establish resemblances in a fragmenting medieval Christian world, but to furnish dependable information with which to buttress the sovereign state whose security rests precisely upon the success with which it has displaced disorder from within its boundaries onto the international plane. Mutual recognition by sovereigns does not rest upon an awareness of sameness, of common cultural roots implying a common identity. Instead, a plurality of sovereigns implies an analytical recognition of factual, territorial separation, combined with a mutual accord of reputation which, so long as it lasts, serves to guarantee some measure of security.

The primary definition of state interest is not a search for resemblances, affinities of religion or dynastic family. Instead, it is a matter of knowing how to conduct one's own affairs, while hindering those of others. Interest is a concept resting upon detachment and separation. Society is composed of a collection of primary, unknowable, self-defining subjects, whose powers of detached, analytical, empirical observation take absolute precedence over any place for knowledge based on passion or empathy, whether oriented towards sameness or difference (Bartelson, 1995: 137–85). Bartelson also recognizes that it is Vattel who first tries to harness the concept of sovereignty in the modern system with a very elemental doctrine of the Law of Nature. According to Vattel's work *Le Droit des gens* (1758), the fact that humankind is divided into separate states does not overrule universal duty. Each nation (the equivalent for state as a corporate entity) may be regarded as a moral person, since it has an understanding, a will and a power peculiar to itself. It is therefore obliged to live with other societies or states according to the laws of the natural society of the human race. The difficulty remains, highlighted by Bartelson, that this universal morality is not immediately binding upon the external conduct of states. He quotes Vattel: 'each has the right to decide in its conscience what it must do to fulfil its duties; a perfect equality of rights among Nations'. Bartelson follows up the contradiction. Without sovereignty, the state cannot be understood as a moral person, but without a wider sense of universal values, this person cannot be sovereign (Bartelson, 1995: 194–5).

The international legal order

Jouannet sees no difficulty in the Vattelian sovereign being integrated into an international legal order. The lack of difficulty is hardly surprising because this new legal order is made by states specifically for their relations with one another (Jouannet, 1993: 447). It is because states have no rights over one another that they have need of a law which recognizes that they are independent and equal (1993: 448). Jouannet appears to see the entire exercise as a taxonomy of what relates or properly belongs to the rights and duties of nations rather than individuals. The idea that there should be rules specifically designed for the character of sovereign states can hardly pose problems of a legally binding character (1993: 451). The aim of this taxonomic exercise is to register a break with the Roman and medieval tradition of law. Now the nation can govern itself without dependence upon what is foreign to it (1993: 454–8). The constant theme of this argument is the corporate character of the sovereign. Because sovereign nations deal only directly with one another, they can only see one another as societies of 'men' of whom all the interests are held in common. It is not a law of nations derived from human nature which rules them, but a law derived from the particular nature of the state (1993: 458–9).

Jouannet admits that Vattel keeps the principle of the subjective appreciation of each state in the application of the law (1993: 472) but considers it unjust to make him responsible for the increasing voluntarism of international law. Voluntarism means that the whole of international law depends upon the continuing consent of states. They can, at any time, cease to accept that a rule binds them and even cease to recognize other states as subjects of the law. Vattel is not responsible for such a view. He merely introduces the logic of Hobbesian and Lockean individualism into international law, in terms of the liberty and sovereignty of states as the foundation of international law (Jouannet, 1993: 475). A doctrine of the autonomy of states is not a doctrine of absolute or unlimited external sovereignty, but neither does it involve submission to a superior juridical order.

The root of the confusion, in Jouannet's view, is to have made a too rapid combination of the question of the application of international law with the decentralized structure of the community of states. There is no compulsory international adjudication. States have to interpret for themselves the extent of their rights. She says that the question of the subjective appreciation of the law is not an aspect or logical consequence of voluntarism in international law, a doctrine that all law is a product of state will, but arises from the way in which the law is applied within a decentralized international legal order. Because international law is interpreted opportunistically, it functions in practice as a series of reciprocal and bilateral interpretations given to it by states.

Vattel simply marks a reflection of a change at an international level which had been occurring generally in legal culture – a movement towards individualization and subjectivization of law, combined with a realist vision of international relations where states have a mission to act to assure their security and preserve their interests. It is not Vattel who introduces this subjectivity into international law. It is simply an unavoidable fact of international law in the absence of any suprastate power. So, in the beginning and middle of the twentieth century, it is not this subjectivist decentralized appreciation inherent in the structure of the international community which is the problem, but the legitimacy of the use of force which accompanies it (Jouannet, 1993: 477–8).

The First World War greatly disturbed the confidence of international lawyers in the viability of a legal order which left appreciation of violations of rights and methods of vindicating them entirely within the discretion of sovereign states. The response which it is intended to highlight, as a reaction to this, comes from within the same legal political tradition as Vattel's – democratic constitutionalism. In the first instance, it does not have to be read as a statement that international organization exists, but rather as a statement of what legal democratic theory would require at the international legal level. The fundamental epistemological condition is that law depends upon what the people express through their constitutional organs, that is through the state. At present, international lawyers are left troubled by the in-between character of an incomplete international institutional order, wherein state sovereignty keeps seeping through.

After 1918 Europeans wished to conceive of the rule of law as being capable of defining the spheres of competence of the state. In Austria the *Lehre vom Stufenbau* (legal ladder steps) approach conceived of an ideal legal structure in terms of state responsibility. Just as order within the state depended upon the capacity to determine the competences of specific state organs constitutionally, so international order depended upon the existence of an international constitution which could determine the competences of the state in international relations. State responsibility was tied to the notion of executive responsibility towards a parliamentary regime, and to reproduce this regime internationally, it was necessary to give priority to international over national law by creating international institutions which could place effective limits on the legal competences of states. Such institutions could function as parliaments supervising states (Stoitzner, 1986: 76).

The chief exponent of the ideal of an international constitutional order was Kelsen. He appreciated the historical perspective which had to be overcome. To argue that state power could look to itself rather than to a constitutional title for its competence to act is to hark back to the spirit of absolutism (Kelsen, 1928: 137). The notion that physical power as such could legitimize an action is to leave the way open to the idea of *raison d'état* in the sense in which a Renaissance disciple of Machiavelli would have understood this: as the capacity of the prince to put his concept of the public safety of the state above all considerations of law and morality. Kelsen's aim is to construct a barrier between modern constitutionalism, democracy guaranteed by positive law, and the historical origin of European states, which was in absolute monarchies (Kelsen, 1928: 138–9). It is the latter who actually consolidated the power which constitutionalism is now supposed to democratize. Kelsen is a theorist of international law who recognizes that there is a danger implicit in the classical notion of the state, whereby sovereignty does create a threat for the obligatory character of international law.

A neo-Kantian epistemological perspective is an essential part of Kelsen's critique of the traditional legal thinking about the state. Power, and hence state power, as an empirical concept, has no legal significance. The notion of command has legal meaning or significance only in terms of a normative order which attributes roles: who may command and who must obey (Kelsen, 1928: 82–3). In international terms, this implies a break with Vattel who took the independence and equality of states as a natural fact. As Jouannet (1993) has said, it was possible to deduce the basic rules of law from the nature of the state. For Kelsen, the coexistence of states is only legally conceivable on the basis of the existence of an exhaustive association which determines the limits of the validity of competences rather than powers which are attributed to states. Such a legal framework puts states on the same juridical plan as their own provinces and communities in their own federal law (Kelsen, 1928: 86). That is to say, on a par with constitutional-administrative law, the state should be considered not as the highest instance, but as a *relatively high* instance, in a scale of juridical instances – hence the metaphor of ladder, or *Lehre vom Stufenbau*.

The difficulty (as Kelsen was aware) remained that power structures of international society did not automatically conform to his ideal construction for the future. Every legal system must be able to say which are its subjects – those who are literally subject to it. A basic question is whether states are dependent upon an international order for their existence or whether they create themselves out of their own forces. Kelsen's response has the appearance of a play on words which is left to plague the whole structure of contemporary international law. The only way to answer the question is to suppose the existence of a legal norm which accepts the legal character of any entity which establishes itself successfully (Kelsen, 1920/28: 230–1, 239–41).

Kelsen insists that the objectivity of a legal order in the sense of its validity, has to be independent of acceptance by its subjects, just as the rule of law at a national level cannot depend upon its subjects. This leads him openly into the construction of a *civitas maxima*, a universal international law which stands over against the rules which states have consented to, and which grounds their validity. This is the same *civitas maxima* which Wolff constructed and which Vattel rejected as nonexistent. It recognizes that the idea of law attaches to the notion of the constitutional state as such, so that the only international legal framework which can adequately encompass the modern state has to be a world constitutional state. This, in the age of modernity, is the only construct which can be a substitute for the medieval notions of a continuing Roman empire with its tradition of legal naturalism, of a *ius gentium*. Kelsen is not at all committed to claiming that such an order exists, but it is the only conceivable juridical pathway to overcome the absolutist, monarchist Machiavellian state at the international level (Kelsen, 1920/28: 239–41, 249–52, 274).

Once this legal ideal is set, the task is to reinterpret the foundations of international law accordingly and to overcome the obvious deficiencies of existing, positive international law, that is merely the legal rules to which states *have consented*, exposed as they are to the dangers of voluntarism. The first stage is easy. One may simply say that treaties are binding, as are rules of general customary law, because there is a basic norm, derived from the idea of a *civitas maxima*, that confers legal validity upon the exercise of state consent which finds expression in such treaties and customs (Kelsen, 1920/28: 261).

Enforcement, war and international law

The problem is not simply the creation of rules of law, but their interpretation and their enforcement. Kelsen and Jouannet appreciate that there are problems with the very idea of a legal order where there are no institutions for the interpretation of the law independent of the states themselves, and equally no mechanisms for the enforcement of legal obligations apart from the states. Kelsen embarks upon two important further arguments, concerning the place of war in the international legal order and the place of the judiciary in the interpretation and in the creation of legal norms. The intention, at this stage, is to explain critically how Kelsen as a representative international lawyer develops his ideas. The final section of the chapter will consider two contemporary international issues which illustrate how the international legal community is not in a position to give expression to Kelsen's legal ideals.

War is a common fact of international life. If international law is to have credibility as a legal order, in Kelsen's view, it must integrate this fact into its interpretative framework. If war is to be evaluated from a juridical perspective, it can only be as a sanction that international law furnishes for the enforcement of law against violators of the law. Traditional doctrine viewed war as permissible. States could wage wars as an instrument of national policy, quite simply to seize territory and resources from other states. Anxious to eliminate such a traditional concept of sovereignty, Kelsen claims that war is regulated by international law (Kelsen, 1920/28: 264). By this Kelsen means that only where a state has suffered an aggression – a violation of its rights – has it a discretionary power to react under international law, a discretion to enforce its right. In this sense war is legally objectivized. War becomes an institution created by the law to put the law into force (Kelsen, 1920/28: 265).

To claim that a state is able, at its discretion, to begin a war, apart from having suffered a legal wrong, would signify the end of the idea of international law. So Kelsen tries to affirm that a state cannot employ the use of force until there has been first a violation of the law. However, the problems of interpretation and application are linked. The lack of an independent instance which can verify objectively whether there has been a violation of law, remains. Yet somehow Kelsen believes that such an objection does not prevent a theoretical construction of war as a coercive act, as a sanction, to enforce international law. He insists upon construing the state which has suffered a legal injury and which responds to it through the use of force, as functioning as an organ of the international legal community. In pursuing this line of argument, Kelsen is determined to replace the traditional concept of sovereignty with a procedural approach to law which ensures that the possibility for initiative for states is clearly regulated (Kelsen, 1920/28: 266).

The underlying motive of this approach to international law remains clear. All law must have a democratic foundation in consent. If legal subjects are to be allowed within an admittedly primitive or decentralized system of law to use force, this can only be in terms which are clearly agreed in advance by the legal community. Hence, the approach which Kelsen adopts to determine whether the minimum conditions of a legal order exist has enormous resonance in the profession and can be said to be the only approach which is conceivable. At the same time, the difficulties which this approach causes are becoming clearer to international lawyers in the light of the two case studies to be offered here – the UN crisis in Bosnia and the Advisory Opinion of the International Court of Justice on Nuclear Weapons.

Kelsen is able to see that a simple prohibition on the use of force is not enough to settle a conflict when states may go to war. Logically it will provide an answer. Either states use force illegally in contravention of the status quo or they act legally by using force to defend it.

However, some mechanism has still to be found to develop and adapt the law in the existing, primitive and decentralized international society. The solution for Kelsen is a system of obligatory jurisdiction which would issue judgements that an executive would be required to implement. This would overcome the obvious fictionality involved in speaking of states which decide to use force to revenge a violation of their rights, as doing anything other than taking the law into their own hands. If a court had to decide whether there had been a violation and could do so in taking a dynamic attitude to the development of the law, the weaknesses of the present system, which favours an easy return to the language of unlimited sovereignty, could be overcome.

It is crucial to such a theory for the development of international law, that its corpus consists of a complete system of general principles which can be applied effectively by a judiciary to concrete situations. Hence the court will not have to say that, with respect to the issue being adjudicated, states have not consented to the development of rules which limit their sovereignty in a particular matter, with the consequence that the court has to declare that there is no law covering the dispute before it. Such an argument would carry with it the implication that one cannot look to courts to overcome the deficiencies in the corpus of rules of existing international law, so that there is no alternative to states meeting together as a quasi-legislature to formulate rules of general application to limit and guide their conduct. Kelsen does not see such meetings as a real political possibility, which is why he prefers the option of obligatory international adjudication. Hence he insists upon a strong role for the judiciary, arguing that the application of a general norm to a concrete case is by its very nature an individualization of the norm. That is to say 'the existing rule is a framework of several different rules. By choosing one of them the law applying organ [the judiciary] excludes the others and thus creates, for the concrete case, a new law' (Kelsen, 1957: 18). The conclusion which Kelsen and the profession generally draw from this argument is that there is only a difference in degree and not in nature between the creation and application of law (Tournaye, 1995: 43–4), and that in this way, the structural weakness of international law can be saved through the judiciary.

The second part of Kelsen's argument was that the judgments of such a dynamic court had to be the starting-point for the action of an international executive such as the Security Council. Kelsen himself demonstrates that this is not what we have. Superficially one might argue that the sovereignty of states is effectively limited by law because the UN Charter is a treaty and under this treaty states are bound by decisions of the Security Council. However, the charter does not tie the council in any way either to decisions of the court or even to international law. The former may decide upon the use of force wherever it considers that a situation constitutes a threat to the peace under article 39 of the UN Charter. It can also leave a decision of the court unenforced. Nor is there anything to oblige the council to consider any disputed question of fact in an impartial or quasi-judicial fashion. The charter foresees what might be called a perfect independence of the court and the council, both principal organs of the UN (Tournaye, 1995: 63).

A state is prohibited by Article 2/4 of the charter from having recourse to the use of force except when its territory is physically attacked. Thus the state is deprived of any effective mechanism for the adjudication and enforcement of its legal rights wherever it considers that there has been a violation. The outcome is that the UN Charter represents a deterioration in the quality of international law in comparison to the classical law. It excludes the individualized sanction for a violation of law imposed by a state acting on its own, but does not replace it with an effective collective sanction. This means that in terms of the minimum conditions for the existence of law, one cannot assume that international law will function (Tournaye, 1995: 70, 77).

It is to be expected that in practice, therefore, states will not refrain from enforcing their rights individually whenever they consider them violated. Given that there is no compulsory international adjudication, should we be able to say that minimum conditions for an international legal order can exist where states act *as if* they are organs of the international community when they defend their rights? Kelsen recognized that it was the minimum condition for the existence of a legal order that it could characterize acts of violence either as illegal or as sanctions against illegal behaviour. International law does not have an objective way, independent of states themselves, of distinguishing between delicts (wrongful use of force in violation of existing legal rights) and sanctions. Kelsen would like to say that we have to suppose that each state decides for itself whether it has been injured and whether the injuring state should incur sanctions. Yet recently a major logical defect of Kelsen's system has been highlighted.

In setting out the logical conditions for a legal order, nothing has been said about the reasons which a state has to give for considering itself injured. The feeble level of explication required of an individual state means that it is impossible for an observing third state to distinguish the 'delinquent' from the 'sanctioner'. This is because it is not possible to follow a rule on one's own. The idea of a rule relies on a common explication of the existence and content of the rule. But we do not have the adjudicative process which could guarantee this. Therefore even from Kelsen's perspective, the minimum conditions for an international legal order do not exist (Pfersmann, 1993: 788–9).

In other words, we have the radical subjectivization of international law which Jouannet admits does come with Vattel's concept of sovereignty. The introduction of sovereignty as a legal concept into international law swallows up the legal character of this order. After considering this critique of international law, it remains to illustrate how it is reflected in actual difficulties of recent practice.

The case of nuclear weapons: the failure of the judiciary

The General Assembly of the UN recently asked the International Court for an advisory opinion on the question as to whether the threat or the use of nuclear weapons is in any circumstances permitted under international law. The court concluded by a majority of one (seven to seven and the casting vote of the president) that while the threat or use of nuclear weapons would be generally contrary to the rules of international humanitarian law,

> in the view of the current state of international law, and of the elements of fact at its disposal, the Court cannot conclude definitively whether the threat or use of nuclear weapons would be lawful or unlawful in an extreme circumstance of self-defence, in which the very survival of a State would be at stake. (Court, 1996: 80)

In her dissenting opinion the British judge, Higgins, points out that what the court did is to declare a *non-liquet*, that there is no legal answer to the question put. The court has not restricted itself to the inadequacy of the facts and arguments concerning the effects of particular nuclear weapons. The reference to the current state of international law is a clear statement that there is no legal answer. Higgins objects that there are general principles of international law relating to self-defence and humanitarian behaviour which could have been used by the court to develop an answer. She says: 'It is exactly the judicial function to take principles of general application, to elaborate their meaning and to apply them to specific situations'. Perhaps the judges are concerned about the contradiction between the practice of states relying upon a doctrine of nuclear deterrence and the existing rules of humanitarian law which exclude indiscriminate and mass destruction. In that case, 'the judge's role is precisely to decide which of two or more competing norms is applicable in the particular circumstances' (Court, 1996: 937).

Higgins herself locates the international problem presented by the existence of nuclear weapons precisely in terms of the continuance of unrestrained state sovereignty. To resolve tensions between competing norms, it is necessary always to bear in mind that it is the physical survival of peoples which is at stake.

> We live in a decentralised world order, in which some States are known to possess nuclear weapons but choose to remain outside of the non-proliferation treaty system; while other such non-parties have declared their intention to obtain nuclear weapons; and yet other States are believed clandestinely to possess, or to be working shortly to possess nuclear weapons ... It is not clear to me that either a pronouncement of illegality in all circumstances of the use of nuclear weapons or the answers formulated by the Court best serve to protect mankind against the unimaginable suffering which we all fear. (Court, 1996: 938)

Higgins has exposed the real weakness of the so-called decentralized international legal order – that states depend, to varying degrees, for their security on a doctrine of nuclear deterrence. This is only a consequence of their legal right to make a subjective assessment that their security is threatened. It is then a certainty that they will decide for themselves how to defend themselves. In the face of these contradictory realities, the judicial imagination has, notwithstanding Kelsen's hopes, proved impotent.

Peace-keeping and peace-enforcement in Bosnia-Herzegovina, and the UN

From the immensely complex crisis in Bosnia-Herzegovina, it is only intended to highlight a small number of elements relevant to Kelsen's expectations concerning the minimum conditions for an international legal order. Where these conditions are not met, it is only to be expected that states will not conform to international law.

The Security Council identified early in 1992 that there had been aggression against the state of Bosnia-Herzegovina, a member of the UN, coming from rump Yugoslavia, and for this reason the Security Council imposed economic sanctions on the latter. The council also reiterated the principle that boundaries could not be changed through the use of force (Weller, 1996: 80). At the same time the Security Council insisted upon maintaining as a matter of legal obligations for members of the UN, an arms embargo on all the parties to the conflict in the state under attack. The council decided that a previous embargo against the former Yugoslavia should also apply to the individual republics upon independence. A very large number of states argued that in the absence of effective international action to safeguard the rights of Bosnia-Herzegovina, her right of self-defence had to be supported rather than restricted (Weller, 1996: 88).

The Security Council formally accorded to states acting on its behalf – the UN forces composed of national armies under a joint command answerable to the UN Secretary General – the authority to take the necessary measures to facilitate the delivery of humanitarian assistance in co-ordination with the UN (Weller, 1996: 97). Furthermore, the same bodies were authorized to take all necessary measures to act in defence of so-called safe areas, where these were the subject of bombardment or incursion (Weller, 1996: 107–8). In practice, the UN forces are well known to have consistently taken the view that they should not take sides in the conflict between the warring parties in Bosnia-Herzegovina. There was always an emphasis upon the agreement of the parties and no special status was accorded to the government of the country (Weller, 1996: 124–39). With respect to Srebrenica, an official British Operations document – a British general was then in command of the UN Protection Force (UNPROFOR) – stated that 'a formula needs to be found to reconcile the belligerent parties' values with the UN's and the world community's interests' (Weller, 1996: 144).

The outcome of such conduct by the UN, its Secretary General and the military forces and commanders in Bosnia-Herzegovina (primarily British and French) was to destroy the legitimacy of the UN. A Declaration on Joint Defence was signed between Bosnia-Herzegovina and Croatia which appealed to the right of self-defence, given the failure of the UN. Turkey declared its support for Bosnia-Herzegovina's right of self-defence with arms, as did the Organization of Islamic States (Weller, 1996: 156–7). Finally, the American initiative to bring about the Dayton Agreements left the implementation of the already mentioned UN Security Council mandates entirely in the hands of NATO to the exclusion of the UN (Weller, 1996: 165).

The conclusion of this incident is, according to Weller, that where a state's territory was to be protected and its population guarded against gross violations of humanitarian law, international organizations and states overwhelmingly rejected the challenge. He points out, with particular reference to the operation of UNPROFOR, that some of the states contributing (including especially the United Kingdom), actively undermined the UN Security Council mandate by claiming that the use of force would constitute intervention in a civil war. This led to the formal refusal of a large number of states to pay regard to the UN's decision to impose an arms embargo. These states were mainly Islamic but supposedly they included the USA as well, albeit in secret (Weller, 1996: 169–75).

Once again the euphemistic legal language of a decentralized international legal community is a cover for the absence of any international solidarity which would protect a state violated in its rights even to the point of threatening its very existence, wherever other states simply do not consider it to be in their interest, that is to say necessary for their own security, to defend the victim state. In this sense Bartelson's epistemology of the meaning of state sovereignty in terms of security and interest remains valid. The concept of legal sovereignty remains in place as a mechanism whereby states can invoke the language of interest and security under a cloak of legality, by offering to put their choice in terms of a legal interpretation of their rights. Through the mist of international court jurisprudence and mandatory resolutions of the Security Council, the spirit of Vattel continues to express the reality of the Renaissance state.

References

Bartelson, J. (1995) *A Genealogy of Sovereignty*. Cambridge: Cambridge University Press.

Court (1923) *Permanent Court of International Justice Reports*, Series A, no. 1.

Court (1996) International Court of Justice Report, *International Legal Materials*, vol. 35. Washington DC: American Society of International Law.

Jouannet, E. (1993) *L'Emergence doctrinale du droit international classique, Emer de Vattel et l'école du droit de la nature et des gens*. PhD dissertation: University of Paris.

Kelsen, H. (1920/28) *Das Problem der Souveränität und die Theorie des Volkerrechts*, 2nd edn. Tubingen: Verlag J. C. B. Mohr.

Kelsen, H. (1928) *Der soziologische und der juristische Staatsbegriff*. Tubingen: Verlag J. C. B. Mohr.

Kelsen, H. (1957) *Collective Security under International Law*. Washington DC: US Government Printing Office.

Pfersmann, O. (1993) 'De la justice constitutionelle à la justice internationale: Hans Kelsen et la seconde guerre mondiale', *Revue Française de droit constitutionelle*, **16**, 761–90.

Stoitzner, B. (1986) 'Die Lehre vom Stufenbau der Rechtsordnung', in S. Paulson and W. Stoitzner (eds), *Untersuchungen zur reinen Rechtslehre*. Vienna: Springer Verlag.

Tournaye, C. (1995) *Kelsen et la sécurité collective*. Paris: Librairie Générale de Droit et Jurisprudence.

Weller, M. (1996) 'Peace-Keeping and Peace-Enforcement in the Republic of Bosnia and Herzegovina', *Zeitschrift für ausländisches Recht und Volkerrecht*, **56**, 7–177.

Willoweit, D. (1975) *Rechtsgrundlagen der Territorialgewalt*. Cologne: Boehlau Verlag.

CHAPTER 7

Political Economy, Sovereignty and Borders in Global Contexts

GILLIAN YOUNGS

Introduction

The study of political economy requires us to probe the interactive nature of political and economic forces in developing a complex understanding of social relations of power. The increasingly international, and more recently global, nature of activity has problematized both the prime conceptual role of sovereign boundaries and the traditionally restricted interest in them. There are two main points which can be made in this respect. Political economy, our understanding of its qualities, its dynamics, and the range of participants and interests involved as well as their interrelationships, requires a greater preoccupation with the question of boundaries or borders than the traditional sovereignty model promotes. The mapping of markets, market shares, transnational industrial and firm structures, and patterns of consumption as well as production and investment, are among the factors to be taken into account. This is as essential to our awareness of the different ways in which states are changing as political entities and actors, internally and externally, as it is to our investigation of the bases and predominant characteristics of the world economy (Youngs, forthcoming). The study of political economy requires more developed spatial sensitivities than the sovereignty model engenders.

The purpose of this chapter is to illustrate why this is the case with regard to the post-1945 international political economy. We will begin by considering the concept of hegemony in the assessment of power in this period, especially in the context of the rise and fall of US economic might. Next we will discuss aspects of inequality in the global era and factors affecting our understanding of them. Finally we will explore how the 'neoliberal' order may be considered to be defining and redefining boundaries, including those between political and economic influences, and assess the impact of the rise of East Asia, including China, as a recent dynamic centre in the world economy. The general premise of the chapter is that sovereignty needs to be addressed not in a timeless but in a contingent fashion that is rooted in considerations of political economy. The story of the post-1945 economy is one of internationalization and globalization, where sovereign power, particularly of the USA, must be understood in terms of political economy. The growing dynamism of East Asia, it is argued, has certainly changed the geographical shape of our thinking about the world or global economy, but it is also raising new considerations with regard to sovereignty and political economy.

Hegemony: the political economy of power

If, as many would argue, sovereignty has dominated traditional notions of state power in international relations, then hegemony is the concept which has been utilized to illustrate and analytically pursue the premise that state power, certainly in respect of the second half of the twentieth century, must be understood on the basis of political economy. It is fundamentally an American tale. The historically notable combination of political, economic and military strength which the USA exercised internationally by the closing stages of the Second World War are well documented (see, for example, Gilpin, 1987; Kennedy, 1989). Few have stated the relevance of the extent and combination of US capacities at this point in history more clearly than Strange in her detailed analysis of structural power in international political economy:

> Without the productive power to supply food and capital goods for the reconstruction of European industry, and without the financial power to offer credits in universally acceptable dollars, the United States could not have exercised the power over the recipients of Marshall Aid that it did. Nor was American structural power based only on dominance of the security structure, the production structure and the financial structure. Its authority was reinforced by the belief outside America that the United States fully intended to use its power to create a better post-war world for others as well as for its own people. (1994: 32)

As the Cold War set in, the USA became identified as leader of the Western capitalist bloc. The liberal principles of political and economic rights and the promotion of freer international trade were advanced through the United Nations (UN) system, which reflected the combined concerns of military, political and economic security. That this situation mirrored so closely American interests should probably not surprise us even from this historical distance (Stubbs and Underhill, 1994a). With the recovery of Western Europe and the beginnings of what is now known as the triad of power in the global political economy (the US,

Europe and Japan) what soon came to concern mainstream analysts of international relations was the kind of hegemony the US maintained, how such hegemony could be considered weakened and what this would mean for world order.[1]

The recent transformation of the General Agreement on Tariffs and Trade (GATT) system into the World Trade Organisation (WTO) is evidence of the enduring relevance of internationalized approaches to trade. However, the emphasis on intellectual property rights (IPRs) and copyright issues characterizing the tensions between the US and China over the latter's entry to the WTO signals the emergence of new forms of protectionism. These may be best understood in market-share as much as state-centred terms, and are more geared towards the so-called preservation of investment and property rights, which may be taking a prime place in contemporary considerations of governance of the world economy (Nicolaides, 1994; Hoekman and Kostecki, 1995). The high level of attention to IPRs is an indication of the changing nature of the *products* being traded on the global market. It also reflects the increase in service-related and knowledge-based materials of all kinds linked to the vast globalizing financial sector and the expanding range of products from computer software to video films and compact discs (Barnet and Cavanagh, 1994; Drucker, 1994).

This illustrates the highly technologized developments in processes of product-origination, production and consumption, and associated marketing strategies. Some of the boundaries which come into play here include who owns what and on what bases, and the implications for global inequalities of the concentration of key technological know-ledges in the industrialized countries and their scientific and commercial infrastructures and interests. We can be sure that the IPR debate will increase in its complexities, and already it is symbolic of major changes in market structures and orientation.

China's resistance in this context and the importance attached to its compliance are indicative of the continuing expansion of the world capitalist economy, particularly with the collapse of the Soviet system, and the controlled capitalist transformation of at least parts of the Chinese economy. Its recent rapid growth rates – for example 14.4 per cent in manufacturing per year between 1980 and 1990 (Agnew and Corbridge, 1995: 140) – and the scale of its current and potential market identify it as *the* key growth economy as we move into the twenty-first century. Agnew and Corbridge (1995: 142–4) have described China as 'an economic colossus' but attach importance to the economic and political tensions which it is yet to address (see also *Journal of International Affairs*, 1996), identifying it in military and economic senses as 'a regional rather than world power'. China's continuing predominantly agrarian nature and the challenges of meeting the basic needs of its population of more than a billion, as well as the contradictory pulls of its centralized authority structures and the decentralizing influences of 'an externally orientated economy', are major issues (Agnew and Corbridge, 1995: 144–5).

There is no doubt that geopolitical and geoeconomic developments in the post-1945 period continue to affect what might be considered significant market borders in terms of both the scope and relevance of different market areas, particularly in the Asian region, and the kinds of products which dominate and thus define how the global market is segmented, and who benefits most from the exchanges undertaken within it. This is one of the reasons that Strange's identification of the four structures of power – security, production, finance and knowledge – and her assessment of enduring US hegemony have proved so powerful within debates about major change in the world market. Her differentiated structural sensitivities offer the possibility of an examination of power in global political economy linked directly to an awareness of what characterizes market as well as state influence. Her framework explicitly emphasizes the interactivity of the four structures, which is especially important with regard, I would argue, to the knowledge structure. Technology is a major force here, drawing our attention to the enduring importance of the military–industrial complex as a source of the dynamics affecting sophisticated, state-of-the-art, security-related products and the diffusion of associated technologies through the generation of new consumer products and services. The notion of the military–industrial complex,[2] perhaps more relevant now than ever, has always indicated how blurred the boundaries are between state and market. One of the most well-known and publicized symbols of this situation is the US-originated Internet, established on a security basis for communications purposes and now at the centre of a globalizing new trend in relatively inexpensive and accessible boundary-breaking communication used by government, business, education and individuals, and helping to create new companies, services and products, as well as areas of competition.[3] The knowledge structure vitally includes the accumulated expertise of transnational activity in which, with their dominance this century of transnational growth, US corporations can be seen to have a historically significant lead. Although over the post-1945 period US transnational corporations (TNCs) have increasingly been joined by those from the other two triad areas, Europe and Japan, and more recently those from growth economies, particularly in Asia, the home-market and overseas experience of large-scale production has placed US-based firms in a distinctive leading role in the global market. This is one of the major reasons why 'hegemonic pretenders' (Agnew and Corbridge, 1995) are regarded as of little significance at this stage.

While major TNCs are key globalizing foci in the knowledge age, this fact has served to concentrate power further in the US through the production structure:

> Not only are these corporations predominantly headquartered in the United States, but the importance of selling on a global market means that even those corporations based in other places – Europe, Japan, Korea – cannot afford *not* to sell on the US market. It is still the largest, richest market under one national set of laws and one national bureaucracy. In short, the technological changes have led to a greater concentration of power in one state. (Strange, 1994: 133)

East Asian dynamism has begun to explode certain myths which have attached to the other main definitive boundary of the post-1945 international political economy – separation of the so-called developed world from the undeveloped and developing countries. The developed sector has been historically formed by the advanced industrialized nations, as they are usually termed, led by the hegemon, the USA, and including other members of the triad in Western Europe and Japan which together with Canada have made up the dominant economic club of the G7. The undeveloped and developing countries were understood in the Cold War period to be all those others in the capitalist system (many of which were part of the post-1945 decolonization process) considered to be at various stages of development on the basis of the Western model of industrialization. It can be argued that the linear development mode of interpreting international political economy has come to dominate since the collapse of the Soviet bloc and the bipolar structure of international relations, with the new sense that there is now one global capitalist system of which all countries are increasingly a part. This is exemplified by Fukuyama's (1992) thesis of 'the end of history', defined as the combination of political and economic liberalism becoming dominant within a growing global community.

However, for many reasons, it can be maintained that far from the end of history being reached in this evolutionary vein, a whole new history of global political economy is being written, one which breaks faith with much of traditional Western development dogma and assumption, and relies heavily on the importance of a new range of boundaries that intersect national and international space and characterize crucial new political and economic trends.

The new global era: inequality reframed

Old notions of the First, Second and Third Worlds are being swept away by the effects of recessionary pressures, global restructuring, new markets and the expanding communications revolution which is raising awareness of the degree to which national economies are no longer, if they ever could truly have been, neatly and meaningfully summed up as *entities* sitting somewhere on the *development scale*. The starkest contrasts between mass deprivation in sub-Saharan Africa and relative wealth in Western industrialized nations[4] continue to dominate our understanding of global inequalities, but they by no means exhaust their full meanings. These require new kinds of spatial sensitivities towards transnational forces.[5] The so-called advanced economies continue to be subject to restructuring through TNC activity, and direct government involvement in this process is firm proof that this is a matter of political economy.

Cerny (1990, 1995 and 1996) has captured the embedded role of states in the contemporary dynamics of global political economy in his arguments related to the notion of 'the competition state', and Runyan (1996) has powerfully depicted the governmental processes which effectively court global capital. These forms of analysis increase our awareness of the extent to which governments, perhaps notably those of the so-called advanced Western states such as the US and Britain, are focusing their attention outside their sovereign boundaries to achieve economic security for their citizens.[6] Often, for example in Western Europe, where access by TNCs to the open market of the European Union is of prime interest, states are in stiff competition for transnational capital, and incentives may include grants, labour skills and costs and infrastructure factors. In these circumstances, workers are exposed to competition explicitly on a transnational basis, and their governments' interests in attracting inward investment can easily end up being aligned with the interests of transnational capital in, for example, driving down production costs to increase profits.[7]

The growth in unemployment levels and the pressure on welfare and health provisions in some of the so-called advanced Western nations has also highlighted another issue underlined by the 1996 United Nations Human Development Report (HDR) that over the last 15 years 'the world has become more economically polarized — both between countries and within countries' (UNDP, 1996: iii).[8] In the case of the USA which ranks second behind Canada in the HDR's league table of human development, there are warnings sounded about increasing income gaps, poverty, job insecurity and the lagging of health care behind economic growth. Between 1975 and 1990, the HDR explains, the wealthiest 1 per cent of the population increased its share of total assets from 20 per cent to 36 per cent, and the number of people living below the poverty line is rising, with the per capita income of the poorest 20 per cent currently less than a quarter of the country's average income. The HDR makes it clear, too, that even in the US economy, where jobs are being created, job insecurity is increasing because many of these openings are 'dead-end, temporary jobs – without security and without a future' (1996: 58). The world economy, according to the HDR's various assessments, features trends which place emphasis on problems of job-creation as well as those of growth. In other words, even in substantial areas of the so-called developed world, it matters what kind of work you can get and its relative levels of security and rewards. It has quickly been recognized that caution and subtlety are required for our understanding of exactly what it means to live in a global era, and that spatioeconomic and spatiopolitical sensitivities are essential in enabling us to identify how inequalities are being reshaped. The globalizing scope of the market, especially the financial market, is challenging both how we might understand state–market relations and, importantly, how we might understand states and markets as political and economic spaces (Bryan and Farrell, 1996). For example, the political meanings of states as increasingly active participants in the processes deepening the integration of national, regional and global markets, need to be recognized and probed. As has been indicated by a number of commentators on the processes of globalization, thinking in such terms is not a matter of blindly claiming that boundaries no longer matter, but of thinking even more deeply about what boundaries mean and even, to some degree, where they might be understood to lie.[9] In this sense globalization studies contest the status of state-centred boundaries which traditional approaches to sovereignty have tended to encourage (Agnew and Corbridge, 1995; Youngs, forthcoming).

The HDR makes clear that there are strong imperatives for thinking afresh in global terms about inequality, and doing so with awareness of the new and old losers within and across state boundaries. The terms of global trade and the flows of global capital remain two central factors in this equation affecting who can gain most from current market conditions, and we need to consider on a global basis geographical trends in both respects, as well as associated developments in new patterns of consumption. The GATT was designed to liberalize trade in industrialized goods and left primary producers in a disadvantaged position (Tussie, 1987). The WTO's emphasis on services and IPR issues, as well as goods, develops this trend further and indicates how technology in its broadest senses is increasingly influential as a motor of knowledge-based production and consumption. As the HDR points out:

Many developing countries have seized globalization as an opportunity. Countries that combine low wages with high-technology skills have out-competed more established countries. In just ten years India has expanded its software development industry, centred on 'Silicon Bangalore', to become the world's second largest software exporter. Other developing countries need to escape their debilitating dependence on exports of low-value primary products by combining their natural resources with their human capital. In the 21st century rapid strides in technology and communications will open the prospect of 'leapfrogging' several decades of development but only for the poor countries that can master the new skills and compete. (UNDP, 1996: 8–9)

Technological priorities have added new dimensions to debates about human capital issues which have become a global preoccupation as much for the so-called advanced economies in considering factors of restructuring as for the centres of the most dynamic growth, for example in East Asia. Linkages of educational and employment paths, proactive emphasis on new technologies as promoted by economies such as Singapore, and reorientation of awareness of social inequalities on the basis of the significance of differing levels of access to technological facilities, including global communications systems, are among the areas of concern. One of the most notable developments in the analysis of global cities and their interrelationships has been the ways in which they highlight new concentrations of rich and poor, including, notably, the information-rich and information-poor (Sassen, 1991; Lash and Urry, 1994).

These concentrations emphasize divisions within as well as across state boundaries. They also suggest the potential for transnational associations on the basis of shared values relating to wealth and knowledge, market access and the freedom of global communication and travel (Lash and Urry, 1994).[10] These kinds of analysis, which are fundamentally addressing factors of political economy in the context of spatiality, recognize that *mobility* is one of the most complex characteristics of the world economy affecting not only people but also the vast and rapid flows of capital and products and the diverse forms of knowledge which generate and sustain these flows and are produced by them.[11] This embraces knowledge, for example, about growth markets, new market niches, advantageous global production structuring and restructuring, and the capacities of public and private research bases and workforces to innovate technologically and to cope with the demands of globally oriented production and marketing.

In some ways it can be argued that such influences appear to be contributing to the merging of state and market interests, continuing to blur the divisions between political and economic spheres. Evidence to support this perspective can, crucially, be gained as much in the context of recent political debates about 'national renewal' in established economies such as the UK (Commission on Social Justice 1994; Hutton 1996) as in the relatively newly emergent economies of South-east

Asia.[12] It would be hard to deny from a Western standpoint that we seem to be living through times when state political interests are articulated frequently and overtly in economic terms, and that these are more often than not placed in direct relation to the world economy and its dominant trends. In a global era, it seems, the relationship between politics and economics is increasingly intimate. Of course, this has always been, to some extent, a well-understood backdrop to critical considerations of state sovereignty, but it now appears not only more complex and central but, and this is equally important, much more explicit.[13]

The 'neoliberal order': just part of the story?

The 'second wave' of globalization studies (Kofman and Youngs, 1996a; 1996b) are bringing a welcome degree of critical sensibility to the risky and simplistic tendencies of a one-world dream of global capitalism spreading wealth and, Fukuyama's 'end of history' thesis would have us believe, the demand for political liberalism. It is hardly surprising that the early advances of capitalism and Western hegemony have established a tendency to link free-market principles with liberal democracy and encapsulate the growth of the world economy in terms which too readily fuse the two. I have argued elsewhere (Youngs 1996a: 31; 1996b) that the 'end of history' approach is 'neo-colonial in turn, a kind of post-imperialist dream or vision of the ultimate triumph of the *West*'.

The geographical shift in dynamic trends within the world economy discussed above signals that our approach to it needs to be oriented firmly towards factors of political economy, that is the interaction of political and economic influences. The West-centric fusion of liberal politics and economics may sum up a significant part of the reality but it can by no means be accepted as a full explanation. The strongest critique of the dominant Western ideology is the Gramscian interpretation of the 'neoliberal' world order. This approach emphasizes 'the growing structural power of capital, relative to labour, and relative to states' (Gill, 1995: 69) and interrogates its dynamics on the basis of the interaction of material and institutional forces and ideas (see Cox 1981, 1994 and 1995). Gill has argued that:

the integration of the world into a single market also involves the disintegration of existing sets of social arrangements and state forms – such that social provision of many basic public goods becomes unsustainable. (1995: 70)

The power drift toward economy in the political economy equation is evidenced in

> a relentless social Darwinism [which] is tending to increase the level of socioeconomic inequality and political marginalization in much of the world, and, dialectically, to generate a growing disillusion with conventional organized politics. (1995: 70)

This interpretation of the dominant principles and characteristics of the globalizing economy is the dark flip-side to the euphoria of the Fukuyama model, which places faith in the old-fashioned expansionist and development model of capitalist growth – a model which the HDR (UNDP, 1996) stresses must be critically regarded by industrialized and new growth economies alike in the interests of sustainability.

I would like to suggest here, however, that we must give due attention not only to the shifts across political economy to stronger influences in economic forms of power in the world order, but also to the nature of politics and political change. East Asia, including China, and its recent dramatic growth and importance in the world economy, is a crucial area in this respect. We do not have to be blind adherents to notions of a new Pacific age to recognize that the geographic shift in significant economic activity to this region in recent years has major implications for our understanding of the global political economy.

Dominant 'neoliberal' forces characterized by so-called 'free market' principles are clearly a key factor in creating a global economy incorporating the 'East' as much as the 'West', but the full implications of this are only just beginning to be recognized. The days when Japan, as part of the triad of world economic power with the US and Europe, was the only main focus of interest in the region are long gone. This is a major development at least in part because Japan, despite its distinctive history, culture and political economy, is part of the 'Western' (G7) club of developed economies. Looking beyond Japan, political values as articulated in state and, to some degree, regional terms, are a central issue. Expressions of contemporary sovereignty in East Asia do not, in general, reflect adherence to a Western liberal model as it is generally understood, whether we are thinking of the most notable example of Communist China or the complex contrasts between autocratic 'democracies' such as Singapore and Malaysia.

Close consideration of the political economy of this region suggests a number of things.[14] First, it is completely misunderstood if regarded as some kind of blank canvas for the play of global capitalism or 'neoliberal' influences of the political as well as the economic kind. Indigenous factors, colonial and postcolonial, questions of ethnicity, established approaches to authority and social cohesion, and religion, are just some of the areas which must be addressed in understanding not only historical forces but also approaches to change in different contexts. Secondly, the rapid and distinctive nature of economic growth in the region is deeply relevant to our understanding of political change within it, and such change cannot be explained on the basis of assumptions tied to the long industrial development trajectories which characterize the histories of the Western capitalist nations. A recent assessment of South-east Asia (Vatikiotis, 1996) has usefully highlighted the degree to which economic success has, in many ways, reinforced and refashioned traditional indigenous influences in political cultures, rather than signalling their abandonment for Western democratic models. The transitions in the region need to be considered in direct relation to its own history, whose key forces include the move from colonial to postcolonial governance and from Cold War to post-Cold War divisions and associations. In the current period, to claim that high-growth economies such as Singapore, Malaysia and Thailand are finding a new place in the globalized economy as well as in East Asia is far from an overstatement. And, it appears, this is supporting regional as well as national interest claims, as demonstrated through the Association of South East Asian Nations (ASEAN) and its growing role in promoting the region politically and economically (Vatikiotis, 1996).

One notable factor linking the past to the present and future of the political economy of this region – one which is gaining attention – is the distinctive role of the overseas Chinese community and its networks in promoting and maintaining prosperity.[15] The build-up to the 'handover' of Hong Kong from Britain to China in July 1997 has seen the further expansion of these networks to produce new geographic concentrations of influence and ownership in cities such as Vancouver, Canada. There is no doubt that the global proportions and economic involvements of the Chinese diaspora has been widening, and students of international political economy will need to give thought to the particularities of these forms of transnationalism, which do not fall neatly into established Western models tending to focus strongly on states and TNCs. We are not talking here purely of the structures and principles influencing investment and trade flows, but also of the motivations and bases for sustaining and doing business.[16]

The history of Hong Kong's economic dynamism, and its deep involvement in fuelling industrialization in China and providing access for Chinese goods to the world market, has a great deal to teach us in this respect. Much has been made, in Western terms, of the free-wheeling, *laissez-faire* nature of Hong Kong's economic environment under colonial governance, and probably far too little of the importance of the strength of the Chinese diasporic business culture's fundamental contribution to the assurance of its success. Not surprisingly, the process of transition to

Chinese rule has placed emphasis on the nature of Hong Kong as a 'polity' in Western terms, but it is clear that the political economy of the territory has always been shaped as much by its predominantly Chinese, multiethnic population as by the Westernizing influences generated by its involvement in the world economy. From a Western standpoint it is too easy to make assumptions about what 'business as usual' means in Hong Kong, to view it as part of the Westernized global economy, to overlook its fundamental role, and the meanings attached to it, in the recent rapid development of mainland China's economy.

Conclusion

There are a range of conclusions to be drawn from this consideration of the global political economy which has focused on some of the major influences in the post-1945 period. The first is that with respect to international political economy and considerations of sovereignty, national borders have been only part of the story. Transnational forces which have increasingly shaped states as well as markets, have been characteristic of the dynamics of a globalizing world. United States hegemony has been a key factor in shaping the international 'neoliberal' order which, in its promotion of a global market, has contributed to the geographical spread of economic growth and associated political developments, including tensions with, as well as supports for, 'neoliberal' tenets. As we move towards the next century, the role of East Asia has been identified as central to the challenges confronting us in understanding political economy, affecting specific definitions of sovereignty at national and regional levels. We cannot take for granted the dominance of the Western liberal model, which itself has come under strain in many respects from globalizing tendencies. The restructuring of developed Western economies cannot be understood outside of assessments of such tendencies, whether they relate to the boom in the service sector and financial markets or the transnational terms of competition affecting employment patterns, work practices and job security.

Definitions of sovereignty must increasingly take account of questions of political economy, and recognize that changing patterns of interaction between politics and economics are at the heart of critical investigations of sovereignty. These are contextual, relating to specific historical circumstances in nations and regions, but the growth of global connections highlights the need to be aware of commonalities as well as differences.[17] One stark development which, in certain respects, transcends sovereign borders is the growing gulf between the most advantaged and the least advantaged in the world. State-centred definitions of inequality offer only a partial view of a world in which market territorialization must increasingly be regarded in transnational as well as national terms, in which localities within states, as well as regional and international groupings of states, are relevant to our understanding of the global political economy.

Notes

1. This has been the basis of the 'after hegemony' (Keohane, 1984) debate in the field of international relations. See also Gilpin (1987); Keohane (1989); Keohane and Nye (1989).
2. See the discussion by Gill and Law (1988: 103–24). See also Gibbons (1996).
3. Governments are also stepping in to assert their sovereign control over access to the Internet from within their countries. Procedures by China and Singapore to block access to Web sites on government blacklists have been widely reported. The global nature of the Internet may make such measures circumventable but this can be costly. See *Asian Wall Street Journal* (11 September 1996).
4. The United Nations Human Development Report 1996 (UNDP, 1996) paints a worsening picture in terms of relative global wealth patterns in noting that in the past 30 years the world's poorest 20 per cent of people saw their share of global income decline from 2.3 per cent to 1.4 per cent while the share of the richest 20 per cent rose from 70 per cent to 85 per cent, doubling the ratio shares of the richest and poorest from 30:1 to 61:1. In sub-Saharan Africa, where declines mostly began in the late 1970s, it states that 20 countries are still below their per capita incomes of 20 years ago.
5. See the discussion of the European Union, territoriality and sovereignty in the context of economic globalization by Anderson and Goodman (1995) and Ruggie (1993).
6. A useful assessment of the changed international climate in which national governments are operating with regard to economic sovereignty was provided by the Commission on Social Justice (1994).
7. One of the most extensive discussions of associated issues has been undertaken by Rupert (1995).
8. For an up-to-date analysis of the situation in the UK, see Hutton (1996).
9. See, for example, Harvey (1990); Dicken (1992); McGrew, Lewis *et al.* (1992); Lash and Urry (1994); and Held (1995). For a critical assessment of the extent and nature of economic globalization see Hirst and Thompson (1996).
10. For an extensive analysis of 'cosmopolitan democracy' see Held (1995).
11. In this author's view we will be increasingly preoccupied with questions of inequality associated with mobility. The divisions between those who are forced to move for economic, political or social reasons and those who can or cannot choose to be mobile on various grounds are likely to prove of

growing importance in an increasingly globalized world; thus attention to
migration has grown substantially in recent years. See, for example, Waever
et al. (1993) and Castles and Miller (1993). Hirst and Thompson have
argued:

> despite the rhetoric of globalization, the bulk of the world's population
> live in closed worlds, trapped by the lottery of their birth. For the
> average worker or farmer with a family, one's nation state is a
> community of fate. (1996: 181)

12. See the discussion by Vatikiotis (1996).
13. Interesting in this respect are Hirst and Thompson's (1996: 170–94)
    arguments concerning the need to think more in terms of 'governance' than
    government, and to recognize that 'states will come to function less as
    "sovereign" entities and more as the components of an international
    "polity"'. See also Rosenau and Czempiel (1992).
14. The following points owe much to the insights of Vatikiotis (1996). See also
    Yahuda's (1996) discussion of Hong Kong–China linkages in political
    economy terms with regard to the former's transfer to the latter by the
    British in July 1997.
15. See also Vatikiotis (1996).
16. In relation to the following discussion of Hong Kong and China, see Wang
    (1995) and Yahuda (1996).
17. Gendered inequalities at a global level are now gaining attention and are
    assessed specifically in the HDR (UNDP, 1996). See also Peterson and
    Runyan (1993) and Whitworth (1994).

References

Agnew, J. and Corbridge, S. (1995) *Mastering Space: Hegemony, Territory and
International Political Economy*. London: Routledge.

Anderson, J. and Goodman, J. (1995) 'Regions, States and the European Union:
Modernist Reaction or Postmodern Adaptation?', *Review of International
Political Economy*, **2**, 600–31.

Asian Wall Street Journal (1996) 'Censoring the Net Isn't Easy, But It Can Be
Intimidating', 11 September, 1, 11.

Barnet, R. J. and Cavanagh, J. (1994) *Global Dreams: Imperial Corporations and the
New World Order*. New York: Simon and Schuster.

Bryan, L. and Farrell, D. (1996) *Market Unbound: Unleashing Global Capitalism*.
New York and Chichester: John Wiley.

Castles, S. and Miller, M. J. (1993) *The Age of Migration: International Population
Movements in the Modern World*. Basingstoke: Macmillan.

Cerny, P. G. (1990) *The Changing Architecture of Politics: Structure, Agency and the
Future of the State*. London: Sage.

Cerny, P. G. (1995) 'Globalization and the Changing Logic of Collective Action',
International Organization, **49**, 595–625.

Cerny, P. G. (1996) 'What Next for the State?', in E. Kofman and G. Youngs (eds)
Globalization: Theory and Practice. London: Pinter.

Commission on Global Governance (1995) *Our Global Neighbourhood*. Oxford: Oxford University Press.

Commission on Social Justice (1994) *Social Justice: Strategies for Social Renewal*. London: Vintage.

Cox, R. W. (1981) 'Social Forces, States and World Orders: Beyond International Relations Theory', *Millennium: Journal of International Studies*, 10, 127–55.

Cox, R. W. (1994) 'Global Restructuring: Making Sense of the Changing International Political Economy', in R. Stubbs and G. R. D. Underhill (eds) *Political Economy and the Changing Global Order*. Basingstoke: Macmillan.

Cox, R. W. (1995) 'Critical Political Economy', in B. Hettne (ed.) *International Political Economy*. London: Zed.

Der Derian, J. and Shapiro, M. (eds) (1989) *International/Intertextual Relations: Postmodern Readings of World Politics*. New York: Lexington.

Dicken, P. (1992) *Global Shift*, 2nd edn. London: Paul Chapman.

Drucker, P. F. (1994) *Post-Capitalist Society*. New York: HarperCollins.

Fukuyama, F. (1992) *The End of History and the Last Man*. Harmondsworth: Penguin.

Gibbons, J. H. (1996) 'National Security and the Role of Science and Technology', *SAIS Review: A Journal of International Affairs*, 16, 1–12.

Gill, S. (1995) 'Theorizing the Interregnum: The Double Movement and Global Politics in the 1990s', in B. Hettne (ed.) *International Political Economy*. London: Zed.

Gill, S. and Law, D. (1988) *The Global Political Economy: Perspectives, Problems and Policies*. Hemel Hempstead: Harvester Wheatsheaf.

Gilpin, R. with the assistance of Gilpin, J. M. (1987) *The Political Economy of International Relations*. Princeton, NJ: Princeton University Press.

Harvey, D. (1990) *The Condition of Postmodernity: An Enquiry into the Origins of Cultural Change*. Oxford: Blackwell.

Held, D. (1995) *Democracy and the Global Order*. Cambridge: Polity.

Hettne, B. (ed.) (1995) *International Political Economy: Understanding Global Disorder*. London: Zed.

Hirst, P. and Thompson, G. (1996) *Globalization in Question: The International Economy and the Possibilities of Governance*. Cambridge: Polity.

Hoekman, B. M. and Kostecki, M. M. (1995) *The Political Economy of the World Trading System: From GATT to WTO*. Oxford: Oxford University Press.

Hutton, W. (1996) *The State We're In*. London: Vintage.

Journal of International Affairs (1996) 'Contemporary China: The Consequences of Change', 49(2).

Kennedy, P. (1989) *The Rise and Fall of the Great Powers: Economic Change and Military Conflict from 1500–2000*. London: Fontana.

Keohane, R. O. (1984) *After Hegemony: Cooperation and Discord in the World Political Economy*. Princeton, NJ: Princeton University Press.

Keohane, R. O. (1989) *International Institutions and State Power*. Boulder, CO: Westview.

Keohane, R. O. and Nye, J. S. (1989) *Power and Interdependence: World Politics in Transition*, 2nd edn. Boston: Little, Brown.

Kofman, E. and Youngs, G. (eds) (1996a) *Globalization: Theory and Practice*. London: Pinter.

Kofman, E. and Youngs, G. (1996b) 'Introduction: Globalization – The Second Wave', in E. Kofman and G. Youngs (eds) *Globalization: Theory and Practice*. London: Pinter.

Lash, S. and Urry, J. (1994) *Economies of Signs and Spaces*. London: Sage.

McGrew, A. G., Lewis, P. G. *et al.* (1992) *Global Politics: Globalization and the Nation-State*. Cambridge: Polity.

Nicolaides, P. (1994) 'The Changing GATT System and the Uruguay Round Negotiations', in R. Stubbs and G. R. D. Underhill (eds) *Political Economy and the Changing Global Order*. Basingstoke: Macmillan.

Pauly, L. W. (1994) 'Promoting a Global Economy: The Normative Role of the International Monetary Fund', in R. Stubbs and G. R. D. Underhill (eds) *Political Economy and the Changing Global Order*. Basingstoke: Macmillan.

Peterson, V. S. and Runyan, A. S. (1993) *Global Gender Issues*. Boulder, CO: Westview.

Rosenau, J. N. and Czempiel, E. O. (eds) (1992) *Governance Without Government: Order and Change in World Politics*. Cambridge: Cambridge University Press.

Ruggie, J. G. (1993) 'Territoriality and Beyond: Problematizing Modernity in International Relations', *International Organization*, **47**, 139–74.

Runyan, A. S. (1996) 'The Places of Women in Trading Places: Gendered Global/ Regional Regimes and Inter-nationalized Feminist Resistance', in E. Kofman and G. Youngs (eds) *Globalization: Theory and Practice*. London: Pinter.

Rupert, M. (1995) *Producing Hegemony: The Politics of Mass Production and American Global Power*. Cambridge: Cambridge University Press.

Sassen, S. (1991) *The Global City: New York, London, Tokyo*. Princeton: Princeton University Press.

Strange, S. (1994) *States and Markets*, 2nd edn. London: Pinter.

Stubbs, R. and Underhill, G. R. D. (1994a) 'Global Issues in Historical Perspective', in R. Stubbs and G. R. D. Underhill (eds) *Political Economy and the Changing Global Order*. Basingstoke: Macmillan.

Stubbs, R. and Underhill, G. R. D. (eds) (1994b) *Political Economy and the Changing Global Order*. Basingstoke: Macmillan.

Talalay, M., Tooze, R. and Farrands, C. (eds) (1996) *Technology, Culture and Competitiveness and the World Political Economy*. London: Routledge.

Tussie, D. (1987) *The Less Developed Countries and the World Trading System: A Challenge to the GATT*. London: Pinter.

United Nations Development Programme (UNDP) (1996) *Human Development Report 1996*. New York: Oxford University Press.

Vatikiotis, M. R. J. (1996) *Political Change in Southeast Asia: Trimming the Banyan Tree*. London: Routledge.

Waever, O., Buzan, B., Kelstrup, M. and Lemaitre, P. (1993) *Identity, Migration and the New Security Agenda in Europe*. London: Pinter.

Wang, E. (1995) *Hong Kong, 1997: The Politics of Transition*. Boulder, CO, and London: Lynne Rienner.

Whitworth, S. (1994) *Feminism and International Relations: Towards a Political Economy of Gender in Interstate and Non-Governmental Institutions*. Basingstoke: Macmillan.

Yahuda, M. (1996) *Hong Kong: China's Challenge*. London: Routledge.

Youngs, G. (1996a) 'Culture and the Technological Imperative: Missing

Dimensions', in M. Talalay, R. Tooze and C. Farrands (eds) *Technology, Culture and Competitiveness and the World Political Economy*. London: Routledge.

Youngs, G. (1996b) 'Dangers of Discourse: The Case of Globalization', in E. Kofman and G. Youngs (eds) *Globalization: Theory and Practice*. London: Pinter.

Youngs, G. (forthcoming) *From International Relations to Global Relations: A Conceptual Challenge*. Cambridge: Polity.

PART 3

BROADENING THE CONCEPT: SELF, SOCIETY AND NATURE

Imagining the Boundaries of a Sovereign Self

LAURA BRACE

Introduction

This chapter seeks to apply the concept of sovereignty to the self, and ask how we can move beyond the liberal conception of the abstracted individual, without drowning the sovereign subject in the ocean of nondifferentiation. Rather than rejecting the concept of sovereignty altogether it attempts to 'maintain its potential' (Clarke, 1996: 2). It puts forward an argument for a relational view of sovereignty, but not one which forces us to abandon a notion of self-ownership or to reject the notion of a boundary as fundamentally flawed. Instead, it hopes to build a vision of a sovereign individual who is partially constituted by her relationships with others, but continues to inhabit her own 'imaginary domain' while recognizing and acknowledging that her domain and those of others may overlap.

Reaching this vision of a sovereign self rests on making a distinction between a territory and a domain. The significance of this distinction becomes clear if we trace its genealogy back to the seventeenth century and explore the writings of Hobbes and Winstanley. In Hobbes we reach the heart of the liberal social contract tradition and in Winstanley we can hear the 'authentic voice' of a utopianism which resembles communitarianism (Sabine, 1937: 494). Their arguments about the nature of the self underpin their contrasting visions of sovereignty and demonstrate the need for all of us to grapple with notions of self-sovereignty. I hope to show that the Hobbesian model of the self is territorial, while we can use Winstanley to help us envisage a self within a domain. Hobbes formulated a vision of separate selves, able to relate to each other through competition and exchange and this vision relied on fixing boundaries around the individual and regarding those outside the boundary as potential invaders. Winstanley's alternative was a rejection of the boundary, an insistence on the importance of unity and community, of relatedness. He used the metaphor of enclosure to demand that the needs of those outside the boundaries be recognized and met and to reject the model of the territorial self.

This chapter sets out to explore the construction of the idea of sovereignty. For both Hobbes and Winstanley, the idea of sovereignty is to some extent a fiction. Hobbes claims that his vision of self-sovereignty arises from men's natural proclivities, and in particular from their natural fear of one another. Winstanley rejects the idea of fear as natural and instead sees it as an artificial construction to justify certain political consequences which include Hobbes's particular vision of sovereignty as exclusion. For Winstanley, it is imagination which creates and sustains the Hobbesian vision of sovereignty and of the self.

Winstanley's own vision of the self involved a struggle for sovereignty within each individual as he or she re-enacted the cosmic drama of the Fall. It was Winstanley who was preoccupied with the image, the metaphor of the hedge and the dam and he saw them as internalized. His ultimate vision of sovereignty was that it could be reclaimed and revitalized as community. He rejected the imagination which for him meant relying on outward objects for comfort and sanctioning the fictions of private property and a separative self.

We need to recognize the importance of imagination in its broader contemporary sense to both accounts. This involves challenging Winstanley's conception of the 'selfish, unwarranted and unexperienced' imagination as people's 'weakness and disease' (Hill, 1973: 220). He saw the imaginary power as hypocritical, and deceitful, making people ignorant and credulous. For him, it was a power perpetuated by teachers and rulers who wanted to prevent the people from daring to use their own understandings. In this chapter, the term 'imagination' is used to mean not the cloak of ideology, but each person's own understanding. It means taking up Griffiths' challenge: 'To change oneself personally and collectively, requires a leap of the imagination, from the current assumptions and patterns into new forms of identity' (Griffiths, 1995: 191).

Both Hobbes and Winstanley were asking their readers to make such leaps and to forge new forms of identity. They were addressing the imagination. Hobbes's state of nature is 'an existential nightmare' (Prokhovnik, 1996: 1718). Winstanley's vision of unity and community may be described in terms of recovery, but this is a way of imagining a future (Reeve, 1996: 1083–92). Both their accounts should alert us to the extent to which sovereignty is a way of imagining the world. It is this process of imagination which in some sense determines our self-perceptions and our articulation of our position in the world and our relationships to each other. Sovereignty is part of this story, part of the way in which we invoke our imaginations (Clarke, 1996: 5).

In imagining self-sovereignty, this chapter invokes the categories of state sovereignty which emphasize the importance of identity and difference. It aims to make the 'space' of the self an object of political knowledge (Bartelson, 1995: 31). In the process this chapter concerns itself with the 'internal boundaries of individuals' (Mehta, 1992: 3). Sovereignty is taken as a kind of double project which has been assumed to involve delimiting and moulding the imagination as well as being concerned with the sovereign's power to coerce and police individual restraint. This brings together the self and the state through its emphasis on demarcating the domestic from the international, the inside from the outside. It is also, significantly, a project of the imagination, a way of 'husbanding' the mind (Mehta, 1992: 99) or of drawing a 'line in water' (Bartelson, 1995: 50) at the level of definition, aided by metaphors and presuppositions. This chapter explores how that line is drawn and the self is enclosed by Hobbes and by Winstanley, and considers how we should resist the process of settling and limiting which is often taken to be inherent in the idea of sovereignty.

Hobbes's concept of the self asserts its identity 'in radical abstraction from the other' (Hoffman, 1995). He encloses the self, trying to create a fortress from within which to resist invasion from the outside. The other is an enemy, any relationship with them will be based on struggle, on competition, on the need to restrain them. This is bound to affect his conception of the relationship between the self and the world. It is the basis for an emphasis on mastery and dominion over others and over the world. For Winstanley, the struggle is internalized, the banishment of the evil other has to take place within each individual so that it can take place in the world. Individual selves will not find themselves in radical abstraction from one another because they are connected by the same story, tied together by the same narrative. They enact the same history as both authors and subjects. This leads him to stress the importance of interaction and community, of reclaiming an 'evenness' between individuals and between humankind and the earth as a common treasury. It is a discourse which acknowledges common interests, allows for the notion of overlapping domains and rejects the idea of mastery and dominion.

This chapter argues for the need to recognize both sovereignty and personhood as processes, as experiences rather than as fixed identities. Even 'natural' Hobbesian selves have to make an effort to keep their identities fixed and permanent: an emphasis on boundaries involves a recognition of their fragility and an emphasis on excluding others means recognizing that there are 'others' who need excluding. Winstanley is much more explicit about the idea of personhood as a process. He argues for the importance of shared experience as the basis for action. It is at this point that his concerns most clearly intersect with feminist projects. This chapter explores the metaphor of the boundary and questions Nedelsky's argument that it should be rejected by feminists. If we revive Winstanley's more subtle conception of the boundary as a damaging dam within ourselves which prevents us from recognizing others, then we no longer need to assume that in Hobbes's conception of the bounded self we have reached the end of the story and fixed our identities.

The importance of metaphor and imagery is central to the arguments of this chapter. Looking at the language employed by Hobbes and Winstanley, and at their use of metaphor in particular, throws a kind of sidelight on the idea of sovereignty and the self. Although neither of them discuss the idea of self-sovereignty directly, they use suggestive imagery. Winstanley constantly invokes the notion of humankind being 'cast out of themselves', and his whole interpretation of the Fall can be reinterpreted as a description of losing and then reclaiming sovereignty over the self. Hobbes's language of mutual fear and security, and the importance of being able to make an accurate estimate of the power of others reflect the more conventional language of sovereignty as exclusion.

Hobbes: subjugating absence

In *De Cive* Hobbes described the atmosphere of mutual fear, distrust and diffidence which characterized the relationships between individuals living in the state of nature. His description recalls the notion of sovereignty in its language which echoes descriptions of relations between states rather than between individuals. It is the language of conflict, predicated on the 'necessity of suspecting, heeding, anticipating, subjugating, self-defending' (Warrender, 1983: 33). The self must be constantly on its guard, alert to the possibility of danger and invasion. The autonomous self is like the autonomous state in Bartelson's discussion of sovereignty, 'a rational inside coping with problems on the outside' (Bartelson, 1995: 42). The defining condition of the individual in the state of nature is that he or she cannot distinguish between the wicked and the righteous, and so must inevitably take the stance of distrust and self-defence.

Constructing dualisms and then privileging one side of the equation involves knowing which side to privilege: knowing who you are requires knowing who you are not. In terms of the boundary metaphor, it is crucial to know who to admit and who to banish. Any relationships between people are bound to be based on suspicion and distrust. This is the logic of Hobbes and the logic of sovereignty. We should note how easily 'subjugating' slips into Hobbes's list of the necessities created by mutual fear and diffidence. This subjugation is part of the impulse to mastery both over the self and over the world. It is part of the model of dominion which Hobbes constructs. Force becomes a necessary part of his construction of sovereignty.

Hobbes argues that people come together and delight in each other's company not by nature but by accident. The self comes first: it exists prior to the artificial construction of relationships with others. In this sense identity is fixed in that the self provides a base from which the person can arm themselves as invader or resister. People seek society not for its own sake, but to receive some honour or profit from it. They meet to trade with one another, for example, and 'a certain Market-friendship is begotten' which is based more on jealousy than on true love (Warrender, 1983: 42). They meet for pleasure and recreation in order to satisfy their own vainglory by making comparisons with the defects and infirmities of others. They 'wound the absent' by condemning and judging them (Warrender, 1983: 42). They can assess the impact of all these actions on their pre-existent self, and they will not necessarily find themselves transformed. It is part of the way Hobbes imagines sovereignty that he can start with a bounded self and move outwards towards others. The metaphor means that owning always comes before sharing (Nedelsky, 1990: 172). The 'inside' has to be rational before it can cope with the problems posed by the outside.

The self in Hobbes is like the state in Hoffman's account. It is a sovereign voice that seeks to banish, exclude and marginalize and so extinguish difference. The self claims a monopoly, the right to exclude competitors and contestants as potential invaders. It reassures itself of its own existence by wounding the absent. Hobbes is clear that individuals come together 'not so much for love of our Fellowes, as for love of our Selves ...' (Warrender, 1983: 43). In Hobbes we find a complex vision of the self which has to legitimate itself in relation to others through notions of honour and glory which consist in comparison. At the same time, Hobbes insists that 'every man must account himself, such as he can make himselfe, without the help of others' (Warrender, 1983: 44). This looks like an assertion that the self owes nothing to the others, those who are on the outside are 'absent'. The Hobbesian self is caught in the same trap as Hoffman's state: it has to legitimate itself through comparison with the absent who it must also seek to wound.

This is a particular way of imagining sovereignty, and it is one which should remind us of Weber's definition of the state as a monopoly of legitimate force over a particular territory. It is a form of sovereignty which is bound to be based on mutual fear and dominion. Great and lasting societies, according to Hobbes, were built not on the basis of mutual good, but of mutual fear. This mutual fear consists partly in the natural equality of individuals and partly in 'their mutuall will of hurting' (Warrender, 1983: 45). The idea of harm comes first. The fiction of sovereignty which Hobbes constructs relies on this notion of the will to hurt; it relies on there being a self to be harmed and an 'other' which has the will to harm it. Such a society based on fear can never be expected to offer security. It must be part of the existential nightmare that this mutual will to hurt can create great and lasting societies: it can be something so fragile and frightening, something which ultimately rests on fantasy and imagination, which holds the whole together. The will to hurt and the fear it engenders involve a vision of sovereignty which is preoccupied with breakdown, with invasion and with identifying the risk the other poses as a natural proclivity present in the self as well as the other. There can be no escape into community or interaction, and no return to a 'lost primordial unity' (Bartelson, 1995: 38).

Hobbes describes the dangers of living in such a state of insecurity. A fiery-spirited man has a will to hurt which arises from vainglory and a false estimation of his own strength. He will challenge others to acknowledge his superiority and require them to honour and respect him. The most frequent cause of desire to hurt each other comes from competition over a scarce resource which can neither be held in common nor divided. The result must be decided by force. Among so many dangers, Hobbes asserts 'to have a care of ones self is not a matter so scornfully to be lookt upon' (Warrender, 1983: 47). Even a temperate man in the state of nature will exercise his will to hurt out of self-defence. Self-preservation is not absurd or reprehensible. Each individual has a natural right to endeavour to protect his or her life and body.

People's natural proclivity to hurt each other derives mainly from 'a vain esteeme of themselves' (Warrender, 1983: 49). The right of all to all things means that one individual has the right to invade and the other has the right to resist. This is bound to result in perpetual jealousies and suspicions. Each person will try hard to 'provide against an enemy invading us, with an intention to oppresse, and ruine' (Warrender, 1983: 49). Hobbes's description of the self in society rests on the metaphor of state sovereignty. He understands and experiences the self in terms of the state. His language emphasizes security; distrust of enemies; the possibility of invasion; the importance of self-defence, and the atmosphere of mutual fear. As Lakoff and Johnson insist, the metaphor goes beyond language to structure our thought processes and conceptual systems: 'The essence of metaphor is understanding and experiencing one thing in terms of another' (Lakoff and Johnson, 1980: 5).

They emphasize that it matters which metaphors we choose. Metaphorical concepts provide only a partial understanding, and in doing this they hide other aspects of these concepts. Using metaphor allows us to pick out parts of our experiences and treat them as discrete entities. We can refer to them, categorize them, quantify them. This is what Hobbes is doing when he discusses the self in terms of its vulnerability to invasion. It is part of the process of excluding the other, of wounding the absent. It allows us to quantify and understand our experience of aloneness, of feeling threatened by others, of having the will to hurt and of acting for our own profit and honour. It describes one possible way of imagining the self and the world: the self as bounded by a hostile world it must seek to conquer and restrain. It suppresses the acknowledgement of relationships, of bonds we have not chosen, of interdependence and shared experiences. It precludes the possibility that an individual may wish to be 'invaded' and the centrality of the boundary metaphor will mean that all sorts of things are experienced as invasion or violation.

Hobbes's description of the self in terms of the state is an indirect expression of the boundary metaphor. Nedelsky explores the enduring power of the image of the boundary through a focus on property. She sees boundary as the central metaphor in understanding and experiencing rights as limits, as a way of keeping others out, and the constitution as a guarantee against invasion. Envisioning property through the boundary metaphor requires a picture of human beings who see 'their freedom and security in terms of bounded spheres' (Nedelsky, 1990: 163). Hobbes's description of human beings living in the state of nature is a description of these bounded spheres, but it is also a description of sovereignty. The two metaphors are almost indistinguishable. They both foster the importance of protection, insulation, a sense of the danger of invasion and intrusion by others. They work on the assumption of a bounded space and invoke the idea of the 'territories of the self' (Nedelsky, 1990: 168). Respect then becomes acknowledging the territory of a person and implicitly conceding to the concepts of jurisdiction, exclusion and legitimate force loaded into the notion of a territory. Hobbes describes a temperate man in the state of nature as the one who will permit as much to others as he assumes to himself — in other words, he acknowledges the equal territory of each person. Intimacy then requires allowing others in, waiving claims over your own territory.

Thus Hobbes encloses the self, the 'rational inside' within a fortress, buttressed by our own sense of esteem and relating to others as outsiders or as absentees. Each person becomes a potential invader and a potential resistance fighter. We understand and experience our selfhood as enclosed, in need of protection against intrusion and invasion. As sovereign selves we are not only powerful, striving for gain and glory, we are also vulnerable and in need of protection. Each person may be a bounded sphere, but the boundary may prove fragile. Hobbes exhorts us to look at fully grown men 'and consider how brittle the frame or our humane body is' (Warrender, 1983: 45). He says this will help us to recognize our natural equality, but it should also remind us of the vulnerability which is an essential part of sovereignty envisaged as protection against intrusion.

This notion of the 'territories of the self', and Hobbes's assimilation of the self to the state, should alert us to the implicit imperialism of the boundary metaphor and to its gendered connotations. McClintock discusses the gendering of the imperial unknown, the way in which men imagined themselves as the 'masters and possessors of nature' (McClintock, 1995: 24). In becoming masters (sovereigns), men needed to cross dangerous thresholds and orient themselves in the new space as agents of power and knowledge. McClintock's point is that the obsession with boundaries betrays not only megalomania, but also paranoia. The metaphor of the boundary hides the 'erotics of engulfment' which is bound to be its counterpart (McClintock, 1995: 24). Hobbes's emphasis on the brittleness, the fragility of the human body is not there by chance, it is central to male anxiety about boundary loss. The obsession with self-defending and subjugating reinscribes the boundary, but this can never be more than 'a strategy of violent containment' (McClintock, 1995: 24).

The Hobbesian self is thus a colonial self:

> This may be seen as the simultaneous dread of catastrophic boundary *loss* (implosion), associated with fears of impotence and infantilization and attended by an *excess* of boundary order and fantasies of unlimited power. (McClintock, 1995: 26)

Men living in the state of nature are 'suspended between a fantasy of conquest and a dread of engulfment' (McClintock, 1995: 27). This is perhaps precisely the region which sovereignty inhabits, where 'territories of the self' come into their own. It is not only unknown lands which need to be discovered, conquered and contained, but also the unknown territories of the self. Sovereignty as it is imagined by Hobbes mediates between the fantasy and the dread. It is about fixing the territory, staking a claim to ownership and enforcing a monopoly. The sovereign self becomes an 'inner legislator', husbanding, enclosing and moulding the imagination (Mehta, 1992: 73).

Winstanley: undamming the self

Winstanley begins by describing each individual as a globe, a perfect sphere: 'every single man, male and female, is a perfect creature of himself; and the same spirit that made the globe dwells in man to govern the globe' (Hill, 1973: 77). While the language still invokes an image of space, of being encompassed, it is concerned with wholeness rather than restriction or protection. The conflict between conquest and engulfment is internal and self-contained. Winstanley's individuals have to choose whether to live off the tree of knowledge which will fill them with fears and doubts or the tree of life which will grant them universal love and pure knowledge. The Garden of Eden becomes his central metaphor for the self.

In the Garden of Eden (which for him represents both each person and humankind as a whole) the weeds of self-love, pride, envy and imagination (in Winstanley's particular sense – see above) have choked the sweet flowers and herbs of the spirit of truth. The most venomous weed is hypocrisy. It is not one of 'the true native inhabitants of the heart' and it must be cast out (Hill, 1973: 215). Mankind, the living earth, is the very Garden of Eden, and within the garden and so within each person there is a tree of knowledge and a tree of life. The tree of knowledge transmits knowledge of good and evil and feeds the imagination. If the living soul feeds on the tree of knowledge he loses his honour, strength and understanding. He is driven out of the garden and lives without God or reason. He 'does not enjoy the kingdom within himself' (Hill, 1973: 221).

Fear is not a natural proclivity or the defining characteristic of humanity. It is imagination which fills each person with fears, doubts and troubles. It stirs up wars and divisions. The selfish imaginary power within each individual creates Hobbesian individuals who can only imagine themselves through their mutual will to hurt, their fantasy of conquest and their dread of engulfment. Winstanley argues that the whole of humankind is eating out of the tree of knowledge and so 'are cast out of themselves' (Hill, 1973: 221). Again, the language of 'native inhabitants', 'kingdom', 'cast out' suggests a domain, a space within which the individual can be sovereign. It is the power of the imagination that 'puts all out of order' (1973: 224). It corrupts the five senses and makes humankind 'walk disorderly'.

This sense of disorder and disjunction is created when people seek to live upon outward things, when they see the world as made up of objects with properties independent of any other people. Individuals corrupted by the imaginary power are incapable of living within themselves, of envisaging themselves as a perfect globe: they are forced to look outside themselves for delight and for knowledge. It is this, and not their natural proclivities or their will to hurt, which makes fear the dominant feature of relations between individuals. Fear is the fruit of the imagination. It tells 'men' to get what they can by any means or face death. It encourages people to see the treachery of others, to imagine them laughing at you, cheating you. Covetousness creates the fear of being crossed by others and the fear of being in material need. It encourages hypocrisy, subtlety and envy. Through your imagination '[t]hou seest how full of hardness of heart and deceit every man is, each seeking to save himself' (Hill, 1973: 230). It makes a man break all his promises and engagements 'and seek to save himself in others' ruin' (1973: 191). This way of thinking, this conceptual system, is perpetuated by the weapons of slavish fear, evil surmising and a sense of misery and despair.

Being cast out and forced to live a life of disorder is a loss of sovereignty. Becoming a Hobbesian self, relating to others through market friendship, or vainglory or by wounding the absent means having ceased to be sovereign. It involves loss, a denial of the true inhabitants of the heart. It is not a natural condition. It should not provide a model for sovereignty because it is a model that is bound to exclude and marginalize not only others, but the true self. As long as I seek to live like this, outside myself, not acting according the freedom of my own spirit then 'I am in bondage, and my eyes are put out' (Hill, 1973: 240). This bondage is the opposite of sovereignty. It involves allowing the imagination to control the narrative and impose its own metaphor of sovereignty.

For Winstanley the essence of the Fall is a sense of a separative self: 'When self-love began to arise in the earth, then man began to fall' (Hill, 1973: 192). The Fall comes from imaginary covetousness, the impulse to seek contentment outside the self. This impulse comes from within each person, it creates a shared narrative which unites each person with one another, and connects the story of the individual to the story of the earth. Each person is a globe and their experience is global. The process of becoming a person is tied to the process of inhabiting the earth. The 'singleness and simplicity' of the original creation and of the original individual was subjected to corruption and change (Hill, 1973: 263). The stronger or elder brother (like the fiery spirited man in Hobbes) imagined that it was fit that he should have a larger part of the earth, and be held in more esteem and acknowledged as superior by the rest. The others consented to these inventions and so mankind fell from its original simplicity to be full of divisions: 'one member of mankind is separated from another, which before were all one, and looked upon each other as all one' (Hill, 1973: 264). This sense of separation from each other is the first step of the Fall.

The second step is the break into outward action, the separation from the earth. The imagination of the elder or stronger brother moved him to enclose parcels of the earth and call those enclosures his own property 'and the younger brother lets it go so' (Hill, 1973: 264; cf. Rousseau, 1973: 84). The final stage is when mankind begins to buy and sell the enclosures of land so that the younger or weaker brother is 'more forcibly shut out of the earth' (Hill, 1973: 264). Buying and selling and private property are part of the Fall. They are the outward expression of the sense of separation, claiming a monopoly, a right to exclude. As Nedelsky points out, the problem of protection of unequal property concerns inequality, power and domination and a focus on protecting the few from the many. She draws attention to the link between protecting private property and protecting a bounded or separative self. Winstanley makes the same connection. The property-owning elder brother's concern to force the weak off the land is also a concern to protect his imaginative self: 'every man seeks himself, and thinks it equity for others to regard him, and is offended at those that do not regard him; and the whole earth is filled with this devouring self-righteousness' (Hill, 1973: 266).

One branch of mankind has taken to itself the liberty to rule over the persons and labours of their fellow creatures. Winstanley is adamant that this is the law of darkness and not a state of nature: 'for nature or the living soul is in bondage to it, groans under it, waiting to be delivered from it' (Hill, 1973: 269). Sovereignty over a bounded self is an artificial creation perpetuated by the equally artificial right to own private property. Both constructions or conceptual systems mean that we think of owning as prior to sharing. Exercising control and choice over outward objects and over others becomes inextricably tied to our notions of autonomy and the idea of selfhood as separateness. Winstanley's concept of imaginary covetousness is the same as Nedelsky's claim that selfhood is 'hammered out in possession' (Nedelsky, 1990: 172). It is this sense of the self that I want to label as territorial.

Nedelsky argues that we need a new metaphor for autonomy and selfhood, one which directs our attention where it belongs. She recognizes the partiality of the Hobbesian description of the sovereign self and insists on the importance of relationship in making human autonomy possible. She wants to shift the problem to interactions between state and citizen and change the conception of the relation between the individual and the collective so that we can see the collective as a source of autonomy as well as a threat to it. In the process, we should give up our attachment to the boundary metaphor which teaches us that 'security lies in walls' (Nedelsky, 1990: 175). It covers up relationships, obscuring them from view by building walls around the individual.

I want to argue that we should complicate the boundary metaphor by exploring Winstanley's conception of the self. We can replace the notion of a territorial self, enclosed by walls, with the notion of a self inhabiting a domain. Such a self recognizes her connection to others through a shared narrative, and is able to act in and on a world shared by others. Winstanley uses the metaphor of the boundary, the hedge, to reject the image of the separative self and to expose relationships based on power and in particular the power to exclude. He describes the particular churches as like enclosures of land 'which hedges in some to be the heirs of life, and hedges out others' (Hill, 1973: 214). He uses the notion of the boundary to focus on the relationships between people and within each individual.

Imagination and covetousness may cast people out of themselves, but there is always the possibility of return. The tree of life has restoring power which can lead mankind into truth 'making everyone to seek the preservation and peace of others as of themselves' (Hill, 1973: 222). It promotes not self-love, but universal love. It casts out fear, envy, pride and vainglory and sets up a new kingdom of righteousness. Each person begins to live within himself or herself and feel love, humility and sincerity. There is '[n]o life like to the life within: this kingdom within is excellent and full of glory' (1973: 229). In his recovery, 'man' will reject outward objects and prefer this inner kingdom to outward riches. He will be saved from within by conquering the spirit of imaginary covetousness.

The great creator Reason made the earth a common treasury. No word was spoken at the beginning that one branch of humankind should rule over another. As a perfect creature, each person has within them their own teacher and ruler. However, once they begin to delight in the objects of creation and become covetous, they look outside themselves for a teacher and ruler. This kills the spirit and brings them into bondage. The teaching and ruling power which corrupts mankind 'dams up' the spirit of peace and liberty 'by filling [the heart] with slavish fears of others' (Hill, 1973: 78). The same process gives the body of the younger brother up to be imprisoned, punished and oppressed by the outward power of another.

This is where the image of the boundary can be usefully revitalized, not to shore it up, but to recognize the existence of a kind of internal boundary, a stoppage, 'the A-dam' which encloses the earth and encloses the mind. It makes men mad, ready to destroy one another to uphold civil property and assert honour, dominion and riches over one another. Adam is the power of darkness 'that stops up the waters and well springs of life' (Hill, 1973: 192). The whole earth is now filled with this Adam, the inward darkness of covetousness, envy, pride and self-love. This is the power which makes men seek to rule over one another and puts one branch of humankind into bondage. It is this dark power which makes everyone love himself or herself at the expense of others and makes mankind begin to loathe and envy each other's freedom and peace. The dam means that 'the union and communion of love within is broke' (Hill, 1973: 196).

Winstanley believes that this union of love within can be reinstated once the boundaries within people, between people and between humankind and the earth have been broken down. The spirit of universal community and freedom will overrun the dam and 'drown those banks of bondage, curse and slavery' (Hill, 1973: 88). They will re-experience a common world, without which they have suffered 'a justifiable and explicable experience of loss' (Reeve, 1996: 1085). Winstanley's vision is of an end to oppression and imaginary covetousness, a reclamation of sovereignty which is a reclamation of oneness, evenness and simplicity. Each person is a globe and inhabits her own domain, but is also partially constituted by her relationship with others because they are tied together by the same narrative, by their common interests and by the world. Their sense of self is to some extent determined by their place in the narrative, their position in the world and their self-perception: their self-domain may be subject to transformation and re-vision. The self is no longer dammed up.

Reclaiming sovereignty

In this section I want to examine what feminists can learn from Winstanley and this vision of oneness and simplicity. His notion of universal love where each person seeks the preservation of others and lives within themselves is a useful and important one for feminists trying to forge new conceptions of the self and of sovereignty. In Winstanley we can see a way through the 'erotics of engulfment' without resorting to the 'fantasy of conquest'. We can follow his conception of the dam and seek to drown the banks of the Hobbesian self, without finding ourselves engulfed and invaded.

Winstanley's recognition of the significance of power relations and his insistence on the importance of the relationship between the enclosers and the enclosed and excluded mean that his relational view of sovereignty lends itself to feminist analysis. His notion that every creature is the upholder of his fellow, knitted together into a oneness through interdependence and shared experience offers a vision which is compatible with feminist projects. The rejection of the idea that one branch of humankind can claim legitimate sovereignty over another through mechanisms of deceit and fear finds its echoes in feminism. Winstanley argues that what matters is self-sovereignty. From there we can work towards unity, community and evenness. We should also pay attention to the way in which he sees the Fall enacted within each individual as part of a shared narrative which ties them to each other and to the earth. It is a narrative which can ultimately take us beyond the Fall. If we feed upon the tree of life, there will be changes wrought within each particular body and 'as this restoring spirit spreads himself in a variety of bodies' the whole creation is brought into unity (Hill, 1973: 224).

The question is whether we need to reject the metaphor of the boundary altogether and leap to a new, unbounded paradigm perhaps like the conception of the person embodied in some notions of care, or whether we can take seriously the rejection of the dam and still leave some sense of an imaginary domain intact. It is important at this point to return to the role of the imagination. Winstanley's imagination, as Hill points out, is not something of which we should approve. It is opposed to Reason which is also Love. It is a distortion of reality (Hill, 1973: 52; and above). In this section I want to look at Cornell's concept of the 'imaginary domain' which she sees as in need of protection: is this a question of simply resetting the boundary? Her central argument is for the need to respect women as persons with their own imagination, and in the process imagination becomes a good, something of which we should approve. I want to argue that it is only terminology which distances Cornell from Winstanley: 'imaginary covetousness' for Winstanley is something which encroaches upon and denies the existence of Cornell's 'imaginary domain', but the significance of recognizing and resisting this encroachment is the same for both, and central to both their projects.

Feminists have been engaged in trying to reimagine the self following critiques of the Hobbesian radically abstracted self as a masculine conception. Held describes the fragility of a conception of the person built on contracts and separation. Her analysis emphasizes the forces of egoism and dissolution which are bound to be at work to undermine a self constituted through contracts. She sees Hobbesian selves as engaged in an endless struggle 'trying, somehow to restrain their antagonisms by fragile contracts' (Held, 1993: 204). Such contractual relations can never be more than a veneer to cover up the mutual will of hurting and the impulse to wound the absent. Contracts can only act as a restraint; they cannot provide a way out of the existential nightmare because they do not require a rethinking of either the fantasy of conquest or the dread of engulfment.

A central strand in the feminist re-visions of the self has been the need to undertake such a reconceptualization. A major tool has been the idea of care. Tronto argues that care requires attentiveness, receptiveness and selflessness. It involves relinquishing the primacy of the needs of the self, making concrete connections with others and questioning assumptions about authority and autonomy. The idea of caring for others, of being attentive and receptive to their needs and of feeling related to them, undermines the notion of the self as a container with a fixed boundary. It makes the idea of invasion and violation much more problematic. It questions whether we should always see relationships with 'others' as potentially threatening to our sense of self. The possibility of 'consensual invasion' comes closer (Nedelsky, 1990: 170). For Tronto we need to question the assumption that morality starts once separative, autonomous selves have already been established – does owning have to come prior to sharing? Thinking about caring for others rather than being obsessed by our own boundaries might help us to think about 'how to meet the other morally' (Tronto, 1995: 106).

Held discusses the possibility of meeting the other morally by rejecting the separative, antagonistic self and forging a vision of the 'relational self' (Held, 1993: 60). For her this means a self built on the basis of recognition, understanding, interaction and interdependence. The boundary is removed to allow us to concentrate on the relations between people, and once we are able to do that, we will find that those relationships are partly constitutive of the self. It is a question, as Nedelsky argues, of shifting our attention away from the boundary, or at least of reconceiving the boundary: 'Boundaries structure relationships. But they structure them badly' (Nedelsky, 1990: 178). They structure them as contractual, as restraints of our natural proclivities. Held calls on us to think about other sorts of relationship such as that between mothering person and child which are not part of the paradigm of a separative self. They do not privilege the idea of contract and consent as the model for self-sovereignty.

We need to ask whether the idea of care involves engulfment. Noddings talks about the need for the carer to be 'engrossed' in the reality of the cared for. She should displace her own interests and become self-less through engrossment. It is essential to the ideal of care and the relational self that there should be 'no inherent boundaries' to the practice of care (Bubeck, 1995: 216). This seems to suggest that by being willing to care and be attentive to the needs of others, individuals can overcome the limitations of the separative self. They can seek the preservation and peace of others and reforge the union and communion of love. In other words, we need to be able to perceive the boundary as a dam in order to be able to work towards dismantling it. Once we have done so, we should be in a position to meet others morally.

Removing the inherent boundaries to care is part of the recognition that human (nonseparative) autonomy is made possible by relationship. In considering sovereignty we need to consider the problems of interaction and interdependence. Boundary imagery will always tend towards the static, directing attention away from the importance of 'constructive relationship' and towards an obsession with protection against intrusion (Nedelsky, 1990: 168). Nedelsky argues that we need reminding that 'boundaries are not just barriers that separate but points of connection and contact' (1990: 176). She suggests the image of the skin to replace the conventional image of the wall because human skin is permeable, constantly changing and sensitive to the rest of the world. Concentrating on the fear of being invaded becomes an excuse not to care, not to concern ourselves with the 'others' in pain and hunger all around us. Held, too, is convinced that a conception of a relational self will help us to care about distant children, future generations and the well-being of the globe.

Removing the boundary and unleashing a flood of care to 'drown those banks of bondage, curse and slavery' looks appealing. It involves recognizing that in Winstanley's terms we are creatures of the Fall and we need to address what it is within each of us that constitutes a dam, and work to remove it. Such a recognition and removal will transform not only our inner kingdom, but also the world. Replacing the separative self with a relational self, aware of the points of connection between the self and others and between the self and the world, will transform both the 'rational inside' and the problems on the outside. But as Bubeck points out, while there may be no inherent boundaries to care, there are boundaries imposed on the practice of care from the outside through belief and value systems built on the barriers of sex, race and class. This is part of Winstanley's point about the power structures which hedge some in and others out.

We need to make use of the metaphor of the boundary to increase our awareness of these power structures and the way in which they structure our relations with others and dam up our sense of self. Cornell's emphasis on the idea of an imaginary domain can help us to do both these things. She stresses the importance of envisioning personhood as a project, a struggle and an endless process. As Winstanley emphasizes the importance of being able to live within oneself, of not being cast out of the self, so Cornell makes the idea of the 'imaginary domain' central to her notion of a person. In order for every individual to have an equivalent chance of becoming a person, we each need the psychic space within which we can imagine and reimagine ourselves on our own terms. The protection of the imaginary domain is a minimum condition of individuation, it means that a person is 'able to imagine herself as whole' (Cornell, 1995: 4). Although Winstanley rejects the imagination as a term, his sense of the importance of wholeness, of the kingdom within and of being able to envisage a future of communion reflects Cornell's sense of the need to foster and protect 'future wholeness' (Cornell, 1995: 43).

Returning to the imagery of an 'imaginary domain' is to return to the image of the boundary, but I hope it is to reinscribe it. We do, as Nedelsky argues, need to refocus our attention on relationships, but I think we need to recognize that those relationships are structured by the metaphor of the boundary and by the social relations of power. Care, for example, takes place within a very specific set of power relations structured by patriarchy, the economy, notions of disability, attitudes towards old age and so on. It may foster the 'relational self' and a sense of relatedness and connection, but it does so within a very specific environment where 'engrossment' can easily be structured as a duty or a necessity rather than a choice. Engulfment becomes a clear and present danger. We need to reclaim some kind of sovereignty from the ideal of selflessness, otherwise we are going to find far too many people getting under our skin.

Conclusion

Cornell's notion of the imaginary domain allows us to resist engrossment without reverting to the notion of a separative self. It is part of the wider recognition of the complexity of our selves, of the potential we have for deviating from relationship norms, of being able to imagine ourselves as different from how we have been constituted or fixed by our social situation. We need to recognize 'the diversity of ways in which we are constituted by our social contexts' (Friedman, 1991: 171) and the 'plurality of partial identities' which we can move back and forth between (1991: 172). The notion of a domain of the self as opposed to a territory should be able to incorporate this plurality, as well as the sense of movement and of overlap between different stages in the narrative.

The process of becoming a sovereign self is always an aspiration, 'a throwing or projecting into the future' (Clarke, 1996: 122). It is never entirely completed, and so the boundary can never become fixed, the territory can never be enclosed. This means that the boundary should never become A-dam, but it does not mean that we should reject the boundary altogether and give up on any idea of being sovereign over our own imaginary domain. This means more than trying to draw a line in water. It involves struggling to 'clear a space' (Cornell, 1995: 99) for the self from which we can recognize both encroachments and enclosures, and so resist both conquest and engulfment.

References

Bartelson, J. (1995) *A Genealogy of Sovereignty*. Cambridge: Cambridge University Press.

Bubeck, D. (1995) *Care, Gender and Justice*. Oxford: Clarendon Press.

Clarke, P. (1996) *Deep Citizenship*. London: Pluto Press.

Cornell, D. (1995) *The Imaginary Domain*. New York and London: Routledge.

Friedman, M. (1991) 'The Social Self and the Partiality Debates', in C. Card (ed.) *Feminist Ethics*. Kansas: University of Kansas Press.

Griffiths, M. (1995) *Feminisms and the Self: the Web of Identity*. London and New York: Routledge.

Held, V. (1993) *Feminist Morality*. Chicago and London: University of Chicago Press.

Hill, C. (1973) *Winstanley: The Law of Freedom and other Writings*. Harmondsworth: Penguin.

Hoffman, J. (1995) 'Postmodernism, the State and Politics', in J. Dowson and S. Earnshaw (eds) *Postmodern Subjects/Postmodern Texts*. Amsterdam: Rodophi.

Lakoff, G. and Johnson, M. (1980) *Metaphors We Live By*. Chicago and London: University of Chicago Press.

McClintock, A. (1995) *Imperial Leather: Race, Gender and Sexuality in the Colonial Contest*. New York and London: Routledge.

Nedelsky, J. (1990) 'Law, Boundaries and the Bounded Self', *Representations*, **30**, 162–89.

Prokhovnik, R. (1996) 'Hobbes's *Leviathan*: Feminist Interpretation and Feminist Theorising', in I. Hampsher-Monk and J. Stanyer (eds) *Contemporary Political Studies*, vol. III. Belfast: Political Studies Association.

Reeve, A. (1996) 'Community, Industrial Society, and Contemporary Debate', in I. Hampsher-Monk and J. Stanyer (eds) *Contemporary Political Studies*, vol. II. Belfast: Political Studies Association.

Rousseau, J.-J. (1973) *The Social Contract and Discourses*. London and Melbourne: Dent.

Sabine, G. (1937) *A History of Political Theory*. London: Harrap.

Singh Mehta, U. (1992) *The Anxiety of Freedom*. Ithaca: Cornell University Press.

Tronto, C. (1995) 'Women and Caring: What Can Feminists Learn about Morality from Caring?', in V. Held (ed.) *Justice and Care*. Boulder, CO, and Oxford: Westview Press.

Warrender, H. (1983) *The Clarendon Edition of the Philosophical Works of Thomas Hobbes*, vol. III: *De Cive*, English Version. Oxford: Clarendon Press.

CHAPTER 9

The Citizen, Her Sovereignty and Democratization: Lessons from Chile

LUCY TAYLOR

The transition from military rule to formal democratic regimes in Latin America gives those who study democracy an almost unique opportunity to observe both the processes of change involved in this movement away from authoritarianism and the political dynamics in the fragile democracies which emerge. This is not only of great value if we are to understand the global trend towards political liberalization, it also enables us to reassess how ideas and concepts associated with democratic theory function in 'actually existing' democracies.

A theoretical approach has a great deal to offer our understanding of democracy and the democratization process; it helps us to understand the interaction, interrelationships and antagonisms associated with democratic concepts. It is perhaps surprising that scholars of democratization have been largely rather reluctant to turn to democratic theory in order to grasp the implications of phenomena and events identified during the transition and consolidation process. Instead, they have tended to analyse democratization in terms of existing actors, their roles and conflicts, and identifiable events. Clearly this very valuable work forms the basis of understanding and analysis, but in the end it tends to be rather country- or region-specific, and in highlighting differences it impedes the transfer of knowledge and understanding to other regions and contexts. The approach taken by this chapter seeks to illustrate that concepts associated with democratic theory might provide a framework to facilitate meaningful comparison and also to show how our understanding of democracy can be enriched by analysing democracies in the making. Specifically, this piece will focus on the experience of Chile during transition to democracy, and it will take as its central topic the issue associated with this volume; sovereignty.[1]

Some theoretical notes

Our understanding of sovereignty is based fundamentally on the work of classic authors, particularly Hobbes and Rousseau. While substantial and contestable differences emerge in these two interpretations of sovereignty, both are agreed that sovereignty requires at its most fundamental and formal level that each person shall give up 'his' freedom and subsume it within the given community. For Hobbes, this 'pact' is framed thus:

> I Authorise and give up my Right of Governing my selfe, to this Man, or this Assembly of men, on this condition, that thou give up thy Right to him, and Authorise all his Actions in like manner. (Hobbes, 1985: 277)

Similarly, for Rousseau

> each one of us puts into the community his person and all his powers under the supreme direction of the general will; and as a body, we incorporate every member as an indivisible part of the whole. (Rousseau, 1968: 61)

For both Hobbes and Rousseau, each loses a modicum of freedom, but regains freedom in equal quantity and quality as freedom is reinterpreted through the sovereign body. In both cases the sovereign is whole and complete, a person cannot suffer under autocratic (i.e. non-sovereign) rule, yet nor can one opt out of the sovereign pact. The persona created by this contract is a political entity known as a citizen who has specific rights and responsibilities in relation to the sovereign body and whose participation in the polity takes the form of a special and new kind of power, sovereign power, which is endowed with a profound legitimacy by virtue of the pact itself and also because sovereign power is both universal and equal.

The nature of the sovereign body is a point of critical divergence, though. For Hobbes the sovereign is embodied in a person or government and the pact requires that people 'conferre all their power and strength upon one Man, or upon an Assembly of Men, that may reduce all their Wills, by plurality of voices, unto one Will' (Hobbes, 1985: 277). This understanding of sovereignty places emphasis on the transfer of sovereign power from the citizens themselves to their representatives through the act of submission and nomination. A contemporary counterpart to Hobbes's interpretation is that offered by Schumpeter. His model of elite democracy also involves citizens agreeing to subject themselves to the decisions of their proxies in government. Although the founding idea that 'the role of the people is to produce a government' (Schumpeter, 1976: 269) echoes Hobbes's understanding of citizen–governor relations, to remain democratic an element of electoral regularity and competition is necessary. Despite the implication that sovereignty is alienated from the citizen at the moment of pact-making or voting, the proviso that all citizens should have the same impact at that moment keeps in place the essential elements of equality and universality. For Rousseau, however, sovereignty remains with the people themselves. It is inalienable from the citizen – 'the sovereign ... cannot be represented by anyone but itself' (Rousseau, 1968: 69); it is indivisible – 'either the will is general or it is not' (1968: 70), and it is also unrepresentable – 'the people's deputies are not, and could not be, its representatives; they are merely agents' (1968: 141). Sovereignty is anchored in the citizenry: it pertains to the citizen as an individual, but in order to exist, every citizen must be able to wield their sovereign power and must do so within the context of a community of citizens. That is, it must conform to the requirements of equality and universality.

These notions of universality and equality, satisfied by each approach, are essential in giving democracy its apparent moral grounding. These are the qualities which persuade many of us that democracy is the 'right way' to rule and that selective exclusion from the political process is unethical. Key to democracy and sovereignty, then, are political rights which provide the mechanisms through which sovereign power can be wielded. Without political rights, we are at the mercy of those who rule our lives. No matter how beneficent the ruler, no matter how complete and equal our ability to wield civil rights, no matter how expansive and progressive our access to social rights, we are still at the whim of those who make decisions (be they for good or ill). In this case, people are better characterized as denizens (those who live within the aegis of a certain state and are subject to it) than as citizens (those who participate in the workings of a certain state and to whom it is subject). In 'actually existing' democracies, these political rights are most clearly and easily identifiable with periodic voting in elections, which embodies, in principle, the equality and universality which sovereignty demands, and satisfies (at the very least) the minimal scope for sovereignty proposed by Schumpeter. In authoritarian regimes, the option of voting for a representative or standing as a candidate for election is commonly denied the citizen and she is usually portrayed as a denizen of the autocratic state; the citizen is stripped of her sovereignty and is made subject to the decrees of a government which has no mandate from the people and thus lacks the formal legitimacy of sovereign representation.

The analysis of politics under the military government of Chile implies that the concepts and mechanisms of citizenship and sovereignty persisted, mutated, were suspended and selectively applied, and in some ways were reinvigorated. Given this more confusing and complex picture, it will become clear that we must take a more flexible approach to the analysis of citizen–governor relations both in authoritarian regimes and, by inference, also in democratic polities.

Electoral sovereignty and legitimacy

The Chilean military took power in September 1973, and General Pinochet maintained a tight grip over politics until 1989. The regime sought to reshape Chilean politics and eventually to install a type of democratic regime which would protect capitalism and the 'Chilean way of life' (Valenzuela, 1978; Roxborough, et al., 1977). One of the reasons why the military intervened was the high level of political polarization and strife, especially the development of 'extreme' left-wing groups during Salvador Allende's socialist government which preceded the coup (Sigmund, 1978). Influenced by the National Security Doctrine and infused with anticommunism, the military formed two conclusions from this context (Garretón, 1989a). First, it was apparent that the civilian political elites were unable to govern this situation and civilian continuation in power would lead to severe dislocation and potential revolution in Chile. Secondly, it appeared clear that the democratic system in place was too 'liberal' and allowed elements which threatened the Chilean nation to reach positions of power. As such, in the short term the civilians should be displaced from power and in the longer term the military should set about tightening and reinterpreting the democratic system to ensure that threatening elements could never again disrupt Chilean political life.

On taking power, Pinochet set about his constriction and transformation of the Chilean polity. The trappings of democratic rule were disbanded; Congress was dissolved; political parties were banned and universities, the judiciary and the bureaucracy were purged of politically undesirable elements. Control of society was ensured through the imposition of a curfew, severe repression of any antimilitary activities and censorship of the press. Society was also to be cleansed and the undesirables eliminated, and this was to be achieved by the arrest, imprisonment, assassination and disappearance of trade unionists, socialists and communists (Davies and Loveman, 1978). Evidently, these policies severely undermined the rights of the citizen. They abrogated substantive civil rights including right to life and the right to a fair trial and legal representation. Political rights were also suspended with the denial of the right to represent and be represented, and political activity in the social sphere was made extremely dangerous through repression and the threat of violence. In this context, the Chilean people were clearly stripped of their formal sovereignty. The choice to be ruled by the military was not made through the expression of a mandate which ensured the equality and universality of that choice; it was imposed from outside and was enforced through violent means. Nor did the Chilean citizenry have any opportunity (until much later) to ratify the 'right to rule' of the military government or to oust the regime. With the suspension of political rights, the mechanism for exercising sovereignty was inoperative.

However, a particularly interesting event took place in 1980. To accompany his transformation of the Chilean polity and his cleansing and restriction of Chilean democracy, Pinochet had implemented a number of Decree Laws, many of which related to the future form and remit of democratic politics. In order to institutionalize these changes and ensure their longevity, he sought to change the constitution. The General could have inserted these changes by decree, of course, but this would have left this crucial reinterpretation vulnerable to being rejected or ignored in the future. It was essential, then, that these changes be made as immovable as possible and this required that the adoption of the new constitution be legitimized. He therefore called on the people to vote 'yes' or 'no' in a referendum which sought to ratify the new constitution. The vote took place under circumstances made dubious by the general air of coercion and repression and murmurs of ballot-rigging, but the voting population indeed agreed to adopt the new constitution.

This episode displays several elements of importance to our understanding of sovereignty under authoritarian rule. First, it indicates that formal sovereignty had not ceased to exist, it had simply been placed in suspension. What had changed under military rule was that the mechanism for the expression of sovereignty had been temporarily blocked. The ability to defrost sovereignty resided with those who had decision-making power (and held the guns). Formal sovereignty was to be turned on or off like a tap, then, but it couldn't be wholly eliminated.

Secondly, despite the fact that the military had suspended the sovereign power of the citizenry, sovereignty was still a reference point for the military, and as a moral and political source of power and legitimacy it could not be ignored. Instead, Pinochet harnessed the idea of sovereignty to serve his cause, even though he held no sovereign mandate or right to rule, and even though at no other point in the proceedings which led to the finished constitution were the people asked to tender an opinion or a vote. The manipulation of sovereignty as an instrument of legitimacy also allowed Pinochet to distort this event by interpreting the vote as a personal endorsement. He felt able to claim that the referendum had ratified his political, economic and social project, had endorsed his 'right' to rule and had stamped approval upon the authoritarian method of government. Nevertheless, Pinochet's recourse to referendum in 1980 implies a tacit acknowledgement that the 'people' *are* sovereign and that a legitimacy grounded in the expression of the sovereign will *does* matter. As such, not only does sovereignty continue to exist as an instrument of government, it continues to wield substantial influence over politics and is understood to do so by those who rule from the barracks.

Third, this strategy was a great success and Pinochet's constitution continues to hold sway, although some slight modifications were negotiated during the transition to democracy (1990 and 1992). By painting this event as a democratic oasis within a desert of authoritarian rule, the constitution referendum stands out as a brief moment of citizen participation. The fact that the 1980 constitution has endured implies that for both military and citizens alike the constitution is imbued with a substantial legitimacy which is born of the sovereign act itself.

These statements might appear obvious if the political context were democratic. However, it is essential to recall that this oasis of sovereign expression occurred within a context of dictatorship where rights were violated, where the people were coerced and repressed and where the mechanisms and institutions associated with democratic rule were nonexistent. To what extent, then, can we call this referendum the act of a sovereign citizenry? Clearly, in some ways we can if we interpret sovereignty as a formal act in which a choice is placed before a community of people and their ability to express a preference is both universal and equal in relation to that issue and at that moment. However, it is equally clear in this case that sovereignty had very little meaning, given a context of repression and given that the opportunity to exercise sovereignty was controlled by coercive elites, rather than by the citizenry or through prescribed, regular opportunities. There is evidently a need to look further than formal mechanisms for the expression of sovereignty and to build into our analysis the structural environment and political climate within which this action takes place. Moreover, we need to ask questions concerning the extent to which the citizen herself has sovereign power. If people cannot claim civil and political rights, would it not be more accurate to classify Chileans during this period as denizens and subjects of the state? Again, this is a tempting option, but as an analysis of citizen participation during the Chilean military period reveals, the dynamics of sovereignty are not necessarily eliminated. They can be reinterpreted and moulded to fit the contours of the authoritarian political context.

Citizen sovereignty and legitimacy

Although the profoundly penetrating and very frightening repression inflicted by the military regime upon the people of Chile successfully restrained antimilitary activities for a long period of time, many sectors of society began to organize and to protest against the regime. Of particular importance in the early stages were the human rights organizations which sought to contain the forced imprisonments and disappearances through legal means by placing habeas corpus petitions and seeking to represent those imprisoned. Sister organizations also sprang up which brought together the relatives of the victims of repression, and these spearheaded the political campaign of denunciation against the military (Frühling, 1983; Lowden, 1995). By the early 1980s, other organizations emerged to challenge military rule, of which the most substantial were the shanty town dwellers' groups. The military regime's economic policy adopted a strident neoliberal strategy and caused mass unemployment and increased levels of poverty (O'Brien and Cammack, 1985). Those most severely affected were the shanty town dwellers who adopted a two-pronged strategy: to organize self-help provision of social needs and to develop a campaign of resistance, both to the economic policies and to the military regime itself. The shanty towns became centres of struggle against the regime which encompassed both this political activity and physical clashes on the streets with the security forces, bombings of military targets and electricity black-outs (Oxhorn, 1991; Leiva and Petras, 1986).

A disparate set of organizations emerged – from women's organizations to communist party theatre groups, from soup kitchens to guerrilla groups – and together they organized and developed a complex and substantial antimilitary campaign. Another set of organizations also emerged during the early 1980s – the women's groups. These also were highly differentiated, some concentrating on intellectual and personal development, others seeking to improve the lot of Chilean women by teaching practical skills to poor women. They too were drawn deeply into national politics, and by 1984 International Women's Day was a key forum for the denunciation of poverty and human rights abuses, and for rejection of the regime in general (Jacquette, 1989; Waylen, 1992). These three broad groups were very diverse, yet they developed a complex and clandestine network of links both within the movements and across the sectoral divides and were all united on one key point – to get rid of Pinochet. Marches and demonstrations became a regular event during the early 1980s and reached a peak in 1983 when a series of one-day stoppages, which included strike action and black-outs, took place once a month and were accompanied by violent action on the streets.

It was said earlier that according to formal indicators at least, the people of Chile ceased to be citizens under the military regime and that their sovereignty was frozen or suspended, to be released only at the behest of those who ruled by force. Yet when we look at this evidence of concerted and widespread activity on the streets in opposition to the regime, we do not see people acting as subjects but as *subjected citizens*. While civil rights were at best partial and precarious, while political rights were nonexistent and while social rights were being undermined by neoliberalism, that is, while the citizen was being stripped of the outer framework of her identity as a citizen, her inner framework remained intact. This inner framework is very closely related to the expectations and fundamental understandings associated with political culture and in particular, the people's understanding of their role in politics. Here, specificities related to political culture often mould these interpretations. The relatively long history of democracy in Chile (which spanned most of the twentieth century), the substantial faith in democratic politics as a solution to national problems (such that even the radical left sought the parliamentary road to socialism under Allende) and the high levels of political education and participation characteristic of Chilean politics all contributed to create a deep democratic culture and a strong sense of citizenship which was not easily eradicated. Thus, under Pinochet's rule, those involved in antiregime activity asserted a set of rights and the concomitant roles which they could not exercise but which they perceived to be legitimate claims. The banners which rose above the marchers make this plain: 'No to Repression'; 'Justice for the Violators of Human Rights'; 'Liberty! Rights! Freedom! Democracy Now!'; 'No to Impunity'; 'Democracy in the Country and in the Home'. These were people who were denied the rights associated with citizenship, but who nevertheless saw citizenship as a political identity and who acted upon that identity outside the confines of the formal political arena which remained in the hands of Pinochet and the military establishment.

The social movements which formed the core (in this earlier period) of the antiregime campaign were clearly engaged in political activity, but the formal arena of politics was closed off to them. Instead, they created an enclave for political activity in the social sphere which expanded as more people became involved and as the intensity of campaigning increased (Garretón, 1989b). In many ways, they created democratic pockets within the authoritarian context. The organizations themselves usually functioned in a democratic manner (representatives were elected, clear structures of accountability were introduced, open meetings were held where a range of views were aired) and the demands and goals were clearly founded on the urgent need for democratic government. They engaged in actively claiming rights (to life, to political participation), and the organizations acted as a vehicle for dissent and put forward competing views of how society should be organized and what should be done. If democracy requires the meaningful presence of rights, competition and participation, then *within the community created by the social movements* democracy could be said to exist. If we have a group of people who feel themselves to be citizens engaging in political activity within the confines of a democratic pocket, can we say that they are exercising sovereign power? The question of sovereignty is a knotty problem. In order to live up to its name, the sovereign must be indivisible and sovereignty must be exercised equally and universally. In an authoritarian context, in which dissent and opposition politics takes place in an informal political arena and is unconstrained by the regulations and institutions of formal democracy, we must ask what sovereignty means and where it resides. If the sovereign is indivisible, what is occurring when we see one set of people participating, claiming rights and exercising political power, while another and much larger group of people refrain from participation and believe it to be misplaced?

The case discussed here indicates that we must take a more flexible and more complex view of sovereignty. We must identify at least two dimensions. The first relates to the sovereign body of which everyone is a member and in which all have equal power but in which sovereign power is conferred wholly or in part upon another external entity which comes to embody sovereign power. This dimension identifies most closely with the Hobbesian and Schumpeterian concept of sovereignty, and it is this body which we most closely associate with elections and formal mechanisms for the expression of sovereignty. Secondly, we must also think of sovereignty as being located in the people, both as an abstract group and as a collection of individuals. This links sovereignty more closely to citizenship and urges us to think about what sovereignty means to the citizen herself. In strengthening the connection between sovereignty and citizen, this dimension identifies sovereignty more closely with the Rousseauian concept of where sovereignty resides. For this person, sovereignty confers the over-arching 'entitlement' to exercise her own political and civil rights in relation to the polity and society. This understanding leads to the conclusion that sovereignty in 'actually existing' polities is best understood as a combination of both the formal and the citizen-based elements.

What has happened, then, to citizen sovereignty under Chilean military rule? We know that in its formal manifestation sovereignty had been suspended with the taking of power by the military, and we understand that (no matter how popular) the military could not lay claim to formal legitimacy as no formal act of the sovereign citizenry had sanctioned their actions or endorsed their right to rule. Yet sovereignty still 'exists' as a tangible quality and as a tool of politics. Pinochet utilized and manipulated it; social movements within their democratic pockets wielded it. If we are willing to accept that sovereignty has a psychological dimension linked to the perceptions associated with political culture and the invisible dynamics associated with legitimacy and influence, then a possible solution to the question 'where does sovereignty reside' emerges. If those who rule are not representatives, the full power of sovereignty reverts to the people themselves. How then can we reconcile the partial manifestation of sovereign power (only some people act as citizens in democratic pockets) with the characteristics of equality and universality demanded by the nature of sovereignty? Perhaps the answer lies in characterizing citizen-based sovereignty as having a *potential* for equality and universality and a *manifestation* which is commonly particular and individualized, a characteristic which emerges from the different willingness of individuals to participate in the political process. This kind of approach to sovereignty which accommodates different dimensions and manifestations and which builds in an understanding of dynamics and change, helps to explain important political phenomena in non-democratic contexts. It allows us to get a firmer grip on the elusive notion of legitimacy under military rule which is expressed by a changing climate of opinion rather than by formal endorsement. It allows us to understand that military claims to be acting with the sovereign consent of the people are not unfounded (military take-overs are often popular at the very beginning) and that campaigns against military rule are rooted in a shift of opinion which carries the weight of legitimacy anchored around a deep understanding of citizenship and sovereignty. In order to change politics and the government, subjected citizens under authoritarian rule cannot exercise formal sovereignty, but they are potentially able to wield their individualized citizen-based sovereignty to great effect.

Dynamics of sovereignty and democratization

This identification of separate dynamics also helps us to understand the complexity of the transition process and the potential antagonism between these two manifestations of sovereign power. The case of Chile again provides us with an intriguing example of the role of formal and citizen-based sovereignty in bringing about the return to democratic rule in 1989.

Perhaps surprisingly, the Pinochet regime put into place a mechanism which would satisfy many of the criteria of the 'electoral' sovereignty. The constitution of 1980, endorsed by the sovereign citizenry, had within it the provision that a plebiscite would be held in 1988 in which sovereignty would again be unfrozen allowing the people to vote 'yes' or 'no' to a further eight years of military rule. Should they vote 'no', then presidential and congressional elections would be put in train for the following year (Angell and Pollack, 1990). This clause does two important things. First, while the original constitution referendum tacitly acknowledged the sovereignty of the citizenry, the constitution which they endorsed explicitly recognizes the existence and over-arching importance of the sovereign citizenry. Secondly, this clause provided an actual future mechanism for the exercising of sovereign power at the ballot box which would be, ostensibly, equal and universal. This introduced an important principle which is the idea of accountability. Clearly accountability tomorrow is no compensation for violations today, yet in terms of our formal 'electoral' sovereignty this brings the regime much closer towards the democratic norm in providing a fixed moment when the regime will be brought to account and when the people will have a substantive choice between authoritarian and democratic rule.

When the moment of the plebiscite came the 'noes' were victorious with 55 per cent. This event indicates two important points. First, this rather bizarre strategy on the part of the military proved the vital impor-tance of electoral sovereignty in that it opened the gates to the formal return to democracy. Moreover, in being orchestrated by the regime, the military was obliged to abide by the result due to the legitimacy of sovereignty itself which the entire process implied. Secondly, however, this meant that 45 per cent of the electorate voted to continue life for a further eight years under authoritarian rule! Although some of those voting 'yes' may have done so for fear of recriminations and repression (especially in rural areas), a substantial proportion of the citizenry rejected democracy; that is, a considerable number exercised their sovereign power to indicate a preference to be ruled over, rather than to rule. The sustained support within the polity for the military (and for the extreme right as their parliamentary proxy) which persists in Chile is a reflection of this first vote. The implications of this are considerable if we regard this plebiscite as an instance which measures the degree of consent to respect the will of the majority. Clearly the plebiscite result indicates that this consent was granted only by a bare majority itself and as such, forms a somewhat shaky foundation from which to construct democratic representative government.

Following our analysis of dimensions of sovereignty, this event clearly had a major impact. It implied, both in the plebiscitary act itself and the outcome of the poll, that a return to formal electoral sovereignty was in train. Yet what of the informal, citizen-based sovereignty which had been returned to the citizenry and had been exercised so effectively by social movement activists? As time went on, the democratic pockets of informal political action solidified and became the arena within which the (banned) political parties of the left and centre began to regroup and to reorganize. These pockets provided the platform from which the parties launched their campaigns and upon which they built structures and mechanisms of formal (though not legal) political activity. A process of colonization was taking place, whereby the political parties took over the mantle of opposition from the social movements and reasserted their status as the favoured and official vehicles for political participation. As such, hierarchal mechanisms were introduced into the antimilitary campaign and semiformal relationships of representation began to form (Díaz, 1993; Espinosa, 1993). This implied a shift away from citizen-based and individualized formations of sovereignty and towards formalized, representative forms; the purpose of citizen-based activity became the restitution of formal sovereignty. Indeed, social movement activists worked at the core of the 'no' campaign canvassing on the ground, urging people to use their vote to rid Chile of military rule, and they continued to play a major role throughout the subsequent elections in 1990 to presidency and congress. These elections were won by President Aylwin, who headed the centre–left coalition, the Concertación, which formed the new democratic government.

At last! Democracy has returned to Chile. Yet it is important that we ask what has happened to the sovereignty of the citizen in the wake of the elections. Clearly, electoral sovereignty has once again become meaningful in the light of free and fair elections, and representatives once more rule with the profound legitimacy bestowed upon them by the act of selection by a sovereign citizenry. Alongside formal sovereignty, people may still wield citizen-based sovereignty, granting or denying a climate of legitimacy, raising demands and ideas both outside and within the framework of formal politics, and assenting to or dissenting from the actions of their accountable representatives. Indeed, they may now exercise this type of individual sovereign power with a great deal more security than under authoritarian rule, and their rights to associate, organize, publish and participate are now guaranteed.

However, a cautionary note must be sounded. Despite the resonance of these assertions, sovereignty is being distorted in two ways. First, the nature of the transition to democracy in Chile has left the military in a strong position of power, and Pinochet remains as head of the armed forces. While Pinochet does not intervene in day-to-day politics, it is clear that he has laid down the minimum standards of political behaviour and policy, which create an encircling perimeter fence constraining the actions of the government. For example, in the winter of 1993 a series of military-related scandals and human rights trials for notorious crimes led Pinochet to stage acts of military theatre on the streets of Santiago (placing troops on 'red alert'; attending meetings dressed in full battle regalia). This created a crisis of government–

military relations in which such threatening behaviour held the government to ransom and forced concessions on human rights. If this military barrier is breached, then serious constraints are placed on the government, and the sovereignty of the people and their representatives is seriously eroded.

Secondly, the return to democracy in Chile has been interpreted by those in positions of power to mean the rebirth of elite democratic structures, an understanding of democratic politics which prioritizes formal electoral vehicles for the expression of sovereignty over and above more informal mechanisms. This has occurred for several reasons, the most prominent of which is the catalogue of demands being voiced at the base, including the call to prosecute the perpetrators of human rights abuses and the need for a substantive redistribution of wealth. The government is incapable and/or unwilling to adopt these policies, given the persistence of Pinochet as a political force and the nature of Chilean economic strategy. Balanced as it is in a delicate position between people and armed forces, the government has sought to create an environment of civil calm and order to ease the worries of both military and foreign investors. Given this, the exercise of citizen-based sovereignty in the informal political arena is marginalized or ignored by the government, and is also portrayed as a threat to political stability and therefore to the new democracy. As such, those who continue to call for justice in relation to human rights violations are subtly branded as extremists who risk waking 'the lions that sleep with one eye open', undermine the security of the people and jeopardize the safe consolidation of democracy. Thus forms of participation and expressions of citizen sovereignty previously deemed highly legitimate during the dictatorship are reinterpreted as inappropriate in the context of representative democracy. Any attempt to dissent is interpreted as a partial withdrawal of legitimacy, which in turn is interpreted by the government as treason against democracy itself.

Citizen participation has declined dramatically in Chile. The shanty town dwellers' movement has all but disappeared, the human rights movement is reduced to a hard core of activists, and the women's movement is in a state of fragmentation. The reasons for this decline are many and varied and yet it is certain that the idea that the mantle of political activity has been taken over by the elites at the apex of politics and the notion that this is as it should be in a modern representative democracy has contributed towards this decline. This conflict between political elites and social movement activists can be interpreted through the lens of sovereignty and understood in terms of the antagonisms between the two dimensions of sovereign power, an antagonism which is found in a wide range of polities, both democratic and authoritarian.

Conclusion

The picture which emerges reflects back on the theoretical points made earlier in the chapter. Sovereignty is not only a power bestowed on representatives through the exercise of mechanisms for measuring consent, following Hobbes and Schumpeter, nor is it only a power vested in individual citizens within the context of a wider citizenry, following Rousseau. Sovereignty in the contemporary world is a complex combination of both dynamics. These dimensions, as this case study has shown, interact and conflict to form a changing concept of citizen power. An analysis of sovereignty which only identifies the formal manifestation of sovereign power is clearly, in the light of the Chilean case, inadequate to allow for a complete understanding of sovereignty under authoritarian rule. If we simply look for formal indicators, then we risk overlooking crucial sites for the expression of sovereign power and crucial dynamics produced by these expressions. Although formal sovereignty has come to dominate citizen–governor relations under democratic rule, pockets of citizen-based sovereign expression persist, and they should not be ignored as political phenomena even though their impact has been weakened. It is important, if we are to understand both the process of democratization and democracy itself, that we seek to identify and monitor each dynamic in its own right, as well as observing the interaction, complementarity and antagonisms between them.

Essential to an understanding of the complexity of sovereignty is the recognition that the absence of democratic structures and the presence of coercive force does not necessarily imply that the phenomena and perceptions associated with democracy have also been eradicated. A citizen is not defined solely by the rights which those who rule grant or abrogate. Rather the quality of being a citizen is primarily defined by the citizen's own perception of her role and what she may claim, defined in terms of the legitimacy she herself feels and the climate of opinion which surrounds her claim. In exercising that role and in the act of claiming, the citizen is unmistakably utilizing a special power which accrues from her identity as a citizen: sovereignty. The absence of a formal mechanism through which she may wield this power thus becomes of secondary importance and alternative mechanisms are readily found. Most effective is the construction or rejection of legitimacy, and it is plain from the case of Chile that authoritarian elites court the consent of the people and manipulate moments of sovereign expression to their own benefit. This implies not only that the people do see themselves as citizens and recognize their sovereignty, but that those who rule by force also acknowledge their character and the power and status this confers. It is important, then, to approach the analysis of both authoritarian and democratic regimes by examining the relationship between citizen and governor, and exploring not only their differences (which are considerable) but also the similarities and continuities which persist despite the existence of very divergent regimes.

The greatest irony, of course, emerges when we examine the strength of citizen-based sovereignty under military rule and the watering-down of this sovereignty in the contemporary democratic context. By its very nature, citizen-based sovereignty cleaves sovereign power to the citizen herself, and it remains undiluted by the negotiation and compromise which accompany representation. If we are to regard strong sovereignty to be a hallmark of a meaningful democracy, it is essential that this dynamic does not become alienated from the workings of a democratic polity. Yet negotiation and compromise remain the key qualities of representative democracy which allow it to function. The enduring and deep legitimacy of formal expressions of sovereign power have been made evident in the case of Chile. However, thinking in particular of the legitimacy which was endowed to the 1980 constitution, we should beware of noting only the act of sovereignty itself. It is essential that analysis of sovereignty contemplates the context within which this occurs and the alternative expressions of sovereignty with which it conflicts. This warning is not only of relevance to authoritarian regimes. We must also bear in mind these elements and dimensions of sovereignty when examining events in established democratic polities.

Note

1. This essay draws on research conducted in Chile over six months in 1993 and 1994 during a field trip gathering material for doctoral studies. Readers are directed to the thesis for more and more detailed information concerning events and facts in the contemporary period.

References

Angell, A. and Pollack, B. (1990) 'The Chilean Elections of 1989 and the Politics of Transition to Democracy', *Bulletin of Latin American Research*, **9**(1), 1–23.

Davies, B. and Loveman, T. (1978) *The Politics of Anti-Politics: the Military in Latin America*. Lincoln, NB: University of Nebraska Press.

Díaz, A. (1993) 'Estructuras y Movimientos Sociales: La Experiencia Chilena Entre 1983–1993', *Proposiciones*, **22**, 13–20.

Espinosa, V. (1993) 'Pobladores, Participación Social y Ciudadanía: Entre los Pasajes y las Anchas Alamedas', *Proposiciones*, **22**, 21–53.

Frühling, H. (1983) 'Stages of Repression and Legal Strategy for the Defence of Human Rights in Chile', *Human Rights Quarterly*, **5**, 510–33.

Garretón, M. A. (1989a) *The Chilean Political Process*. Boston: Unwin Hyman.

Garretón, M. A. (1989b) 'Popular Mobilization and the Military Regime in Chile: The Complexities of the Invisible Transition', in *Power and Popular Protest: Social Movements and the Transition to Democracy in Latin America*. Berkeley, Los Angeles and London: University of California Press.

Hobbes, T. (1985, 1st edn 1651) *Leviathan*. Harmondsworth: Penguin.

Jacquette, J. (1989) *The Women's Movement in Latin America*. Boston: Unwin Hyman.

Leiva, F. I. and Petras, J. (1986) 'Chile's Poor in the Struggle for Democracy', *Latin American Perspectives*, **13**(4), 5–22.

Lowden, P. (1995) *Moral Opposition to Authoritarian Rule in Chile 1973–1990*. Basingstoke: Macmillan.

O'Brien, P. and Cammack, P. (eds) (1985) *Generals in Retreat: The Crisis of Military Rule in Latin America*. Manchester: Manchester University Press.

O'Donnell, G., Schmitter, P. and Whitehead, L. (eds) (1986) *Transitions from Authoritarian Rule: Prospects for Democracy*. Baltimore and London: Johns Hopkins University Press.

Oxhorn, P. (1991) 'The Popular Sector Response to an Authoritarian Regime: Shanty Town Organisations since the Coup', *Latin American Perspectives*, **18**, 66–91.

Rousseau, J.-J. (1968, 1st edn 1762) *The Social Contract*. Harmondsworth: Penguin.

Roxborough, I., O'Brien, P. and Roddick, J. (1977) *Chile: The State and Revolution*. London: Macmillan.

Schumpeter, J. (1976) *Capitalism, Socialism and Democracy*. London: Allen & Unwin.

Sigmund, P. (1978) *The Overthrow of Allende and the Politics of Chile 1964–1976*. Pittsburgh: Pittsburgh University Press.

Taylor, L. (1996) Social Mobilization and Political Participation: Chile and Argentina. PhD Dissertation; University of Manchester.

Valenzuela, A. (1978) *The Breakdown of Democratic Regimes: Chile*. Baltimore: Johns Hopkins University Press.

Waylen, G. (1992) 'Rethinking Women's Political Participation and Protest: Chile 1970–1990', *Political Studies*, **40**, 299–314.

'Does She Do Queening?': Prostitution, Sovereignty and Community

JULIA O'CONNELL DAVIDSON

> If the liberal vision [of the person] is not morally self-sufficient but parasitic on a notion of community it officially rejects, then we should expect to find that the political practice that embodies this vision is not practically self-sufficient either – that it must draw on a sense of community it cannot supply and may even undermine. (Sandel, 1992: 89)

The notion of sovereignty refers to the rightful exercise of power over self and others. It therefore has to be imagined in relation to a set of assumptions about human nature and sociality, for we cannot decide what powers we can rightfully exercise over others, or what powers they can exercise over us, without first determining our proper relation to them. Furthermore, the very way in which 'power' itself is understood reflects a set of assumptions about human interdependence since 'theories of power are implicitly theories of community' (Hartsock, 1985: 3). Feminist theorists of power, such as Hartsock (1985), Young (1990), Pateman (1988) and Cornell (1995), have therefore insisted that power cannot be abstracted from the social relations in which it is embedded and through which it is reproduced. This chapter represents an attempt to apply a relational understanding of power to a particular social practice, that of prostitute use, and to the notions of sovereignty and community which underpin it.

In the course of research on prostitution and sex tourism over the past three years, I have interviewed some 200 Western men about their prostitute use, and there are two stories about why men use prostitutes which I have heard over and over again. The first is an upbeat tale about the client's sense of inclusion, his sense of mastery, his sense of being constituted as a full sovereign individual through his prostitute use. The second is a tale of woe. It centres on his fear of exclusion, and it is a story of grief and loss. These two stories are not told by different individuals. The same client tells both stories, typically beginning with the first, then moving on to the second when his prostitute use is interrogated more closely. Both stories are, among other things, stories about sovereignty, for in discussing their prostitute use, clients tell tales about the kinds of power which they believe men have a right to exercise over their own, and other people's, bodies, minds and selves. Stories must also have a setting, and clients' tales about their prostitute use are set in a social world that is imagined in a very particular way. Examining the way in which clients imagine their world (who is included in their 'community' and on what conditions, who is excluded from it and why) is also relevant to debates about the way in which sovereignty is constituted.

In this chapter, I want to argue that clients' stories are not simply the products of warped or aberrant individual minds but are instead informed by, and consonant with, both the liberal political tradition and widely accepted ideas about gender. The sovereign self of liberalism is imagined as unencumbered by 'his' social relations, as a person incapable of constitutive attachments. To imagine such a person is not to conceive of an ideally free and rational agent, rather it is 'to imagine a person wholly without character, without moral depth' (Sandel, 1992: 88). This chapter aims to show how perfectly this captures the soulless existence that clients imagine for themselves.

Classic tales: the Natural Born Client and the sovereign individual

One explanation that clients typically offer for their prostitute use draws upon the idea of male sexual 'needs'. Some men view themselves as lacking the physical or social charms necessary to meet these 'needs' in noncommercial contexts (they say things like, 'When I was younger I could always pick a girl up at a disco or something, but now I'm older and getting a bit thin on top, like, put on a few pounds, they won't look at me'). Because prostitution affords them instant access to a selection of females, they can, as one man put it, get their 'sex drive out for the night'. Other clients describe their prostitute use as a quick and simple expedient in situations when no other 'outlet' is available. For instance, a sailor told me that he was visiting a red-light district in a port town because 'I'm a man, I have biological needs. I've been on ship for months without a woman. I had to have one.' There are also clients who have wives or girlfriends from whom they are not physically separated. They tend to explain their prostitute use as a function of rather more specific sexual 'needs' which would otherwise go unsatisfied ('I'm a masochist, and my wife couldn't, well, I wouldn't ask her to'; or 'I need something that's just purely sexual, just to meet my needs with no complications') or else as a response to their wife/partner's lack of sexual interest in them. Finally, there are clients who say that they use prostitutes as a means of satisfying a 'natural' impulse to have sex with as many different females and as often as they possibly can.

As well as naturalizing their own prostitute use, these ideas about male sexuality allow clients to simultaneously construct the sexual licence and/ or services alienated by the prostitute as a 'good' or 'commodity' which satisfies a perfectly understandable and reasonable demand on the part of the 'consumer'. Such assumptions allow the client to tell a story in which prostitution performs an important social function. As the following quotes from clients show, prostitution is imagined as soaking up excess male sexual 'urges' which would otherwise lead to rape, marital breakdown and all manner of social disorder:

> Prostitution should be legalized. You shouldn't have anyone telling adults what they can and can't do sexually. In fact, it's a bad thing for governments to try to tell people what to do, because if you repress them, then they'll find a way. They'll go out and rape someone. It's the same as telling children they can't have chocolate, it's bad for their teeth. What do children do? They want it all the more and you find them stealing it. People always want what they can't have. It's human nature.

> If there was no sex commerce what/where would sex loneliness go? Deeper inside to become converted into a much messier distortion of life potentiality I fear.

> Men are the hunters. It's men that chase women, you don't find many women chasing men. It's the way things are. In the old caveman days, if you wanted a woman you just grabbed her, and that was the end of it. It's the animal kingdom. That's why you need prostitution, it's why it's the oldest profession there is in the world.

The idea of powerful male sexual 'needs' enables clients to picture prostitution in radical abstraction from the power relations which underpin it. It naturalizes their own prostitute use to the point where saying they are entering into a social relationship with the prostitutes they use appears as far-fetched as saying they enter into a social relationship with the toilets that serve as receptacles for other biological 'functions'. Discourse about a biologically based male sexual 'drive' has been largely discredited in academic circles (see Weeks, 1986, for an excellent critical review), and even if we were to accept the notion that human males are afflicted by powerful, biologically rooted sexual 'appetites', this would in no way constitute a direct explanation for prostitute use. It would leave unanswered questions as to why some men do not use prostitutes, even when they are 'deprived' of other sexual 'outlets', and why those who do use prostitutes are not indiscriminate as to how their 'need' for sexual 'release' is satisfied and by whom. No one would attempt to account for the demand for *nouvelle cuisine* through reference to hunger as a biological drive, and it would be a stranger 'hunger' still that could only be satisfied if quails' eggs were served up by costumed waiters of a particular sex, age, physical build and racialized identity. It is equally fatuous to try to explain the demand for the extensive and varied range of commercial sexual services through reference to biological imperatives for sexual 'release'. Biology is enabling, not determining.

The story of the Natural Born Client does not describe a biological reality. Regardless of its logical and empirical flaws, however, it does serve to naturalize and defend prostitution as a form of commodity exchange, and for the purposes of this chapter, what is significant is the remarkable similarity between the clients' view of what lies behind the commodity exchange of prostitution, and certain classical liberal theorists' view of what lies behind more general forms of capitalist commodity exchange.

Classical liberal discussions of sovereignty start from the proposition that human beings are naturally competitive and self-interested, and for this reason need safeguarding from each other. Hobbes, for instance, holds that in a state of nature, each man would use all means available to him to possess, use, and enjoy all that he could get. By agreeing (on condition that all men do the same) to a social contract which creates a political society or state, and transferring rights of law-making and enforcement to that state, individuals can, it is argued, simultaneously retain powers of sovereignty over themselves, and be restrained from invading and destroying others. The legitimacy of the liberal democratic state hinges upon its role as enactor of laws which preserve and protect the 'natural rights' of its citizens, rights which include possessing property, disposing of their own labour and exercising sovereignty over themselves, their own minds and bodies. The powers enjoyed by the state are thus viewed as a condensation of the wills of a mass of individuals, each of whom has an equal interest in the construction of a legal juridical framework which safeguards life, liberty and estate.

According to this story, contractually organized commodity exchange is central to the preservation and protection of sovereign rights. No individual or group holds the power to snatch or commandeer goods or resources from another. Instead individuals must voluntarily contract to alienate property in peaceable and mutually advantageous exchanges. As Marx puts it, in the fiction of capitalist commodity exchange:

A and B recognize each others as owners, as persons, whose commodities are permeated by their will. Accordingly, the juridical concept of the

person comes in here, as well as that of freedom in so far as it is contained
therein. Neither forcibly takes possession of the property of the other;
each disposes of it voluntarily. (Marx, cited in Sayer, 1991: 59)

This logic extends to the wage–labour contract, for according to
liberals, a person's labour is a commodity which can be freely alienated
like any other commodity. The abstract, sovereign individual of
capitalism cannot be invaded by another's will, even when she or he is
denied access to any means of subsistence other than wage labour.
Sovereign individuals are free because no monarch, lord or state
apparatchik can command their labour, person or property – each
juridical subject is safeguarded against threats to self-sovereignty by the
contracts which regulate social interaction.

A parallel story is told by clients about a sexual contract and the
institution of prostitution. Clients insist that men have natural sexual
appetites. Male sexual desire is imagined to be rooted in man's animal
nature and men are afflicted by a sexual 'drive' akin to hunger or the
need to evacuate the bowels. To imagine men as possessed of sexual
'needs' (as opposed to wishes) is to construct women as embodying a
resource (their female bodies) which is vital to men's physical and
psychological well-being. Clients assert that, unless they are restrained
in some way, men's competitive struggle for access to this 'resource'
will wreak chaos and destruction. By agreeing to enter into some form
of social contract (again, on condition that all men do the same) and
allowing sexual access to the female body to be controlled and
regulated through a combination of legal and customary devices, the
terrible consequences of men's competitive struggle can be averted.

Because clients view the formal and tacit rules which govern sexual
life in their society as akin to the 'social contract' imagined by liberal
theorists, that is as a distillation of their individual wills, they typically
attach a good deal of legitimacy to this form of sexual governance.
Prostitutes' clients are thus far from progressive thinkers on questions of
gender or sexuality. Most of them want their own wives or girlfriends
to practise monogamy; they make extremely derogatory comments
about women whom they deem to be 'promiscuous'; they happily use
the term 'pervert' to describe those whose sexual preferences differ from
their own; they believe that flogging or hanging should be reintroduced
for those whom they define as rapists and paedophiles; they believe that
'real men' should conform to extremely macho stereotypes of
masculinity; they are typically deeply homophobic, and so on. In short,
clients are not usually men who challenge the existing status quo so far
as either sexuality or gender are concerned, in fact it is precisely that
status quo which clients (along with functionalist sociologists and socio-
biologists) believe is safeguarded by the institution of prostitution.

They reason that first, prostitution is a necessary defence against the threats to the established order which would inevitably result if some men's sexual 'needs' were left unmet (men whose 'appetites' are not satisfied might return their 'natural state' and go about seducing or raping other men's wives, mothers and children). By ensuring that access to sexual 'resources' can be contractually arranged across a market, prostitution prevents this nightmare world of rape and seduction becoming reality. Second, and equally significant, the institution of prostitution ensures that despite being 'contractually' bound to restrain themselves sexually by rules which they themselves have agreed, men do not lose control over their own bodies. There is always an 'outlet' for their sexual 'urges'. As one British man said of his visits to red-light districts in Thailand:

> Over there, you don't have to worry about going out and getting someone, because you know any time, day or night, you can have anyone you want within seconds. You feel so powerful, you feel you're in control of your sex life.

In other words, because prostitution allows men to purchase sexual licence as a commodity, it furnishes them with full 'sovereignty' over their own bodies, minds and selves, in just the same way that entering into any other commodity exchange enables consumers to exercise 'sovereign' powers.

Liberal theorists' classic stories about the social contract and individual sovereignty have been subject to powerful critiques by both Marxists and feminists. Marxists have argued that liberal democracies are neither creations nor creators of isolated, solitary, 'sovereign' individuals, for 'it is not the single, isolated individual who is active in historical and political processes, but rather human beings who live in definite relations with others and whose nature is defined through these relations' (Held, 1983: 24). The insights which Marxist and feminist theorists have offered into the ways in which relations of domination are both reproduced and concealed by various fictions about sovereignty can also be applied to the tales clients tell about the sexual contract and prostitution, for these are tales which simultaneously entrench and naturalize patriarchal social relations (see Brace and O'Connell Davidson, 1996). On closer inspection, it becomes apparent that the story of the Natural Born Client is one which also both reflects and reproduces the boundaries of an imaginary community.

Sovereignty and the boundaries of community

The clients I have interviewed are, to different degrees, preoccupied with ideas that can be understood as a legacy of the Cartesian dualism which has shaped Western thinking. This legacy implies that reason can be sharply demarcated from emotion and that desire poses a fundamental threat to reason and morality (Seidler, 1987; Jaggar, 1989). Clients believe that male sexual desire is rooted in man's animal nature and that it is a mark of 'civilization' for a society to control and regulate its subjects' sexual behaviour through a multiplicity of formal and informal rules and conventions. Yet they simultaneously believe that to restrain men's natural sexual 'appetites' is to prevent them from expressing that which makes them truly masculine. The sexual contract to which they imagine themselves party (a contract which is constituted through these rules and conventions) is something which, at one level, goes against 'nature'. As has been seen, prostitution becomes an institution which allows men to escape this impasse.

Prostitution involves the exchange of sexual licence and/or sexual labour across a market, and it is usually (but not always) organized and constructed as a commodity exchange like any other. In order to imagine the prostitute–client transaction as a commodity exchange, clients have to treat sexuality as though it were something which can be detached from the person. The prostitute's sexuality becomes something which she can freely alienate, and the client's sexuality is also imagined as somehow estranged and divisible from his real self. He enters into the exchange merely to 'control' his sex life or satisfy his sex drive. One client even compared his sexuality to a vehicle which the owner has to maintain, describing his visits to prostitutes as being 'a bit like taking your car to the garage to get it serviced ... you're paying for the services of an expert, someone who really knows what they're doing'. Thus 'sexual needs', which are in reality nothing more than productions of the human imagination, are invested with a life of their own and viewed as an external force driving the client to behave in particular ways.

Patterson has observed that in the course of human history there have been two polar extremes in terms of how power is exercised:

> One has been the tendency to acknowledge human force openly, then to humanise it by the use of various social strategies such as fictive kinship, clientship and asymmetric gift exchanges. The other extreme has been the method of concealment, in which coercion is almost completely hidden or thoroughly denied. Indeed, it is even presented as the direct opposite of what it is, being interpreted as a kind of freedom. (1982: 81)

By telling himself that prostitution is a commodity exchange (he and the prostitute meet freely in the marketplace and voluntarily contract to dispose of their property), the client can conceal his own power from himself. This means he can also overlook certain facts about the person to whom he secures sexual access, facts which would often make sexual contact with her illegitimate in terms of the rules and conventions which, in noncommercial contexts, he himself would endorse. The prostitute may be extremely young, a child even. She may be another man's wife or girlfriend or pregnant by another man. She may be being coerced into prostitution by a husband, boyfriend or pimp. She may even be debt-bonded or otherwise enslaved to a brothel-keeper. But because his relationship to her is constructed as a commodity exchange, the client does not feel morally compelled to interrogate what lies behind her sexual 'consent'. He can simply think in terms of an exchange of 'values', *x* amount of money for *x* sexual benefit (and clients do really talk about 'value for money').

Although clients seek to justify and defend the power they exercise over prostitutes as power over commodities, rather than power over persons, and to tell themselves that this is a commodity exchange like any other, I would argue that at another level, they are quite conscious of the fact that they enter into the contract precisely in order to exercise personalistic, and not materialistic, power over the prostitute. Clients know that in reality they contract, as Pateman (1988) observes, for the use of a human embodied self, for the right to temporarily command what is embedded in and cannot be detached from the prostitute's person. Indeed, they complain bitterly when, in their view, the prostitute fails to keep to 'her side of the bargain' by refusing to give them this kind of command. To quote one client:

> [Some prostitutes] they just lay there, like a dead fish on the slab. They just lay there. I don't know how you can get any satisfaction with a woman just lain there like that. You might as well go home and have a wank.

In the prostitution contract, the client seeks to exercise sovereign powers not only over his own self, mind and body, but also over the prostitute, who in entering the contract must temporarily relinquish sovereignty over her own person. Furthermore, few clients really accept that the prostitute's sexuality can be estranged as a 'thing' or 'commodity' separate from her person. In fact, quite the reverse. Clients tend to buy into very traditional ideas about gender and sexuality, and so demarcate 'good' from 'bad' women, 'Madonnas' from 'whores' through reference to notions of sexual 'purity'. A female who sells sexual licence and/or access to her person is considered by clients (as well as by many non-prostitute-using men and indeed by many women) to be dirty, mercenary, dishonoured.

All this tells us something about the kind of community to which clients imagine themselves as belonging. Let us look more closely at what is assumed in clients' notions of sovereignty. To imagine all men as possessed of sexual 'needs' and all women's bodies as a 'resource' necessary to men's well-being would actually be to construct a zero sum model of sovereignty. If men 'need' sexual use of female bodies, then they cannot attain full sovereignty over their own bodies and selves unless they are guaranteed access to this 'resource', and if men were given this guarantee, then women would necessarily be denied sovereignty over their own bodies and selves. Clients do not want to follow through the logic of this zero sum model of sovereignty, a logic which would leave their own daughters, their own mothers and grannies as 'fair game' for any man experiencing an urgent 'biological need'. They therefore adopt a rather more complex model of sovereignty within which women, though denied full subjecthood, are nonetheless included as members of the imaginary community. The rules and conventions which govern sexual life in that community may be patriarchal, constructed by and for men's 'benefit', but they do also afford women a limited degree of control over men's sexual access to their persons. If men generously agree not to rape women, for instance, the corollary is that women are accorded the right not be raped and so a degree of protection from rapists. The story of the sexual contract which clients tell thus implies the existence of a community which incorporates women. The women in this community cannot exercise sovereign rights over their own bodies and selves in the same way that men can, but they are nonetheless entitled to protection from those forms of invasion which are outlawed by the sexual contract which men have established.

Clearly, if prostitute women were imagined as part of this 'community', then men's access to them would be circumscribed in the same way that their access to nonprostitute women is circumscribed, and prostitution would no longer function to 'safeguard' the status quo. Prostitute women thus have to be imagined as outside the community. Because they 'agree' to sell their sexuality as a commodity, prostitutes are held to have placed themselves outside the remit of the socially agreed rules which govern sexual life. They are expelled and excluded from the community, and thus the rape, even the murder, of prostitute women does not evoke the same degree of popular outrage as the rape or murder of women who are covered by the rules, and the sexual abuse of a child is adjudged differently according to whether it takes place within a commercial or a noncommercial context. Equally, the sexual use of women who would normally be considered 'off limits' (for instance, because they are pregnant, visibly ill or injured) becomes acceptable when those women are prostitutes. The exercise of personalistic power to command sexual access and services from females who are included in 'the community' is considered transgressive, but exercising personalistic power over the prostitute is viewed as perfectly acceptable – implicit in 'the deal' even.

The extent of the prostitute's exclusion from the imagined community can be graphically illustrated by a story told by a British sex tourist in Thailand. This man, like many of his compatriots, was quite happy to sit through live sex shows in which prostitutes (some of whom are debt-bonded, some of whom are under the age of 16) pull strings of metal bells, scarves, or razor blades from their vaginas in front of an audience of leering men. He would also happily visit brothels where women and children are lined up, numbered and displayed in order that clients can 'select' an anonymous, visibly objectified and disempowered female body for his sexual use. And although he claimed to disapprove of the sexual exploitation of children, neither he, nor any of his 'mates' had ever challenged another sex tourist about their abuse of prostituted children. He told the following story:

> When I was in Ko Chang there was this old Austrian bloke, must have been 70 at least, and he was enticing the dogs into his beach hut, tempting stray dogs in there with food. It was fucking disgusting. Anyway, someone told the police and they had words with him, but I was telling this bloke at the bar one night and I pointed the bloke out to him and he just walked over to the Austrian bloke and punched him in the face. He said 'You dirty fucking poofter' and he floored him. He says to me after, 'He comes to paradise and what does he do? Fucks dogs'.

In other words, it was easier for this man to imagine dogs as part of his community, covered and protected by rules pertaining to sexual life, than to include prostitutes amongst those worthy of protection. The prostitute's exclusion can also be seen in the fact that while clients often deem particular sexual acts to be 'unnatural' or 'perverted', it is the act itself, rather than the commanding of a prostitute to perform it, which is considered transgressive. There are men, for example, who would not dream of even asking their wives to perform acts of coprophilia, let alone think it right to coerce their wives into so doing, and yet they will telephone prostitutes' receptionists to ask 'Does she do queening?' in rather the same tone of voice that they would inquire of a car sales representative 'Does she do 0 to 60 in 8 seconds?' It seems to me that the power to decide when and where to defecate is very much the kind of power which 'individuals' exercise over themselves. For an individual to be in a position to command another adult human being to defecate in a particular place, in a particular way, at a particular time, is for them to exercise a type of power over that human being which would normally be viewed as an illegitimate invasion of sovereignty. Because prostitution is contractually organized as a commodity exchange like any other, the buyer of this or any other type of sexual 'service' can tell himself that his own actions are quite legitimate. He is simply behaving as a sovereign consumer in a free market behaves. Because the prostitute who sells this 'service' is considered dishonoured, socially dead, and imagined as outside the community, the client can also tell himself that she has surrendered her right to self-sovereignty.

The woeful tale of the client's exclusion

Behind the story of the Natural Born Client, there is another tale which men tell about their prostitute use. This story is also about their masculinity, but this time the focus is on how their gender has exposed them to exclusion, grief and loss. The prostitute users I have interviewed invariably describe a childhood in which they suffered repeated and humiliating attacks upon their gender identity. They report frequent incidents in which they were physically chastised or verbally reprimanded for not being sufficiently 'manly'; they describe having been told not to cry, not to display emotional vulnerability or physical fear; having been expected to perform well in competitive sports, and so on. I doubt that this distinguishes clients in any significant way from non-prostitute-using men, but it does appear to be significant to the sexual hostility prostitute-using men express towards women, for clients typically move from descriptions of this kind of childhood to express enormous resentment of women. They will tell you that life is easier for women, and in particular, that it is easier for women to achieve intimacy and to give and receive care from others. Mothers are allowed to get close to their children, fathers aren't. Women can have intimate friendships with other women, men can't. Women do not have financial and economic responsibilities, they are 'taken care of', but no one 'takes care of' men. Girl children are given advice and helped to prepare for their future role as wife and mother, boy children are abandoned to their fate and left to work it all out for themselves. In the words of one interviewee, a 55-year-old man:

> Mothers train their daughters, they prepare them ... They teach girls how to look pretty, tell them how to sit, how to cross their legs. They teach them how to be attractive and how to please a man. But they don't teach boys anything. Boys are neglected, and then, next thing you know, you're expected to be a man, to be in charge. You're expected to know what women want. They expect you to fight in wars, go out and fuck whores, be a real man. The mother's even happy if her son dies for his country so long as she gets a flag, all neatly folded, and a letter saying that her son

was brave. She doesn't care if he goes out and fucks some dirty whore. She just says 'Good, that shows he's a man'. Boys get nothing. They might be hurt, but they have to hide it, they're not allowed to cry. And no one tells them how to please women. The boy reaches the age of 15 or 16, he has biological urges, he needs to find a girlfriend. So what happens? He goes out and gets humiliated. Girls are just laughing at him ... Men are like yo-yos, emotionally they're controlled by women. It's always women who hold the strings.

In this story, the client presents himself as emotionally victimized, neglected, vulnerable and misunderstood, and describes non-prostitute women as powerful, vindictive, careless. The sexual contract, which appeared to reflect the common will and to guarantee freedom in the tale of the Natural Born Client, is now presented as oppressive and unfair. It accords too much power and control to the 'good' women (mothers and wives) upon whom men depend for love, care and emotional support. As another habitual prostitute user put it:

You get the gold-diggers, the women who'll do anything to get a bloke because he's got a few bob, and once she's got in, that man is caught, because if he tries to get out, she'll take him to the cleaners. It's a web ... I found when I was married, I felt caged ... Men are very insecure in relation to women. They want the woman for security, at the same time they feel insecure in the marriage because they know they can be taken to the cleaners any time. And I honestly feel that the prostitution side ... it's because they're ... trapped.

In this way, clients shift from explaining their prostitute use as a simple consequence of biologically given male sexual 'drives' and start to explain it as a consequence of the 'excessive' social and emotional power exercised by women. A recurring theme in the stories of woe which clients tell about their prostitute use is that men are weak and non-prostitute women are strong. 'Good' women are berated for their power to 'incite' sexual desire and then 'withhold' sexual access, for their power to refuse unconditional emotional support, for their ability to withdraw freely from intimate relationships – in short, for being autonomous individuals. Vengeance thus becomes central to a client's sexual excitement. Stoller (1975) suggests that perversion is essentially a gender disorder constructed out of a triad of hostility: rage at giving up one's earliest bliss and identification with the mother; fear of not succeeding in escaping out of her orbit; and a need for revenge for her putting one in this predicament. In word and deed, compulsive prostitute users express rage at not being able to command, at will, the adoring and indulgent gaze of any woman they choose. Adult women who are their economic, social and/or legal equals are perceived as hugely threatening simply because they are in a position to control themselves – to exercise choice over whether or not to meet a man's demands. For a woman to be in a position to exercise choice is for her to assert her separateness, her free will, her capacity to withdraw freely from the relationship and so to arouse these men's infantile rage.

The client's tale of woe highlights the value of the work of psychoanalytic feminists such as Chodorow (1978), DiStefano (1991) and Butler (1995) who argue that for male children, gender socialization as currently practised entails relinquishing intimacy and identification with the mother, something which often involves a very exaggerated, early and brutal form of 'de-differentiation' of self. As well as the grief of relinquishing 'femininity' (imagined as the right to care and be cared for), male children's gender socialization involves accepting 'masculinity', something which, to varying degrees, is equated with success in a competitive struggle over real and/or imagined 'resources'. Boys must learn to reconstruct their mother as Other, they must reject their own longing to be intimate with/identical to the mother/feminine, they must conquer their own longing to give and receive care and so somehow come to terms with themselves not just as separate from other people, but also as separate from their own emotions, feelings and desires. In this sense, boy children's gender socialization can be seen as a process of accepting and adopting the Hobbesian model of the 'territorial self' discussed by Brace (chapter 8 in this volume).

If 'femininity' is imagined as the right to care and be cared for (that is to acknowledge one's relation to others), and 'masculinity' rests on rejection of such 'femininity' (that is to deny one's relation to others), then it is small wonder that sexual relationships often represent such difficult terrain for men. As Seidler (1987: 97) notes, little boys are required by culture to displace their own feelings of need, emotionality and dependency with a quest for the prestige, power and status that is associated with a masculine identity, and:

> It is the nature of this displacement from emotional lives and needs for dependency which has so deeply formed masculine sexuality. Often it is closeness and intimacy which are feared; men experience any compromise of their independence, defined as self sufficiency, as a threat to their very sense of male identity.

With a prostitute, clients can manage their sexual and emotional life in any way they choose. They can treat the prostitute as nothing but a sexually objectified body, they can play-act intimacy and romance, they can command the prostitute to perform in ways which allow them to conquer their fears. This can be done without incurring obligations or expectations, and with little threat of any real mutual dependency developing. Furthermore, with a prostitute, clients experience none of their usual rage and frustration about their inability to control their own and other people's sexual behaviour. The prostitute woman's sexual behaviour is controllable through the reductionist medium of money, and, equally important, other men's sexual behaviour is no threat to the client's masculinity in relation to the prostitute. In fact, prostitution reverses men's usual fears about competing with other men for power, prestige and status. In relation to a man's privately owned wife or woman, even past or imaginary lovers represent evidence of his inability to control her sexuality absolutely, and all men are threatening (in many popular songs men are warned that if they love a beautiful woman, they had better watch that their friends do not steal her). But in relation to a prostitute, it is a question of the more the merrier. The client need not fear his fellow men, indeed the more men who fuck her, the more confident the client can be that her sexual behaviour is something he too can control. This image of the prostitute's sexuality as something which can be controlled by anyone and everyone is often very explicitly eroticized in pornography and in clients' sexual fantasies.

Prostitution also provides a forum in which men's fantasies of unbridled sexual access can be momentarily realized. Here, a man can transcend and dominate the constraints imposed upon his sexual behaviour by his age (old men can buy access to young women, young men can buy access to older women), by his physical appearance and/or personal demeanour (men who are nasty, brutish and short can purchase access to women who would otherwise turn them down) and by his racialized identity (white men can secure access to black and Asian women, Asian men can secure access to white women, and so on). Again, I would argue that this teaches us something about the very particular way in which clients imagine sovereignty and community.

The client's tale of woe is a story which centres upon both a longing for and a dread of intimacy. This is a story in which men fear entering into close and dependent relationships with women because they know that in so doing, they risk being infantalized, engulfed, out of control, open to rejection and humiliation. The dread of intimacy is above all a fear of boundary loss, a fear that the dependency which goes hand in hand with intimacy will leave them vulnerable to invasion by another's will. The client's tale of woe is also a story about community, then. It is set in an imaginary community in which 'good' women exercise certain powers of sovereignty, for if women were wholly excluded from and completely denied subjecthood in the imaginary community, they could never be in a position to engulf, control, reject or humiliate men. Prostitution can only offer intimacy without dread if prostitute women are sharply differentiated from their 'respectable' sisters. Prostitute women must be expelled and excluded from the client's imaginary community if prostitution is to mediate between men's fantasies of domination and their dread of engulfment.

Ambiguities and contradictions in the clients' tales

There is a sense in which the two stories told by clients about their prostitute use are but two sides of the same coin, for masculinity is socially constructed as both dominance and denial. Prostitute use is held up as a way in which both fantasy and dread can be successfully managed, and both stories therefore end happily. But the truth is that there is a gap between clients' real, lived experience of prostitute use and the stories they tell about it, and this should alert us to the danger of assuming that reality is identical with the discourses used to discuss it (see Seidler, 1987; Moore, 1994; McNay, 1994). In real life, clients' prostitute use does not always have a happy ending, for in practice, their notions of masculinity, sovereignty and prostitution are riddled with contradictions.

Take for example, clients' idea that where prostitution is organized as a contractual commodity exchange, they can become sovereign consumers. In this discourse, clients are empowered and masterful. But their lived experience often teaches them that the contract is a double-edged sword. Because sexuality, like human labour, cannot be detached from the person, no contract can, on its own, ensure that property rights are fully alienated. A prostitute may contract to allow a client sexual access to her person, but since he cannot detach what he has bought from the prostitute herself, he remains dependent upon her co-operation (or upon the use of force) to 'consume' his purchase. In some political, institutional and economic contexts, arranging the prostitute–client exchange as a commodity exchange like any other actually places the prostitute in a position to control and limit the degree of personalistic power exercised over her.

A successful entrepreneurial prostitute who sells sexual 'services' as she would sell any other kind of services can (under certain circumstances) simply refuse to grant various forms of access to her person (see O'Connell Davidson, 1995a; 1996). When a client asks 'Do you do queening?', she can say 'No'. Clients often experience this kind of power on the part of the prostitute as profoundly threatening. The prostitute becomes as able as her 'good' sisters to refuse him, and the following quote from one client is revealing. He explained that he 'hated' prostitutes. He had used prostitutes all over the world, and he hated European and North American prostitutes in particular:

It's all businesslike. It's by the hour, like a taxi service, like they've got the

Men want more than just a body, they want one they can control

meter running ... There's no feeling. If I wanted to fuck a rubber doll, I could buy one and inflate it ... A prostitute in Europe will never kiss you. In Canada, it's ridiculous. You know, if you go with a prostitute and you don't pay her, you know what? They call it rape. You can be in court on a rape charge.

Many clients respond to this by seeking out prostitutes who are disempowered and unable to set limits on the contractual exchange (for instance, prostitutes who are controlled by a third party or who are forced by extremes of poverty to accept whatever terms the client offers – see O'Connell Davidson and Sanchez Taylor, 1996a, b). But the more vulnerable the prostitute, the more obvious it becomes to the client that he is exercising personalistic power in order to extract sexual services/access from her, and the less he is able to see himself as obeying the 'rules' of the sexual contract (rules which prohibit the use of force to obtain sexual access). This intensifies his paranoia – if he himself does not obey the rules, what guarantee is there that other men will obey them? And if the 'contract' breaks down, the spectre of invasion and engulfment once again becomes very real and threatening.

Note

I have conducted research on issues of control and consent in the prostitute–client exchange in Britain (O'Connell Davidson, 1996), on the attitudes and practices of British sex tourists in Thailand (O'Connell Davidson, 1995b) and, with Jacqueline Sanchez Taylor, I have undertaken fieldwork for ECPAT (End Child Prostitution in Asian Tourism) in Latin America, the Caribbean, South Africa and India, the primary aim of which was to investigate the attitudes, motivations and identity of men who sexually exploit prostituted children (O'Connell Davidson and Sanchez Taylor, 1996a; 1996b).

References

Brace, L. and O'Connell Davidson, J. (1996) 'Desperate Debtors and Counterfeit Love: The Hobbesian World of the Sex Tourist', *Department of Sociology Discussion Papers*, no. S96/3. University of Leicester.

Butler, J. (1995) 'Melancholy Gender/Refused Identification', in M. Berger, B. Wallis and S. Watson (eds) *Constructing Masculinity*. London: Routledge.

Chodorow, N. (1978) *The Reproduction of Mothering*. Berkeley, CA: University of California Press.

Cornell, D. (1995) *The Imaginary Domain*. New York and London: Routledge.

DiStefano, C. (1991) *Configurations of Masculinity: A Feminist Perspective on Modern Political Theory*. Ithaca: Cornell University Press.

Hartsock, N. (1985) *Money, Sex and Power: Toward a Feminist Historical Materialism*. Boston: Northeastern University Press.

Held, D. (1983) 'Central Perspectives on the Modern State', in D. Held, J. Anderson, B. Gieben, S. Hall, L. Harris, P. Lewis, N. Parker and B. Turok (eds) *States and Societies*. Oxford: Blackwell.

Jaggar, A. (1989) 'Love and Knowledge: Emotion in Feminist Epistemology', in A. Jaggar and S. Bordo (eds) *Gender/Body/Knowledge*. New Brunswick: Rutgers University Press.

McNay, L. (1994) 'Foucault, Feminism and the Body', in *The Polity Reader in Social Theory*. Cambridge: Polity.

Moore, H. (1994) *A Passion for Difference*. Cambridge: Polity.

O'Connell Davidson, J. (1995a) 'The Anatomy of "Free Choice" Prostitution', *Gender Work and Organisation*, **2**(1).

O'Connell Davidson, J. (1995b) 'British Sex Tourists in Thailand', in M. Maynard and J. Purvis (eds) *(Hetero)sexual Politics*. London: Taylor & Francis.

O'Connell Davidson, J. (1996) 'Prostitution and the Contours of Control,' in J. Weeks and J. Holland (eds) *Sexual Cultures*. London: Macmillan.

O'Connell Davidson, J. and Sanchez Taylor, J. (1996a) 'Child Prostitution and Sex Tourism: Beyond the Stereotypes', in J. Pilcher and S. Wagg (eds) *Thatcher's Children*. London: Falmer.

O'Connell Davidson, J. and Sanchez Taylor, J. (1996b) 'Child Prostitution and Sex Tourism', *Research Papers 1 to 7*, ECPAT International, 326 PhayaThai Rd, Bangkok 10400, Thailand.

Pateman, C. (1988) *The Sexual Contract*. Cambridge: Polity.

Patterson, O. (1982) *Slavery and Social Death*. Cambridge, MA: Harvard University Press.

Sandel, M. (1992) 'The Procedural Republic and the Unencumbered Self', in T. Strong (ed.) *The Self and the Political Order*. Oxford: Blackwell.

Sayer, D. (1991) *Capitalism and Modernity: An Excursus on Marx and Weber*. London: Routledge.

Seidler, V. (1987) 'Reason, Desire and Male Sexuality', in P. Caplan (ed.) *The Cultural Construction of Sexuality*. London: Tavistock.

Stoller, R. (1975) *Perversion: The Erotic Form of Hatred*. London: Karnac.

Truong, T. (1990) *Sex, Money and Morality: Prostitution and Sex Tourism in Southeast Asia*. London: Zed Books.

Weeks, J. (1986) *Sexuality*. London: Tavistock

Young, I. (1990) *Justice and the Politics of Difference*. Princeton, NJ: Princeton University Press.

Ecology and Animal Rights: Is Sovereignty Anthropocentric?

ROBERT GARNER

The debate within political theory about sovereignty is, as this book has sought to show, a many-faceted one. However, whether or not sovereignty can be divorced conceptually from the state and from its traditional unitary and hierarchical character, the vast majority of political theorists persist in seeing sovereignty as a human-centred project. Thus, the notion of individual rights against the state and civil society refers to the human individual alone, and even more radical conceptions of sovereignty, focusing on the individualized free and autonomous self, are equally anthropocentric.

Over the past three decades or so, this human-centred approach to political theorizing has been increasingly challenged by a new generation of scholars who insist that questions of rights, responsibilities and duties apply beyond the human species. This chapter seeks to consider their arguments. Initially, here, we need to make a distinction between those whose claims focus upon the moral standing of nonhuman animals and those who want to argue for a genuine environmental ethic incorporating the whole of nature within the moral universe. It will be suggested that, whilst it is difficult to accord any moral standing to nonsentient elements of nature, it is equally difficult to deny animals, primarily on the grounds of their sentiency, a much higher moral status than the orthodoxy is presently willing to accept. As a consequence, this requires an adjustment to the anthropocentric nature of political theory in general and the study of sovereignty in particular.

The challenge to the moral orthodoxy

At this point, it is useful to define the constituent units of the natural environment and provide a relatively brief description of the various philosophical positions held in relation to them. I have described this

Table 11. 1 The continuum of recognition

CATEGORY	ANTHROPO-CENTRISM	SENTIENT-CENTRISM	ECOCENTRISM
HUMANS	intrinsic	intrinsic	intrinsic
NONHUMAN ANIMALS	(a) extrinsic (strong version – Descartes) (b) intrinsic (weak version – moral orthodoxy or animal welfare)	intrinsic	intrinsic
LIVING, BUT NONSENTIENT NATURE	extrinsic	extrinsic	intrinsic
INANIMATE OBJECTS	extrinsic	extrinsic	intrinsic

elsewhere (Garner, 1993: 10) as the 'continuum of recognition'. There would seem to be four major categories to which we might attach moral concern, and three major positions each dependent upon the application of one of two theories of value. These are shown in Table 11.1.

It will be apparent that the weak version of the anthropocentric approach has held sway in political theory. Only Bentham, and to a lesser extent Mill, amongst the mainstream figures of modern political thought have considered rejecting an anthropocentric approach (see Clarke and Linzey, 1990: 135–40). Even these two utilitarians, however, failed to appreciate the implications their focus on sentiency would seem to have for the moral status of nonhuman animals (implications which, as we shall see below, Singer did recognize). Besides Mill and Bentham, the major political theorists have been anthropocentric and productivist, arguing – Marx being a classic case in point – that nonhuman nature has value only when humans have worked and altered it (there have been recent, largely unconvincing, attempts to rescue Marx from this fate, of which the most notable is Benton, 1993).

In the West, the traditional ways (since, in Britain's case, the nineteenth century) of thinking about, and behaving towards, non-human animals has been based on a weak form of anthropocentrism. The strong version, associated most notably with Descartes (see Ryder, 1989: 55–8), holds that, since nonhuman animals are machines, they cannot feel pain and therefore we have no obligations to them. I am not aware of any serious thinker who would want to maintain this position now. Rather, the vast majority would accept that since nonhuman animals are capable of feeling pleasure and pain, thereby having an interest in pursuing the former and avoiding the latter, we have a duty to take account of their inherent value. However, it is argued, since humans are worth more morally, we are entitled to sacrifice the interests of nonhuman animals (for example by eating them or using them in scientific experiments) provided that any suffering inflicted is necessary in terms of the resulting value to humans. Because of their greater capacities which go beyond mere sentiency, however, we are not entitled to treat humans in the same way as beings whose interests can be sacrificed if by so doing we further the general aggregate good. Such a position has been concisely described by Nozick as 'utilitarianism for animals, Kantianism for people' (Nozick, 1974: 35–42). The law relating to nonhuman animals in Britain and elsewhere is built on the assumptions of this approach. Thus, the law does not judge, in isolation, what we do to nonhuman animals and also the *purpose* of what we do. The very same infliction of suffering which would result in a prosecution if the animal were a family pet, would be allowed in a laboratory if it was judged that the benefits (to human health or whatever) were sufficient.

This moral orthodoxy has been seriously challenged in recent years, not just at the academic level but also in terms of the rise of a movement which seeks to deny that humans have a right to utilize nonhuman animals, whatever the purpose (Garner, 1993: ch. 2). It would be wrong to assume that there has been a homogenous body of work. Many philosophers in the radical camp have developed significantly different nuances of argument (see, for instance, Linzey, 1987; Rollin, 1981; Midgley, 1983; Clark, 1984). Nevertheless, for ease of exposition, it is appropriate to focus on the two best-known radical challenges to the moral orthodoxy, those provided by Regan (1988) and Singer (1990).

Both Singer and Regan argue that nonhuman animals deserve a higher moral status than the orthodoxy allows, although they reach this conclusion from very different routes. Singer, as a utilitarian, argues that the criterion for moral inclusiveness is sentiency. Unlike Bentham, however, Singer goes on to insist that since both humans and nonhuman animals are capable of experiencing pleasure and pain, there is no reason to deny that their interests should be treated equally. Singer argues that adopting this position makes most of our present uses of nonhuman animals (including raising and killing them for food and utilizing them for experimental purposes) illegitimate.

For his part, Regan, as we shall see below, has criticized Singer for failing to provide a theory which will protect nonhuman animals in the way he wants it to do. His own contribution differs in two fundamental respects. In the first place, he argues for a deontological rights-based approach (one which holds that certain moral duties are absolutely binding irrespective of consequences) to provide protection for both humans and nonhuman animals. Second, Regan suggests that nonhuman animals do not, as he had argued in his earlier work (Regan, 1975), possess rights on the grounds of their sentiency but because they have a level of mental ability which provides them with autonomy.

This is based upon his assertion that at least some species of nonhuman animals have a significant degree of mental complexity (Regan, 1988: 73–5, 94–9). Thus, for Regan, mammals one year of age or older are self-conscious, have a memory, are capable of having an emotional life and act so as to fulfil their beliefs and preferences. They can be considered 'individuals'. As a consequence, some nonhuman animals, like all adult healthy humans, have a welfare which is capable of being harmed by inflictions of pain and deprivation. The ultimate deprivation is death, since it forecloses all possibilities of finding satisfaction in life. The implications of this analysis are far-reaching. If nonhuman animals have a degree of autonomy so similar to humans that they can suffer in similar ways to humans, then it is illegitimate to inflict suffering upon them if we are not prepared to sanction the same possibility for humans. That is, if humans have rights on the grounds that their capacities entitle them to self-sovereignty, then so too must at least some nonhuman animals.

Ecocentrism

Regan and Singer's approaches may seem radical enough, but a genuine environmental ethic, described in our continuum of recognition as the ecocentric approach, wants to go further still. Not only are nonhuman animals to be included as equal partners in the moral universe but the whole of nature is deemed to have intrinsic value, a value which is not reducible to its use for humans. Thus, we should protect the natural environment not just because it is of value to us but also because it has an interest in not being harmed. The inspiration for this position is widely accredited to the American writer Leopold and later to the philosopher Naess (Leopold, 1949; Naess, 1973), and it has now become a central feature of the so-called 'dark green' approach to environment-alism which exists as a challenge to the dominant anthropocentric or 'light green' reformist approach (see Dobson, 1990).

Whilst ecocentrism shares with the Regan and Singer approaches a desire to remove humans from their moral pedestal, there are significant differences. Not only do ecocentrics seek to incorporate the whole of nature − sentient and nonsentient, living and nonliving − within the moral universe, they also tend to emphasize the moral value of whole ecosystems or species rather than the individuals within them. As Goodin points out:

> I simply do not think that caring about animals one-by-one is what the environmentalist movement is − or ought to be − most centrally all about. The whole point of a self-styled ecology movement, surely, is that we must learn to see things in their largest possible contexts. In those terms, it is global forms of the issues that really matter. (Goodin, 1992b: 2)

Leaving aside the difficulties ecocentrics face when seeking to distinguish morally between the various parts of nature (see below), which Goodin does not address in the above passage, it is easy to see why ecocentrism is anathema from an animal rights perspective. Thus, Leopold's classic formulation of ecocentrism, that 'a thing is right when it tends to preserve the integrity, stability and beauty' of the natural environment and 'wrong when it tends otherwise' (Leopold, 1949: 217), leaves open the possibility that we may have to sacrifice the interests of individuals (including humans) in order to maintain the stability of the whole. From a rights perspective, this position is illegitimate precisely because it does not respect the sovereignty of the individual. Indeed, for Regan, it is a version of 'environmental fascism' (Regan, 1988: 362).

Can nature have inherent value?

There are severe problems with the ecocentric position. Even if we accept that the integrity of the natural environment should be prioritized above the interests of the individuals within it (a very big if, particularly if our concern is to maximize the sovereignty of individuals), we are still left with the vagueness of the theory which leads to doubts about its practicability. In particular, it is not clear to what we are according moral standing. Is it to species, to ecosystems or to the concept of diversity itself? (See Johnson, 1991, who attaches moral standing to ecosystems, and Martell, 1994, ch. 3, who discusses the issue further.) In addition, are we to adopt an egalitarian approach which does not distinguish morally between the various parts of nature? The problem with this is obvious. To cope with it, some ecologists have invoked the moral relevance of sentiency. Thus, Fox states that:

> the central intuition of deep ecology does not entail the view that intrinsic value is spread evenly across the membership of the biotic community. Moreover, in situations of genuine value-conflict, justice is better served by not subscribing to the view of ecological egalitarianism. Cows do scream louder than carrots. (Fox, 1984: 199)

This brings us neatly to the second, and most fundamental, problem with ecocentrism. On what grounds can we accord moral standing to nonsentient nature? The problem here, of course, is that moral standing and inherent value presupposes some recognition of harm on the part of those being harmed. We accept some moral responsibility for nonhuman animals precisely because we recognize their capacity to suffer. We cannot make the same assumption for trees or rocks or ecosystems or species. Because of this, it does not seem sensible to say that we can wrong nonsentient nature in the same way that we can wrong a sentient being. Sentiency, then, would seem to be the benchmark for moral standing and, therefore, for sovereignty. As Singer points out: 'There is genuine difficulty in understanding how chopping down a tree can matter *to the tree* if the tree can feel nothing' (Singer, 1983: 123).

Environmental philosophers have devised a variety of solutions to this problem, including arguments based on appeals to intuition (Attfield, 1983) and the development of an ecological consciousness (discussed in Dobson, 1990: 57–63). These kinds of argument are spiritual in orientation, based on the assertion that only if we experience the power and beauty of nature (thereby dispensing with a search for what Dobson calls 'a code of conduct' and replacing it with 'a state of being') will we come to respect nature's value. Whilst I do not wish to belittle the spiritual dimension of environmentalism, such arguments are by definition open to competing intuitions which can be equally compelling. It is difficult to justify environmental protection using such arguments when, for example, we are faced with claims that there is a choice between a certain degree of environmental degradation and material sacrifices, particularly when these sacrifices are demanded of those in already poor developing countries. Indeed, insofar as such stark choices exist, it is possible to see how *human* sovereignty can be damaged by an emphasis on protecting the natural environment.

Another common approach is to develop a continuum between a hard-headed anthropocentrism at one end of the spectrum and a pure ecocentrism at the other. Eckersley (1992: 33–47), for instance, puts forward a fivefold categorization which includes three anthropocentric approaches (resource conservation, human welfare ecology and preservationism), the latter representing a position closer to the ecocentric ideal than the other two. Goodin's 'Green theory of value' argues that nature's value lies in its very naturalness from whose existence we derive satisfaction (Goodin, 1992a: 26–41). This remains anthropocentric because the value of nature still derives from the satisfaction *we* derive from it as opposed to something internal to it. Nevertheless, Goodin wants to argue that this position, where nature has value 'in relation to us', is less anthropocentric than saying that nature only has value 'for us'. This distinction is also made by Dobson, who refers to a legitimate, and inevitable, 'human-centred' anthropocentrism and an illegitimate 'human-instrumental' version, and by Vincent, who makes a similar distinction between a 'light anthropocentrism' and a 'hard-nosed exploitative' anthropocentrism (Dobson, 1990: 63–72; Vincent, 1993: 254–5).

The problem with these types of argument is that it is difficult to see how a qualified ecocentrism can exist. That is, something either has inherent value or it does not. All the above arguments, therefore, remain anthropocentric because it is humans who are putting a value upon nature. The problem remains that these human-imposed values are subject to competing human claims which, it might be argued, are equally valid. For example, if Goodin tells me that I should not cut down trees because he derives satisfaction from knowing that they are there, I can simply respond by saying that I have a different set of values – concern, for example, for human material well-being – which will be furthered by chopping the trees down. Without an additional argument to the effect that cutting down a tree is to wrong the tree, Goodin's argument is on shaky ground.

Short of a convincing argument for granting moral standing to nonsentient nature, there is a tendency to focus on human-prudential grounds for environmental protection. We should, for instance, protect the rain forests not because they have inherent value but because they provide vital functions as sinks for carbon dioxide, the absence of which will cause problems for us (in the shape of the increased likelihood of global warming and a reduction in biodiversity). Likewise, human prudential grounds could also be employed to justify protecting nonhuman animals and the habitats they depend upon. In this way, nonhuman animals are protected not because we recognize their inherent value and therefore respect their sovereignty, but because we value them for economic or aesthetic reasons.

Such prudential arguments are compelling, particularly because there is a strong case for the claim that environmental protection is not necessarily incompatible with economic growth (see Weale, 1992). Ultimately, though, the search for a genuine environmental ethic remains important, albeit theoretically problematic, since only when we respect nature for what it is by recognizing its sovereignty, irrespective of its value to us, can its protection against the human species be assured. Equally, the protection of nonhuman animals can only be guaranteed if we recognize their sovereignty. Unlike nonsentient nature, as will be shown in the next section, the theoretical case for granting this sovereignty to nonhuman animals is built on much stronger foundations.

Sentiency, autonomy and the case for animal rights

Whilst it is difficult to justify according moral standing to nature, most would accept that we owe some obligations to nonhuman animals. The question is what obligations do we owe to them? The radicals, such as Regan and Singer, want to argue, as we have seen, that there is no justification for treating nonhuman animals as morally inferior and, insofar as we do so, we are guilty of what Ryder has referred to as speciesism, discriminating in favour of the human species on the grounds of species membership alone rather than on any morally relevant criteria (Ryder, 1989: 5–12). How plausible, then, are the arguments for granting nonhuman animals a much higher moral status than the orthodoxy is prepared to allow?

The first step is to examine what derives from granting that nonhuman animals are sentient, and crucially whether sentiency alone is enough to allow us to accord sovereignty to them. Advocates of the moral orthodoxy accept that nonhuman animals are sentient but because humans have greater mental capacities – rationality, a language capability, free will, self-consciousness and so on – it is argued that they are morally more important. Thus, whilst we should try to ensure that nonhuman animals live, as far as possible, a pain-free happy life, we do not, as in the case of our relationship with other humans, have to respect their autonomy (Townsend, 1976; McCloskey, 1979; Leahy, 1991; Carruthers, 1992). The possession of autonomy – a term used to describe the human ability to be sovereign or self-governing; to have beliefs and preferences upon which we act – provides an *a priori* justification for noninterference which does not apply, it is argued, in the case of nonhuman animals. As a consequence, the life of a human is more important than the life of a nonhuman animal, and we are entitled to sacrifice the interests of the latter if by so doing we benefit the interests of the former.

The nature of the human benefits we are entitled to promote by sacrificing the interests of nonhuman animals is a matter of, often heated, debate, and this explains why there is a genuine politics of animal welfare whereby the animal protection movement seeks to justify more stringent laws on the grounds that a particular practice inflicts unnecessary suffering. For example, it is possible to campaign for the abolition of fox hunting or fur farms on the grounds, not that animals have rights, but that the suffering caused by such practices does not justify the benefits derived by humans. Conversely, defenders of such practices argue that animal advocates exaggerate the amount of suffering inflicted and underestimate the benefits gained by humans in the process. The key point to note here is that the moral orthodoxy does accept that there comes a point, wherever it is drawn, when it is acceptable to inflict suffering and/or death upon nonhuman animals.

There are at least three major responses we might make here (the following arguments are based on the account in Garner, 1993: 12–26). In the first place, even if we accept the dichotomy between autonomous humans and sentient nonhumans, its moral relevance is not as clear-cut as the moral orthodoxy would have it. It would seem to be the case that the possession of autonomy does entitle a being to differential treatment from one that is merely sentient. A being with complex wants and desires can clearly be harmed in ways (through, for instance, captivity or death) which a mere sentient being could not. This would seem to legitimize, in particular, the painless killing of animals. Interestingly, Singer himself recognized this when he pointed out that:

> to take the life of a being who has been hoping, planning and working for some future goal is to deprive that being of the fulfilment of all those efforts; to take the life of a being with a mental capacity below the level needed to grasp that one is a being with a future – much less make plans for the future – cannot involve this particular kind of loss. (Singer, 1990: 21)

It is not so clear, however, why inflicting pain on a nonhuman animal is any more justified than inflicting pain on a human. A nonhuman's capacity to experience pain, then, is as great as a human's. The weakness of the moral orthodoxy is the assumption that the identification of one characteristic which humans possess and nonhumans do not, is sufficient for the claim that *all* human interests are morally superior to *all* the interests of nonhuman animals. As Rachels (1983: 278) convincingly argues, 'the characteristics one must have in order to have a right vary with the rights themselves'. So, to have the right, for instance, to freedom of worship requires the possession of characteristics – the ability to understand religious beliefs – necessary for worship to have some meaning. The right not to be tortured, on the other hand, is justified merely on the grounds that it causes pain. If we accept this critique of the moral orthodoxy, as I think we must, it follows that if we hold that humans have a right not to have pain inflicted upon them in order to promote the greater good, then the same must apply to nonhuman animals. This does not mean, however, that it is necessarily wrong to kill animals painlessly whether or not humans are likely to benefit. This, of course, has important implications for the way in which we treat animals. Singer wants to claim that the prohibition on pain would rule out most of the ways in which we exploit animals. Whilst this is probably true, there are important exceptions. The use of permanently anaesthetized animals in scientific procedures, for instance, would appear to be morally legitimized. Likewise, shorn of the worst excesses of factory farming, the raising and painless killing of animals for food would also be permissible. Much depends, here, on the definition of pain employed. If the concept is broadened to include suffering in all of its manifestations — taking into account boredom, frustration and so forth — human exploitation of animals would be constrained to a much greater extent than if only physical pain was included. We would also be obliged to show here that animals can suffer frustration and boredom and be able to identify the circumstances in which this is likely to happen.

However we define pain, the critique of the moral orthodoxy outlined above does not allow us to grant full sovereignty to nonhuman animals. Whilst the widespread adoption of such a position would undoubtedly improve markedly the position of animals, we would still be morally entitled to utilize them for our purposes even to the point of taking their lives. Indeed, given that the absence of constraints on our freedom to exist is surely a crucial component of any meaningful notion of sovereignty, it is doubtful whether this first critique of the moral orthodoxy allows us to accord sovereignty to nonhuman animals.

There are two additional responses to the moral orthodoxy, however, which provide much stronger grounds for according sovereignty to nonhuman animals. The first of these is the so-called 'argument from marginal cases' — a term originally coined by Narveson (1977), who is critical of the approach. Here, it is accepted that the autonomy possessed by humans is morally significant, but then we need to ask what kind of moral obligations are owed to those humans — infants and the so-called 'human defectives' — whose mental capabilities are on a par with, or lower than, a healthy adult mammal? To treat human defectives differently from nonhuman animals would seem to be a classic example of speciesism.

Answers to this problem have been less than satisfactory. Human infants, of course, can be dealt with easily enough on the grounds that they have the capacity to become autonomous adult humans, but this still leaves human defectives. Some — for instance, Townsend (1976) — have resorted to the claim that what matters is the general characteristics of a species and not the exceptions. The problem here is that individual characteristics are crucial in assessing what is right and wrong in particular situations, and treating human defectives differently from nonhuman animals does indicate an illegitimate form of speciesism.

The most adequate response to the argument from marginal cases is to accept that we should treat human defectives differently from normal healthy adult humans. This is the approach adopted by Frey (1983, 114–15; 1987: 57–8). To a certain extent, of course, it is the case that human defectives are treated differently from other humans in the case, say, of the use of scarce medical resources. There is a world of difference, however, between letting a seriously retarded human being die peacefully rather than administering expensive medical treatment and actively inflicting pain and suffering on an individual for the benefit of others. Frey does accept this and admits that if we are prepared to use nonhuman animals in such a way then it is difficult to see why we should not use human defectives in a similar fashion.

To contemplate using human defectives in such a way is deeply disturbing and challenges our moral intuition. For the pro-animal philosophers, this is the whole point of the exercise. If we are not prepared to treat human defectives as means to our ends, then we should not use nonhuman animals in the same way. If, that is, we are prepared to grant rights to all humans, then there would seem to be no logical reason why we should not grant them to nonhuman animals too. This argument also serves as a response to the oft-stated claim that animals cannot have rights because only moral agents – those who can recognize right from wrong and act accordingly – can be the holders of rights since only they can understand what it is to be granted rights and what it is to respect the rights of others (McCloskey, 1979). If this were the case, we would then be committing ourselves to the position that infants and human defectives cannot have rights either when clearly we do recognize them in practice. If we accept that human infants and defectives have a right to life (as we generally do), then we must accept that nonhuman animals do too. Further, since such a right would seem to be a crucial component of what it is to be a sovereign individual, then we must also accord such a status to nonhuman animals.

The final response to the moral orthodoxy, which, if accepted, would further establish nonhuman animals as sovereign individuals, is the claim that autonomy applies not just to humans but also to at least some nonhuman animals. As we saw, this is the approach adopted by Regan. For Regan (1988: 94–9), nonhuman animals, like humans, are 'subjects-of-a-life' having inherent value as beings whose lives are characterized by beliefs and desires and thus the capability of acting intentionally to satisfy their preferences. These are lives worth living, lives that can be harmed by pain, suffering, frustration and death.

Assessing the validity of Regan's claims is enormously difficult. Clearly, it is much too simplistic to equate full autonomy with humans and mere sentiency with nonhuman animals. Most advocates of the moral orthodoxy would concede that all mammals are capable of suffering that goes beyond mere pain. Hence, animal welfare concerns often involve trying to ensure that nonhuman animals in captivity are provided with conditions that allow them enough room and environmental enrichment to avoid frustration and boredom. Regan's assessment of nonhuman animal capabilities, of course, goes much further than this. Most critics have argued that his assessment is 'seriously overstated' (Narveson, 1987: 24) and have sought to put forward what they regard as a more realistic account of the capabilities of nonhuman animals, usually along the lines of the moral orthodoxy position.

Frey (1987) provides probably the most convincing direct challenge to Regan. Frey equates autonomy with control, the ability of a being to organize her life in order to achieve a set of clearly set-out goals. Insofar as her life plan is obstructed by others or by her own failures (through the pursuit, for instance, of 'first-order' desires such as eating, drinking, drugs and so forth), she is not autonomous. For Frey, nonhuman animals are incapable of this type of autonomy ('control' autonomy). Rather they have an impoverished version, what he calls 'preference autonomy'. This latter form is based around the pursuit of a limited number of first-order desires which denies them 'means to that rich full life of self-fulfilment and achievement' (Frey, 1987: 61).

Regan recognizes that even though a version of autonomy can be applied to nonhuman animals, humans have greater mental capacities. He responds by invoking the argument from marginal cases. Thus, autonomy as control may not apply to nonhuman animals, but then neither does it apply to marginal humans. The problem here is that, as we have already seen, Frey is prepared to admit that some human lives *are* more valuable than others and that, for some humans, the control version of autonomy does not apply. It is by no means certain, therefore, whether Regan's case for a higher moral status for nonhuman animals is any stronger than those based on sentiency alone. More specifically, employing the argument from marginal cases allows us to accord sovereignty to nonhuman animals without any additional arguments seeking to show that they are autonomous individuals on a par with humans.

Sovereignty and rights

The final part of our discussion about the moral status of nonhuman animals focuses upon what follows from accepting Regan and Singer's claims that animals ought to be granted a higher moral status, and the consequences, in particular, for sovereignty. Here, the debate, as in moral philosophy generally, has centred around the distinction between rights and utilitarianism.

Singer's approach is utilitarian. Thus he argues that what matters in determining a moral judgement is the overall level of preference satisfaction. Unlike traditional utilitarianism, however, he takes the view that since nonhuman animals are sentient, their interests ought to be considered equally with those of humans. This utilitarian approach has been attacked by Regan, who argues that it does not provide the level of protection for animals that is afforded by rights theory. This is a familiar critique, of course, of the consequentionalist implications of utilitarianism. Rights theory, its advocates insist, is based upon the dignity of the individual, respecting, that is, an individual's sovereignty. As Rollin, another advocate of extending rights to animals, points out, rights are:

> moral notions that grow out of respect for the individual. They build protective fences around the individual. They establish areas where the individual is entitled to be protected against the state and the majority *even where a price is paid by the general welfare*. (Rollin, 1981: 28)

It is not clear that Singer's utilitarian analysis could guarantee that meat-eating or scientific experimentation upon nonhuman animals would be prohibited. This would be a matter for empirical examination. Thus, if it could be shown that carrying out painful procedures on some nonhuman animals would have hugely beneficial consequences, in terms, say, of the discovery of a cure for a debilitating or fatal disease, then on utilitarian grounds it would seem to be justified. Singer responds in three different ways to this. In the first place, he seems to think that suffering is inflicted upon animals for largely trivial reasons. 'The overwhelming majority of humans', he writes:

> take an active part in, acquiesce in, and allow their taxes to pay for practices that require the sacrifice of the most important interests of members of other species in order to promote the most trivial interests of our own species. (Singer, 1990: 9)

Now, whilst this might be true in the case, say, of fox-hunting or even meat-eating — although even this is not certain given the economic benefits these practices generate — it is clearly not the case if it can be shown that human lives can be saved by medical discoveries involving the use of nonhuman animals. Singer would no doubt respond to this by claiming that the above examples are speciesist. Thus, we are entitled to consider sacrificing the interests of nonhuman animals in order to promote the general welfare but only if, according to his nonspeciesist version, we include humans within the cost–benefit analysis. We are not then entitled to sacrifice the interests of nonhumans if we are not also prepared to sacrifice the interests of humans, and, since our moral intuition suggests that we would not be prepared to treat humans in such a way, why should we use nonhuman animals as means to our ends?

The fact remains, however, that Singer is a utilitarian, and it is curious that he does not simply adopt a rights-based position, as Regan does, in order to overcome the problems identified above. The answer, I think, lies in Singer's concern for the inflexibility of the rights position. Here, he has clashed head-on with Regan (see Regan, 1985; Singer, 1985). Thus, Singer is prepared to sanction the sacrifice of the interests of some nonhuman animals (or humans) if the general good will obviously be promoted in a substantial way.

Regan is unwilling to accept the sacrifice of individuals for the greater good but he gets into difficulties when he comes to discuss what we should do in the event of a choice between competing rights. The problem becomes more acute when he includes nonhuman animals in the equation. In this context, Regan adopts a so-called 'lifeboat' exercise where a number of humans and a dog cannot all survive. Who is to be thrown overboard? His conclusion, that the dog should go because the death of a nonhuman animal 'though a harm, is not comparable to the harm that death would be for any of the humans' (Regan, 1985: 49) is enormously problematic. Transfer this example to the laboratory and it provides a justification for using nonhuman animals for the pursuit of life-saving medical advances. Regan, it seems, gets into this difficulty because of his reliance on moral intuition which, he suggests, would sanction the sacrifice of the dog. Even without this conclusion, though, the inflexibility of the rights position becomes apparent and some criteria would have to be adopted to deal with it. The crucial point to note is that only a rights-based approach, which protects individuals against the community, accords the dignity and respect that must be accorded to sovereign individuals.

Conclusion

This chapter has tried to show that it is illegitimate for discourse on sovereignty in particular, and political theory in general, to focus exclusively on the human species. It is difficult to justify granting any moral standing to nonsentient nature, let alone the kind of standing required before sovereignty can be applied. Developing a genuine environmental ethic, providing a case for the inherent value of non-sentient nature, would, however, make the case for environmental protection significantly stronger.

In the case of sentient nonhuman animals, there is a cast-iron case for jettisoning the moral orthodoxy in favour of an ethic which recognizes their dignity and worth as sovereign individuals. This follows from merely accepting that nonhuman animals are sentient beings with the capacity to suffer in ways equivalent to humans. As a result, arguments focusing on a notion of sovereignty centring on the autonomous individual need to hurdle the species barrier between humans and nonhumans which has been shown to be a construct of little moral relevance. Likewise, the dignity of sentient humans and nonhumans necessitates protection by an ethic which prevents crucial interests being sacrificed to the general welfare. Only a system of cross-species rights can guarantee this outcome.

References

Attfield, R. (1983) *The Ethics of Environmental Concern*. Oxford: Basil Blackwell.
Benton, T. (1993) *Natural Relations: Ecology, Animal Rights and Social Justice*. London: Verso.
Clark, S. (1984) *The Moral Status of Animals*. Oxford: Clarendon Press.
Clarke, P. and Linzey, A. (eds) (1990) *Political Theory and Animal Rights*. London: Pluto Press.
Carruthers, P. (1992) *The Animals Issue: Moral Theory in Practice*. Cambridge: Cambridge University Press.
Dobson, A. (1990) *Green Political Thought*. London: Unwin Hyman.
Eckersley, R. (1992) *Environmentalism and Political Theory*. London: UCL Press.
Fox, M. (1984) 'Deep Ecology: A New Philosophy of Our Times', *The Ecologist*, **14**, 199–200.
Frey, R. G. (1983) *Rights, Killing and Suffering*. Oxford: Oxford University Press.
Frey, R. G. (1987) 'Autonomy and the Value of Animal Life', *Monist*, **70**, 55–67.
Garner, R. (1993) *Animals, Politics and Morality*. Manchester: Manchester University Press.
Goodin, R. (1992a) *Green Political Theory*. Cambridge: Polity Press.
Goodin, R. (1992b) 'The High Ground is Green', *Environmental Politics*, **1**, 1–8.
Johnson, L. E. (1991) *A Morally Deep World*. Cambridge: Cambridge University Press.
Leahy, M. P. T. (1991) *Against Liberation: Putting Animals in Perspective*. London: Routledge.
Leopold, A. (1949) *A Sand County Almanac*. Oxford: Oxford University Press.
Linzey, A. (1987) *Christianity and the Rights of Animals*. London: SPCK.
Martell, L. (1994) *Ecology and Society*. Cambridge: Polity Press.
McCloskey, H. J. (1979) 'Moral Rights and Animals', *Inquiry*, **22**, 23–54.
Midgley, M. (1983) *Animals and Why They Matter*. Athens: University of Georgia Press.
Naess, A. (1973) 'The Shallow and the Deep, Long Range Ecology Movement: A Summary', *Inquiry*, **16**, 95–100.
Narveson, J. (1977) 'Animal Rights', *Canadian Journal of Philosophy*, **7**, 161–78.
Narveson, J. (1987) 'On a Case for Animal Rights', *Monist*, **70**, 42–54.
Rachels, J. (1983) 'Do Animals Have a Right to Life?', in H. B. Miller and W. H. Williams (eds) *Ethics and Animals*. Clifton, NJ: Humana Press.
Regan, T. (1975) 'The Moral Basis of Vegetarianism', *Canadian Journal of Philosophy*, **5**, 181–214.
Regan, T. (1985) 'The Dog in the Lifeboat', *New York Review of Books*, 17 January.

Regan, T. (1988) *The Case for Animal Rights*. London: Routledge.

Rollin, B. (1981) *Animal Rights and Human Morality*. Buffalo, NY: Prometheus.

Ryder, R. (1989) *Animal Revolution: Changing Attitudes Towards Speciesism*. Oxford: Basil Blackwell.

Singer, P. (1983) *The Expanding Circle: Ethics and Sociobiology*. Oxford: Oxford University Press.

Singer, P. (1985) 'Ten Years of Animal Liberation', *New York Review of Books*, 17 January.

Singer, P. (1990) *Animal Liberation*. London: Cape.

Townsend, A. (1976) 'Radical Vegetarians', *Australasian Journal of Philosophy*, **5 7**, 85–93.

Vincent, A. (1993) 'The Character of Ecology', *Environmental Politics*, **2**, 248–76.

Weale, A. (1992) *The New Politics of Pollution*. Manchester: Manchester University Press.

Index